ROUTLEDGE LIBRARY EDITIONS: WOMEN IN SOCIETY

Volume 11

RAPIERS AND BATTLEAXES

RAPIERS AND BATTLEAXES

The Women's Movement
and Its Aftermath

JOSEPHINE KAMM

Foreword by
MARY STOCKS

Routledge
Taylor & Francis Group

LONDON AND NEW YORK

First published in 1966 by George Allen & Unwin Ltd

This edition first published in 2025
by Routledge
4 Park Square, Milton Park, Abingdon, Oxon OX14 4RN

and by Routledge
605 Third Avenue, New York, NY 10158

Routledge is an imprint of the Taylor & Francis Group, an informa business

British Library Cataloguing in Publication Data
A catalogue record for this book is available from the British Library

ISBN: 978-1-032-87216-2 (Set)
ISBN: 978-1-032-85157-0 (Volume 11) (hbk)
ISBN: 978-1-032-85159-4 (Volume 11) (pbk)
ISBN: 978-1-003-51684-2 (Volume 11) (ebk)

DOI: 10.4324/9781003516842

Publisher's Note
The publisher has gone to great lengths to ensure the quality of this reprint but points out that some imperfections in the original copies may be apparent.

Disclaimer
The publisher has made every effort to trace copyright holders and would welcome correspondence from those they have been unable to trace.

RAPIERS
AND
BATTLEAXES

THE WOMEN'S MOVEMENT
AND ITS AFTERMATH

JOSEPHINE KAMM

FOREWORD BY MARY STOCKS
(BARONESS STOCKS)

London
GEORGE ALLEN & UNWIN LTD
RUSKIN HOUSE MUSEUM STREET

PRINTED IN GREAT BRITAIN
in 11 point Baskerville type
BY SIMSON SHAND LTD
LONDON, HERTFORD AND HARLOW

ACKNOWLEDGEMENTS

My grateful thanks are due to Miss Vera Douie, OBE, Librarian of the Fawcett Library, and Mrs H. V. Horton, Clerk to the Trustees, for their help and encouragement, for many useful suggestions, and for reading this book in typescript. I should also like to thank the Fawcett Society for permission to reproduce illustrations Nos. 2–8.

J.K.

FOREWORD

BY BARONESS STOCKS

Josephine Kamm has produced a factual and carefully documented account of the women's movement and its subsequent achievements, while at the same time bringing the whole story to life by her frank and perceptive character studies of its leading participants. And unlike many of those who have tackled this subject, she has done full justice to the part played by the Pankhursts in bringing the suffrage agitation into the forefront of public consciousness while at the same time stressing the importance of the constitutional and democratically organized body under the leadership of Mrs Henry Fawcett, which preceded the militant movement by many years and survived to carry the campaign for the vote to completion fourteen years after the dissolution of the militant organization.

There is, however, one aspect of the constitutional struggle for the vote of which only veterans like myself, who lived through it can be fully aware: its educational value to women in the technique of democratic government and political agitation. The policy of Mrs Fawcett's organization was not dictated from the centre—it was hammered out year by year at annual conferences of the whole organization. It was not always plain sailing. There were differences of opinion on election policy—on the personnel of the annually elected executive committee—on the organization's response to the war situation in 1914—later, on its attitude to family allowances and proportional representation. All these matters were discussed in the branches before their chosen delegates came up to annual conferences. When they did, they had, for many years, the example of Mrs Rackham's incomparable chairmanship, steering them through the intricacies of amendments and resolutions—and the guidance of two successive parliamentary secretaries: Ray Strachey and Eva Hubback, who knew the parliamentary machine from the inside and were on easy terms with the personnel of government departments.

What the delegates learned in annual conference was reflected back into the branches all over the country. Visiting those branches many years later it could be observed that the women who had once played their part in the suffrage agitation were now playing their part on education committees, borough councils, magisterial benches, were taking the lead in organizing Women's Citizens Associations, Women's Institutes, League of Nations Union branches, thus reflecting in British public life the lessons they had learned in the democratic agitation which made them voters. This, then, in addition to the individual achievements chronicled in the final chapters of Josephine Kamm's inspiring book, was a bequest of the suffrage agitation to posterity—and posterity owes it to the great organization over which Millicent Fawcett presided during its most significant years.

CONTENTS

ILLUSTRATIONS

Chapter I

BIRTH OF A MOVEMENT

_____

It is usual to date the birth of the women's movement from the publication in 1792 of Mary Wollstonecraft's *A Vindication of the Rights of Woman*. In fact, the movement had been born many years earlier although its champions were neither as forceful nor notorious as the ill-fated Mary Wollstonecraft. In 1739, for example, an outspoken and controversial pamphlet appeared. It was called *Woman not Inferior to Man: or, short and modest Vindication of the natural Right of the Fair Sex to a perfect Equality of Power, Dignity, and Esteem, with the Men*. The author called herself 'Sophia, a Person of Quality', but her identity has never been revealed. She may well have been the studious, original Lady Mary Wortley Montagu, who complained that women 'are educated in the grossest ignorance',[1] and wrote long letters of advice on the education of her grand-daughters. Or she may have been another, less famous woman, Lady Pennington, whose *Unfortunate Mother's Advice to her Absent Daughters* was published in 1761. In her youth Lady Pennington had maintained that friendship without lovemaking could— and should—exist between men and women. This 'advanced' theory, which the girl insisted on putting into practice, was considered so shocking that she was forced into a loveless marriage; and her husband, tiring of her, used her friendship with men as an excuse for depriving her of her children. Hence the poor woman's need to address them in print.

'Sophia', whoever she may have been, protested vigorously against the subservient position of women. 'Was every individual Man to divulge his thoughts of our sex', she wrote, 'they would all be found unanimous in thinking, that we are made for their use, that we are fit only to breed and nurse children in their tender years, to mind household affairs, and to obey, serve and please our masters, *themselves*, forsooth.'[2] She herself, she added graphically, had been 'accidentally witness to the diverting scene of a journeyman taylor's beating his wife about the ears with a neck of mutton, to make her know, as he said, her *sovereign lord and master*.'[3]

It was quite natural for Sophia to complain about the ignorance of women: as she knew very well, the lack of an adequate education would help to keep them in a state of subjection. 'It is a very great absurdity, to argue that learning is useless to *Women*, because forsooth they have not a share in public offices, which is the end for which *Men* apply themselves to it. . . .' This fallacious argument could only end in a vicious circle. 'Why is *learning* useless to us? Because we have no share in public offices. And why have we no share in public offices? Because we have no *learning*.'[4] If men were less envious of women's talents and ability, they would long since 'have been as accustom'd to see us filling public offices, as we are to see them disgrace them: and to see a lady at a bar, or on a bench, would have been no more strange than it is now, to see a grave judge whimpering at his maid's knees; or, a lord embroidering his wife's petticoat.'[5]

Sophia's pamphlet formed the first part of a book. The second part (it may also have been Sophia's work) purported to be written by a man to prove his natural right to lord it over woman. The third part, again signed by Sophia, offered 'a plain Demonstration of Women's natural Right even to Superiority over the Men in Head and Heart; proving their Minds as much more beautiful than the Men's as their Bodies are; and that, had they the same advantages of Education, they would excel them as much in Sense as they do in Virtue.'

Such arguments made very little impact on society. To the vast majority of men—and to most women—the idea of equal rights was not only ridiculous but positively blasphemous. 'I am not sounding an alarm to female warriors, nor exciting female politicians,' declared worthy, puritanical Hannah More in 1779. 'I hardly know which of the two is the most disgusting and unnatural character.'[6]

Hannah More, whose writings were extremely influential,

typified the conventional views of her day. The fight for women's rights, she wrote elsewhere in the same book, 'has recently been revived with added fury . . . ; the imposing term of *rights* has been produced to sanctify the claims of our female pretenders, with a view not only to rekindle in the minds of women a presumptuous vanity dishonourable to their sex, but produced with a view to excite in their hearts an impious discontent with the post which God has assigned them in this world. . . . A little Christian humility and sober-mindedness are worth all the wild metaphisical discussion which has unsettled the peace of vain women, and forfeited the respect of reasonable men.'[7] Few women, and fewer men, were prepared to quarrel with such a verdict.

As the eighteenth century drew to its close a few faint women's voices were raised in protest against the post which God had apparently assigned to them. But world-shattering events were needed to shake the majority out of their comfortable torpor. The Industrial Revolution led to a gradual change in the status of women of the middle and lower classes. In prosperous middle class households the work was now done by ill-paid domestic servants, and the skills and crafts of former years were replaced by cheap manufactured goods. This situation, which led to boredom and frustration among the unoccupied single women, stimulated the more energetic to action. Among the lower classes there was a growing tendency for women and girls to abandon cottage crafts for work in factories and mills. Had they remained at home they would soon have been put out of business by the far greater power and productivity of industry.

Meanwhile, the incidence of the French Revolution had implanted in the minds of men and women the ideals of freedom and equality. Conditions in France and England, of course, were very different. When, for instance, Napoleon remarked that he disliked women who meddled in politics, he was, we are told, put smartly in his place by Madame de Condorcet, wife of that apostle of sex-equality, the Marquis de Condorcet. 'You are right, General,' she replied; 'but in a country where their heads are cut off, it is natural they should wish to know the reason why.'[8]

In England, where no heads rolled, the thought of emancipation was a magnet to the intellectually thwarted women of the middle classes. They lived in a state of subjection—economic as well as intellectual—and now, if ever, was the time to break through. As Ray Strachey, author of the standard book on women's movement, put it: 'Of course there would have been no need for a Women's Movement at all had not this subjection existed.'[9]

The disabilities which woman suffered had not primarily been designed with subjection in view. As Sir William Blackstone had stated in his *Commentary on the Laws of England* (1765–9) they were intended for the most part 'for her protection and benefit, so great a favourite is the female sex in the laws of England.' Thus, if a married woman committed any crime in her husband's presence, apart from murder or high treason (and 'treason' was extended to cover a number of offences), she was presumed to have committed it under his coercion and was therefore deemed guiltless. 'By marriage', wrote Blackstone, 'the very being or legal existence of a woman is suspended, or at least it is incorporated or consolidated into that of the husband, under whose wing, protection and cover she performs everything. . . . ' This meant that while a married woman could get away with almost any crime and was not responsible for her own debts, she had no legal claim to any of her possessions: her property, her earnings, even her children, all belonged to her husband, as Lady Pennington had already discovered. 'The incorporation and consolidation were complete,' wrote Ray Strachey, ' "my wife and I are one, and I am he"; and since there was no divorce obtainable for a woman before 1857, [an injured husband could obtain it by Act of Parliament] there was no way of escape save death.'[10]

To an intelligent woman as unconventional and hardly treated as Mary Wollstonecraft (1759–1797) the legal tie between husband and wife was abhorrent. As a child and as a young woman she suffered great hardships in a man-directed world. She was the second of the six children of a thoroughly unattractive alcoholic, who dissipated a fortune, bullied his wife, and, as he wandered restlessly from place to place, sank lower and lower in the social scale. After her mother's death in

1780 Mary, who had championed and protected her in life, left home to become in succession a paid companion, school teacher and author. In her book *Thoughts on the Education of Daughters* (1787) she inveighed against the smattering of superficial subjects which passed as education among the daughters of the middle classes; and she maintained that a sensible and patient mother was a better teacher for her girls than a schoolmistress or governess. This book, though crude and bombastic, contained the germ of her later treatise. She was paid only ten guineas for it. Needing money, she took a post as governess in the family of Lord Kingsborough; but was dismissed when her pupils began to show obvious signs of affection for her.

She then went to London where she earned a living as reader, translator and adapter to her publisher, the bookseller Johnson. It was through Johnson that she met another of his readers, William Godwin; but there was no friendship between them until later, after Mary had lived for a time in France and endured still further sufferings and misfortunes.

In France, Mary was deeply stirred by the ideals of liberty, equality and fraternity; and in her famous book *A Vindication of the Rights of Woman* she naturally claimed equal educational opportunities for men and women, so that women might become reasonable and reasoning beings and genuine companions to men. 'Make women rational creatures and free citizens, and they will quickly become good wives and mothers,' she wrote, 'that is if men do not neglect the duties of husbands and fathers.'[11] And again: 'Let woman share the rights, and she will emulate the virtues of man; for she must grow more perfect when emancipated, or justify the authority that chains such a weak being to her duty.'[12] Mary Wollstonecraft made no vast claim, as Sophia had made, for the superiority of her sex. She did not, she wrote, wish women 'to have power over men, but over themselves.'[13] And she returned to this point again and again in a rambling book which shows every mark of having been hurriedly put together (according to Godwin it took her only six weeks). The *Vindication*, like its author, is flamboyant, passionate and sentimental; and yet it remains a sincere and moving plea for a genuine partnership between men and women in place of the prevailing partnership which was based on their sexual relationship.

While she was living in France Mary Wollstonecraft had formed a liaison with an American, Gilbert Imlay, and their daughter Fanny was born in 1794. Imlay was a faithless lover; and Mary was distressingly in love. When he abandoned her she returned to London, where she twice attempted suicide, once by flinging herself into the Thames. She was rescued, and not long afterwards re-met Godwin. The liaison which followed was quite unlike the tempestuous, unhappy affair with Imlay; and perhaps for the only time in her life Mary knew contentment. Both she and Godwin disapproved of marriage on principle but they did, in fact, marry in 1797 in order to legitimize their child who was born a few days later. The unlucky Mary Wollstonecraft Godwin did not long survive the birth of her daughter—also called Mary—who later became Shelley's second wife.

The *Vindication* naturally aroused the most violent disapproval, and hatred and odium were heaped on its author's head. Mary Wollstonecraft was accused, among other things, of atheism and of advocating sexual licence. Horace Walpole called her a hyena in petticoats; Hannah More could not bring herself to look at the book but condemned it unread. It was indeed far too frank and unconventional to make any sort of appeal except as a scandalous document; yet in due course when the scandal had died down it became the keystone of the women's movement.

The actual birth of the movement was preceded by the selfless lives of a number of women who found in original devoted work full scope for their craving to be of use in the world. Among these forerunners was Elizabeth Fry (1780–1845) who worked throughout her adult life to alleviate the sufferings of women prisoners and started a school in Newgate prison for the women and their children. Hannah More (1745–1833) was another, despite her sneers at the protagonists of equal rights. She advocated a sound though intellectually limited education for the daughters of the upper and middle classes; and, with the help of her sister Martha, she ran schools in a remote country district for the children of the poor. The

training she offered the children of the poor was uncom-
promisingly religious and utilitarian: the children were not
taught to write; instead, they were reared 'in habits of industry
and piety.'[14] Sarah Trimmer (1741–1811), a leading figure in
the Sunday School Movement, was also among the forerunners.
So, too, were Mary Somerville (1780–1872), one of the leading
scientific writers of her day; and Harriet Martineau (1802–76),
a champion of women's education. The greatest figure of them
all was Florence Nightingale (1820–1910), who might, had she
been so disposed, have played an important part in the
emancipation of her sex. Yet despite her personal achievements
and the panacea in nursing she provided for herself and other
frustrated women, Florence Nightingale was never an advocate
of equal opportunities. 'I am brutally indifferent to the rights
and wrongs of my sex,' she wrote to Harriet Martineau in
1858;[15] and she refused to give Miss Martineau permission to
use her *Notes* as the text of a sermon on pioneer women.

When Florence Nightingale found her panacea she revealed
at the same time the degree of economic dependence of women
on men. Women of the upper and middle classes had no
means of earning a living except as governess or paid companion. Married women were dependent on their husbands:
single women on their parents; and the death of a father might
well leave his unmarried daughters destitute.

The economic situation was different among the working
classes. Women laboured as hard and as long as men, but their
rewards, if they went out to work, were a good deal less. In
every sphere of life the notion that woman was inferior to man
still passed entirely without question except among the
eccentrics, and nobody bothered much about them.

Queen Victoria was no upholder of women's rights; yet
during the first twenty years of her reign the first rumblings
of the coming fight were heard. Women's suffrage was in fact
mentioned in the original draft of the Charter of Rights and
Liberties framed by the Chartist Movement which was
inaugurated about 1838. The reference was later deleted on
the grounds that its adoption might have a deleterious effect
on the claims of working-class men; but at least the question
had been raised; and as a result several women's political

associations were formed which actively promoted the aims of that Charter during the brief period in which the Movement flourished.

In the meantime, the subject had been raised elsewhere. In 1831, for example, the *Westminster Review* published an article advocating the enfranchisement of women. The anonymous author was a young woman; and when the article was reprinted some forty years later she confessed that she had been so appalled by her temerity that she had taken to her bed in a 'decline'. The article would never have been sent in had not her doctor insisted on its completion as a form of occupational therapy. In 1832 another article appeared in the *Westminster Review*, written this time by a Member of Parliament; and in the same year a Member presented a petition in the House of Commons. Women's suffrage, he said, might 'be a subject of mirth to some hon. gentlemen,' but the question was 'one deserving consideration.' The petition, which emanated from a wealthy Yorkshire woman, Mary Smith, prayed that 'every unmarried female possessing the necessary pecuniary qualifications should be entitled to vote for Members of Parliament.'[16]

Had the honourable gentlemen taken Mary Smith's petition seriously the struggle for political emancipation might well have been less protracted and bitter: but there is no record that it produced any effect on them at all; and the question was not raised again in Parliament for many years.

Outside Parliament, however, women were cutting their political teeth. Some of them joined the Anti-Corn Law League founded in 1836; and although their co-operation was confined to money-raising social functions they were permitted to attend meetings and to listen to speeches on 'tariffs, salaries, profits and monopolies.'[17] In later years many of these women were to be found in the ranks of the first women's suffrage committees.

There was one form of political dabbling in which women had indulged through the centuries: this was the influence they exerted on public affairs through their husbands and lovers. The influence of scheming women could be important; but it was seldom beneficial and was sometimes pernicious; and it was frequently used as an argument that women already possessed all the political power they required.

The intervention in the 1830's, however, of a much-wronged and maligned young woman, had a decisive effect on the position of married women: it also caused an open scandal which rocked the political world and threatened to unseat the Prime Minister. The woman responsible for it all was not a supporter of women's rights. She was Caroline Sheridan (1808–1877), one of the lovely, fascinating, witty grand-daughters of the dramatist. As a small girl she had apparently not been prepossessing. 'Well, that is not a child I should care to meet in a dark wood!'[18] her grandfather is reputed to have said. At that time her face had been dominated by her enormous black eyes; but as a young woman she was opulent and strikingly beautiful, with dark hair, an olive complexion and regular features. The actress Fanny Kemble spoke of her blinding beauty and the sweetness of her contralto voice, and she was only sixteen when George Norton, younger brother of Lord Grantley and the brother of one of her school friends, announced his intention of asking her to marry him.

Caroline was not in love with George Norton; but when she was nineteen she married him, possibly because of a disappoint-ment in love or else because she thought she would be totally eclipsed when her younger sister Georgiana, loveliest of the Sheridan girls, entered society. George Norton, who was neither fashionable nor rich, was heir-presumptive to his brother. He was quite good-looking, though short and thick-set; but cold in manner, slow, dull and obstinate, entirely unsuited to be the husband of an impulsive, warm-hearted young woman. Where Caroline was romantic and generous George Norton was petty, resentful and cruel; yet, for all her charm, Caroline was self-centred and tactless, and although she had many devoted friends and admirers she had a fatal propensity for making influential enemies. George Norton also made enemies; and the only other characteristic the couple shared was an inability to live within their income.

The marriage, which started badly, soon developed into a dog fight, with politics as the largest bone of contention. George Norton was a Tory, the Sheridans ardent Whigs; and even when he entered Parliament his wife never tried to hide her Whig partialities. At the outset he was besottedly in love:

but Caroline's chief interests were her three little sons to whom she was passionately devoted; her writing (she made a name for herself as a poetess, novelist and the editor of a magazine); and the famous people who thronged her little house in Storey's Gate, Westminster. Her most constant visitor was Lord Melbourne, a member of the Whig Government at the time, whom she first met when she wrote asking him to use his influence to find her husband a job.

Caroline and Lord Melbourne, who was old enough to be her father, were soon on friendly, affectionate terms; and it is scarcely surprising that George Norton was irritated, if not by the friendship, at any rate by some of his wife's indiscretions. On one occasion at a party given by the French Ambassador she is said to have kicked Lord Melbourne's hat over his head, to the amazement of the diplomatic corps. Yet, despite their familiarity, the pair always insisted that there was nothing but friendship between them.

Meanwhile, George Norton was becoming increasingly abusive and physically cruel. Caroline ran home to her family, who welcomed her with open arms. Her husband persuaded her to return; but the quarrels and the dog fights continued, and in the spring of 1836 they came to a head. While Caroline was visiting her sister George Norton sent the three children and their nurse to the house of a relative with orders that their mother should not be allowed to see them. He then prepared to take his revenge in divorce; and he brought a suit for the alienation of his wife's affections against the man he could injure most—Lord Melbourne, who by this time was Prime Minister. In so doing, he believed that could strike a blow against the Whigs, gain heavy damages, and utterly discredit his wife.

The case, which was tried in June 1836, aroused tremendous excitement. There was not a vestige of proof that Caroline had committed adultery with Lord Melbourne or with any other man; and the case was dismissed without the jury retiring from the box. But, if George Norton was baulked of his revenge, the trial had not done his wife an atom of good beyond establishing her innocence. Although her good name had been smirched and she continued to be the object of spiteful gossip, she had not been represented at the trial because she was not legally a party to the suit and, as a married woman, she could neither sue nor be sued. It was only after the trial that the full gravity of her situation was brought home to her. She could—and did—live with members of her family; but in law her property and every penny she possessed, even the money she earned from her writing, (all of which would have been her own had she remained single) belonged to her husband. Infinitely worse, however, was the fact that the children belonged to him unconditionally; and without his permission she might never see them again until they came of age. Indeed, had she been pregnant at the time the law would have allowed him to take the baby from her as soon as it was born.

After the trial George Norton, still in his way in love with his wife, begged her to come back. While he still hoped for a reconciliation Caroline was allowed an occasional glimpse of her children, who looked to her anxious eyes both ill and unkempt. When he realized that Caroline would never return he struck again; and there was a distressing scene in which the shrieking children were torn from their mother and packed off to George Norton's sister in Scotland.

By his cruelty and his obstinate refusal to allow Caroline to see the boys again George Norton made an enemy of John Bayley, his counsel at the Melbourne trial. Bayley, who had been doing his best to mediate between husband and wife, was so revolted by Norton's intransigence and his behaviour to a woman who cared nothing for her property but only for the welfare of her children, that he severed his connection with his client.

Caroline now began to fight back with the only weapon she possessed—her pen; and she gave up her other work to devote herself to the writing of pamphlets which sought to change the law. 'It is the cause of all the women of England,' she wrote. 'If I could be justified and happy tomorrow, I would still strive and labour in it; and if I were to die tomorrow it would still be a satisfaction to me that I had so striven. Meanwhile, my husband has a legal lien (as he has publicly proved) on the copyright of my works. Let him claim the copyright of THIS. . . .'[19] She had found an ally in a young sergeant at law,

Thomas Noon Talfourd, who had appeared as junior counsel for Lord Melbourne in the trial and had every sympathy for those mothers who were unjustly deprived of their children. After certain delays Talfourd, who was Member of Parliament for Reading, introduced his Infants' Custody Bill into the House of Commons in 1838. The Bill passed the Commons but was thrown out by the Lords.

During the month in which the Bill was being debated in the Lords the *British and Foreign Review* published a scurrilous attack on Caroline, linking her name with Talfourd's in a very obvious manner, calling her a 'she-devil' and other terms of abuse, and upholding her husband's point of view. Distressed and furious as she was, Caroline could not bring an action for libel against the paper. Instead, she did the only thing she could and wrote a letter to the *Examiner* which was also reprinted in *The Times*. Six months later she wrote *A Plain Letter to the Lord Chancellor on the Infant Custody Bill*, in which she set down with force and reason the arguments in favour of the Bill. Because she feared her own name would carry no weight Caroline signed the pamphlet 'Pearce Stevenson'. It was sent to every Member of Parliament and every peer; and it undoubtedly assisted the cause; for the Infants' Custody Bill was reintroduced and became law in the summer of 1839. Under the Act it was decreed that mothers against whom adultery had not been proved should be allowed to keep their children under seven and have access to their older children at stated intervals.

After the passage of the Bill George Norton became more amenable, and Caroline was now allowed to have her sons with her from time to time. To her intense grief the youngest died at the age of eight from tetanus after a fall, caused she believed by the carelessness of his father's relatives; but her reunions with the other two brought her the greatest joy.

Yet her life was far from easy. She was extremely sociable by nature and never managed to live within her income, and George Norton continued to take every opportunity of helping himself to the funds to which the law entitled him. She was still a fascinating, attractive woman and strongly affectionate but she could never marry. Her closest friendship of these years— indeed, the closest friendship of her life—was with the statesman Sidney Herbert; but their romance ended with his marriage to another woman. It was not, perhaps, fortuitous that he married soon after his name and Caroline's had been linked in a much-publicized rumour that she had betrayed secret information to *The Times*. Caroline herself seems to have been unaware of the rumour, which was quite without foundation; but years later George Meredith gave it credence in his novel *Diana of the Crossways*, for whom Caroline served as the model.

When Caroline's sons came of age she saw much more of them, especially of the elder, Fletcher, an endearing young man but very delicate, who entered the diplomatic service and died from tuberculosis at the age of twenty-seven. Brinsley, the younger son, was less malleable and more troublesome. He, too, was tubercular and he settled in Italy where he married a peasant girl and had two children by her. By an odd quirk of circumstance Caroline, who had fought so passionately for the right to her own children, was entrusted with the care and education of her grandchildren.

George Norton died in 1875; and two years later, at the age of sixty-nine, Caroline married an old and trusted friend, Sir William Stirling Maxwell, who was some years her junior. And yet, with a degree of calm happiness at last within her grasp, she died within three months of her marriage.

Caroline had never concerned herself with the equality of the sexes. 'I for one', she had written in her letter to the *Examiner*, '(with millions more) believe in the natural superiority of man, as I do in the existence of God . . . I never pretended to the wild and ridiculous doctrine of equality.'[20] From her own bitter wrongs she sought to change the law and the Infants' Custody Bill owed much to her persistence. Two more of her pamphlets, *English Laws for Women in the Nineteenth Century* (1854) and *A Letter to the Queen* (1855) influenced the passage of a Bill to reform the Marriage and Divorce Laws which became law in 1857. Under the new law it was stipulated that a deserted wife should be protected in the possession of her earnings from any claims her husband might make. And, among other clauses, the courts were empowered to direct the payment of separate maintenance allowances to a wife through her trustee; a separated or divorced wife was permitted both to inherit and bequeath her own property as though she were single; and a wife separated or divorced from her husband was given the power to enter into contracts in her own right and to sue, or be sued, in civil proceedings. These concessions, small as they were, reflect Caroline Norton's bitter experiences and show that her rebellion had not been in vain.

In the meantime, a year after the passage of the Infants' Custody Bill and seventeen years before the Marriage and Divorce Laws Bill, attention was drawn in a dramatic fashion to the ridiculous disabilities under which English women laboured. In 1840 the World's Anti-Slavery Convention convened by the British and Foreign Anti-Slavery Society was held in London; and to the shocked amazement of the all-male British delegation there were four women among the American delegates. The brazen quartette were promptly relegated to a curtained gallery and forbidden to speak during the proceedings, whereupon their leader, William Lloyd Garrison, who had arrived in London later than his colleagues, declared that he preferred to join the ladies and refused to take part in the ensuing discussions.

The American women, incensed by their reception, returned home to work for—and achieve eight years later—the first Women's Rights Convention. In England the idea was slow to germinate and spread, and it was opposed at every stage by women as well as men. An influential and prolific author, Mrs William Ellis, made it her business to underline the need to keep woman safely in her subservient rôle. 'In the case of a highly gifted woman', she wrote, 'even where there is an equal or superior degree of talent [than that] possessed by her husband nothing can be more injudicious, or more fatal to her happiness than an exhibition of the least disposition to presume upon such gifts. Let a husband be once subjected to a feeling of jealousy of her importance . . ., and her peace of mind and her free agency are alike destroyed for the rest of her life; or, at any rate, until she can convince him afresh, by a long continuance of the most scrupulous conduct, that the injury committed against him was purely accidental and foreign alike to her feelings and her inclinations.'[21]

By this time the unorthodox were beginning to make themselves heard. In 1843, for example, a woman writer, Mrs Hugo Reid, demanded absolute political and educational equality between the sexes in her book *A Plea for Women*. This book, the forerunner of a host of suffrage leaflets, impressed all but the converted as a piece of wild eccentricity. Nevertheless, the suffrage question was raised from time to time in public and in the House of Commons. During the Anti-Corn Law agitation Richard Cobden declared at a public meeting in Manchester that he would like to see women have the vote. In 1848 he supported a motion in the House of Commons to give the vote to all householders, women as well as men. Disraeli, who had not yet held government office, spoke in favour of the motion. 'In a country governed by a woman', he said, 'where you allow women to form part of the estates of the Realm . . ., where you allow women not only to hold land but to be ladies of the manor and to hold legal courts—where a woman by law may be a church warden and overseer of the poor—I do not see, where she has as much to do with State and Church, on what reasons, if you come to right, she has not the right to vote.'[22]

Disraeli might, as a private Member, support the suffrage; it was to be quite another matter when he took office. Cobden's motion was dropped; and it had no immediate result unless 'the great care with which the word "male" was inserted into the voting clauses of subsequent Poor Law and Local Government Bills can be attributed to this cause'.[23]

The first real champion of the women's cause was J. S. Mill, the brilliant and precocious son of a father who had claimed in an article on government in the *Encyclopaedia Britannica* of 1823 that women were fully represented by their husbands. Mill's long friendship with Harriet Taylor (it apparently was no more than a friendship until in 1849 her husband died and she was free to marry him) quickened his sympathy for the politically down-trodden women. In 1851 Harriet Mill wrote an article on *The Enfranchisement of Women* for the *Westminster Gazette*; and in this, Mill maintained, lay the germ of his own famous work *The Subjection of Women* (1869). Mill's theme resembles Mary Wollstonecraft's *Vindication*; but Mill expressed it with less heat and superior clarity and logic. 'The object of this essay', he declared, 'is to explain . . . the grounds of an opinion which I have held from the very earliest period when I had formed any opinions at all on social and political matters . . . That the principle which regulates the existing social relations between the two sexes—the legal subordination of one sex to the other—is wrong in itself, and now one of the chief hindrances to human improvement; and that it ought to be replaced by a principle of perfect equality, admitting no power or privilege on the one side, nor disability on the other.'[24]

In 1861, three years after his wife's death, Mill advocated women's suffrage in his treatise on *Representative Government*; but in *The Subjection of Women* he demanded not only the suffrage but the emancipation of women from the state of subservience in which they had languished for so long.

Chapter II

THE PHILANTHROPISTS

The forerunners of the women's movement had shown how women of the leisured classes could, if they were so minded, help the needy. If few could follow the splendid trail of Elizabeth Fry, there were many who could with safety and propriety support the work of a Sarah Trimmer. Potential Sunday school visitors need not, she declared, 'apprehend any disagreeable consequences'[1] in their contact with the children of the poor: provided they conducted themselves in a well-bred manner their very presence would help to improve the standards of hygiene and behaviour of their pupils without endangering their own superior position in society.

Duty towards their parents came first in the lives of these would-be do-gooders. Apart from this duty, given willingly or unwillingly, Sunday school teaching or district and cottage visiting formed the sole outlet for their energies; but during the eighteen-fifties and sixties there were many girls whose parents refused to allow them to do any sort of work and condemned them to remain in enforced idleness. Charitable work when it began was a haphazard affair, but it was gradually transformed into organized philanthropy. There was an immense amount to do, and where the need was greatest women pressed forward to fill it. They were conspicuous for their patient, courageous work in the most trying conditions and above all, perhaps, for their total lack of self-consciousness.

Among these new pioneers two at least were outstanding— Mary Carpenter (1807-77) and Louisa Twining (1820-1912).

Mary Carpenter was the eldest child of a pious Unitarian divine, Lant Carpenter, headmaster of a Bristol boys' school. She and her sister were educated in their father's school where they received a sound classical and scientific training which placed them well ahead of the vast majority of girls of their age. For some years after she left school Mary continued to study, and in 1829 she and her mother opened a girls' school in Bristol. But teaching middle class girls did not satisfy the yearnings of a young woman who longed to be of use in the world. Her life was rooted in her religion, and her religion demanded of her service to the under-privileged. The starting-point of her career was a meeting with an American philanthropist, Dr Joseph Tuckerman of Boston, who visited Bristol in 1833. He drew her attention to a wretched looking little boy who rushed out of a dark alleyway as they passed by in the street. That boy, remarked Dr Tuckerman, ought to be followed to his home and something concrete done to help him.

From her childhood onwards Mary Carpenter had been known in the family as 'motherly'. So now, quite naturally, she gravitated towards work for the children of the poor. In 1835 she founded a Working and Visiting Society in Bristol and remained its secretary for twenty years; and when in 1846 she realized that nothing at all was being done for the so-called 'gutter' children she started a 'ragged' school in the Bristol slums. Her pupils were abjectly poor. Some were homeless and parentless; and the homes of the more fortunate were squalid in the extreme. The children formed a wild and lawless gang, unaccustomed to discipline of any kind. Some seemed mentally retarded; yet under their teacher's benign influence they made more progress than she had at first thought possible. It was an inspiring sight, wrote her friend, the stout, amusing suffragist and anti-vivisectionist Frances Power Cobbe (1822–1904), to watch her 'teaching, singing, and praying with the wild street-boys, in spite of endless interruptions caused by shooting marbles into hats on the table behind her, whistling, stamping, fighting, shrieking out "Amen" in the middle of the prayer, and sometimes rising *en masse* and tearing, like a lot of bisons in hobnailed shoes, down from the gallery, round the great school-room, and down the stairs out into the street. These irrepressible outbreaks she bore with infinite good humour.'[2]

Good humour, patience, and love were the chief characteristics which Mary Carpenter brought to her work. Soon she had

1. Mary Wollstonecraft

2. Emily Davis and Elizabeth Garrett presenting the first Women's Suffrage Petition to J. S. Mill, 1866

extended its scope by starting a reformatory school for boys in John Wesley's old house at Kingswood, near Bristol; and later she opened a similar school for girls in an Elizabethan building known as Red Lodge not far from her own home. She worked on the principle that the introduction of children who would otherwise be criminals to the influence of healthy home surroundings would give them the necessary impetus to go straight and thus become useful members of society. She loved her delinquents and she trusted them: the difficulty was to find assistants willing to give her unconventional methods a fair trial. 'We must not attempt to *break* the will', she wrote, 'but to train it to govern itself wisely; and it must be our great aim to call out the good, which exists even in the most degraded, and make it conquer the bad.'[3] Her methods were amazingly successful. Before long her delinquent boys and girls could be trusted to go shopping in Bristol with money in their pockets, and although they might have absconded very few of them did so. There were lapses, of course. On one occasion Mary Carpenter learned that two of her former girls, having failed to keep straight, were in prison in Winchester. She went at once to visit them; and the moment they saw her one of them cried out in relief, 'Oh, Miss Carpenter, I knew you would not desert us!'[4]

Mary Carpenter was both moved and amused by such touching evidence of faith. One of her strongest attributes was a sense of humour which never deserted her even at the most trying of moments. In one of her reports she laconically recorded the return of a delinquent who had absconded from Kingswood. 'He came back', she wrote, 'resembling the prodigal in everything except his repentance!'[5] And at all times, said Frances Power Cobbe, 'the events of the day's work, if they bordered on the ludicrous (as was often the case), provoked her laughter till the tears ran down her cheeks'.[6]

Initially, Mary Carpenter's reformatory work, which had financial backing from certain rich philanthropists, had no legal sanction; she herself had no power to deal with absconders, and the majority of juvenile delinquents were still given prison sentences from which most of them emerged to a life of crime. The success of her methods and her persuasiveness in argument

were largely responsible for the passage of the Youthful
Offenders Act of 1854, which authorized the establishment of
reformatory schools under the aegis of the Home Secretary. This
was a personal as well as a public triumph for Mary Carpenter:
by nature the most modest and retiring of Victorians, she had
forced herself to give evidence before a Select Committee of the
House of Commons, although the ordeal made her shake with
fright. Thereafter, however, her complete involvement in her
work enabled her to speak in public with self-possession and
fluency. She became a frequent contributor to the discussions
of the Social Science Association, which was founded in 1857
and held an annual congress at which current social problems
were debated; and she spoke with authority at meetings of other
societies. She was also interested in the establishment of industrial schools, where boys and girls from poor homes could
receive a useful industrial training. She opened two such
schools in Bristol, one for boys and one for girls, with the object
of convincing the Government that more could and should be
done on these lines; and the Industrial Schools Acts of 1857,
1861 and 1866 owed much to her ideas and example.

After the death of her parents Mary Carpenter had moved
to a house close to the girls' reformatory school; and in 1858,
not content with mothering her problem children and agitating
on their behalf, she adopted a child who had been left in the
charge of a missionary. 'Just think of me with a little girl of my
own!' she wrote with glee. 'About five years old, ready made to
my hand, and nicely trained, without the trouble of marrying,
etc.—a darling little thing, an orphan. I feel already a *mère de
famille*, and am quite happy in buying little hats and socks, and
a little bed to stand in my own room, out of my own money.
It is a wonderful feeling.'[7]

From girlhood onwards she had been troubled about the
condition of women and girls in India; but she was over sixty
before she found time to go and see things for herself. She paid
four visits to India, studied prison reform and opened a girls'
school in Bombay; and on her return from her last visit she
founded the National India Association with the object of
extending the knowledge of India and its needs. She also studied
the reformatory systems of European countries; and at the age

of sixty-six visited America and Canada to investigate prison conditions.

At home, she supported among other women's causes the movement for higher education; and one of the last acts of her life was to sign a memorial to the Senate of London University praying for the admission of women to medical degrees. A month later, on the evening of June 15, 1877, she said her usual goodnight to her adopted daughter and went upstairs to bed. Some time before morning she died quietly in her sleep.

The movement for the enfranchisement of women did not at first make a strong appeal to Mary Carpenter, although later she signed a number of petitions in its favour. 'I don't talk about my rights, I take them'[8] she had said: and this remark aptly sums up the life's work of a brave and practical visionary.

Running parallel with Mary Carpenter's work is the work of her near-contemporary Louisa Twining, the originator of Workhouse Reform. Louisa Twining was one of the nine children of a prosperous tea merchant, a scholarly man and a member of the Royal Society and the Society of Arts. Her home life was secure and happy, and there was no need for her to work; but she and her elder sister Elizabeth (1805–89) both felt they owed a debt to society. Elizabeth Twining, who wrote a number of religious and philanthropical books, organized mothers' meetings in London and was concerned in the establishment of Bedford College for women in 1849.

Louisa's career was with a lower stratum of society. She possessed the energy and drive of Mary Carpenter, together with a lively intelligence and a probing mind. She was drawn into district visiting by way of friendly calls on a retired nurse of the family who lived in the parish of St Clement Danes. When she went to see the old nurse she sometimes called on her neighbours, and was shocked by the conditions in which they lived. But she was still more shocked by the state of the Strand Union Workhouse, to which one of these old people retired. In 1853 when Louisa Twining first saw it, the Strand Union was a noisome place. One of its drawbacks was a laundry in the cellars which filled the building from one week's end to the next with the steam and smells from the paupers' washing. Workhouse food was disgusting and totally inadequate:

the wards were a jumble of the aged, the depraved and the drunken. There were no proper arrangements for nursing the sick, who were housed in rooms in the main building and cared for—when they were cared for at all—by elderly inmates who happened to be sufficiently sober at the time and could be bribed for their pains with beer and extra food. For laying out the dead and for specially unpleasant tasks a small glass of gin was expected as an additional bait. The mortality rate, especially among mothers and children, was appallingly high; while the combined sounds of carpet-beating which went on all day outside one of the men's wards, the tinker's shop which was situated outside another, and the women's insane ward immediately beneath the lying-in ward, effectively deprived the inmates of rest. Even worse than the physical conditions in Louisa Twining's eyes was the dreadful loneliness and monotony of the existence. Coffin and shroud-making was the only occupation of the inmates; and the frequent arrival of the parish hearse to remove a corpse the only break in the monotony.

The Strand Union was typical of the workhouses of the time: in some conditions were even more scandalous; yet no improvements or alleviations were thought necessary. Louisa Twining had quickly taken it on herself to go about among the 500 inmates of the Strand Union bringing small gifts with her. When, however, she applied to the Poor Law Guardians for permission to recruit a band of volunteers to help her she was curtly informed that voluntary efforts would endanger the discipline of the workhouse and create an inconvenient precedent. Undeterred by the rebuff, Louisa Twining put on her best bonnet and cloak and took a cab to Whitehall to interview the Guardians. She was extremely nervous, a fact which was not lost on the hall-porter. 'You need not be afraid, ma'am', he told her; 'you will find they are very nice gentlemen indeed.'[9]

Kind they may well have been; but Louisa Twining had to nag at them for more than a year before they gave a reluctant consent to organized workhouse visiting, and then only on condition that it was carried out quietly and unobtrusively. As soon as the necessary permission had been obtained an orderly band of women turned up, 'carrying snuff, tobacco, tracts, hymnbooks, and spectacles to the aged poor'.[10] They were as quiet and unobtrusive as the Guardians could wish, but they kept their eyes wide open and once outside the workhouse they were free to speak and write about the offensive conditions within.

In the meantime, Louisa Twining had written a paper on *The Condition of our Workhouses* for the 1857 congress of the Social Science Association: it was the first time the subject was debated in public. She followed this up with a paper on *Workhouse Management* for the 1858 congress, and with letters and articles for the Press which attracted a great deal of notice and led to the formation of a proper Workhouse Visiting Society.

An important aspect of Louisa Twining's self-imposed task was her agitation for the better accommodation of the adolescent girls who were herded in the women's wards with their drunken and depraved seniors. The solution seemed to her and to her friends to lie in the establishment of industrial schools in which these girls could be trained and to which they could return when out of work. She emphasized this point in 1860 in evidence to the Newcastle Commission which had been set up to enquire into the state of popular education; and in 1862, partly as a result of her representations, an Act was passed which empowered Boards of Guardians to finance the maintenance of the young in certified homes. By this time Louisa Twining had herself opened a home in London for girls who would otherwise have had to return to workhouses after periods of domestic service. She lived in the home and managed it for many years, finding to her 'grief and disappointment' how little could be done to combat 'the inherited wickedness, vice, and drunkenness of generations'. And she came to the conclusion that 'the fearful tempers' with which she occasionally had to deal 'were, without doubt, forms of insanity owing to the same causes'.[11]

Louisa Twining was equally concerned with the destitute and incurably sick, who often languished for years in the ordinary workhouse wards, with no comforts, and no care beyond the doubtful attentions of the so-called pauper nurses. In 1861 there were only two hospitals for incurables, some 80,000 of whom still endured a living death in English workhouses. Louisa Twining was not the first in this field: recom-

mendations had already been made by Frances Power Cobbe
and her friend Margaret Elliot, daughter of the Dean of Bristol,
that the patients should be housed in special wards, regularly
visited, and provided with essential comforts. But she took up
the work with her usual energy and enthusiasm and for
twenty-eight years was the chief social worker in a home for
'incurable women', as the sufferers were appropriately called.

Gradually other workhouse abuses were being reduced or
abolished; and after 1875, when for the first time women
became Poor Law Guardians, further ameliorations were made.
Louisa Twining was a member of the Kensington Board of
Guardians from 1884 to 1890; and, after her retirement at the
age of seventy-four, she was still acting as chairman of the
executive committee of an organization for the recruitment of
women Guardians. Like Mary Carpenter, she could look back
on a lifetime of endeavour and achievement.

Today, of course, it is customary to equate the desire to serve
still evinced by a small minority of the population with the need
to get rid of a burden of guilt. Be that as it may, to women like
Mary Carpenter and Louisa Twining, bulwarked as they were
by their piety and the conviction that what they did was right,
the effort to live up to their own ideals was always a battle.
The sights, the sounds and the smells of the squalor, poverty and
the moral and physical degradation to which they were continually exposed must have been very hard to endure; yet to
their eternal credit they not only endured but overcame them.

The work of these devoted women could not have been
carried on without financial help. Louisa Twining's home for
workhouse girls was one of many supported by the most
generous of all the benefactors of good causes, the Baroness
Burdett-Coutts (1814–1906).

Angela Burdett, the youngest child of Sir Francis Burdett,
was born in London. Her mother was one of the three daughters
of the prosperous banker Sir Thomas Coutts, all of whom made
brilliant marriages. Coutts, who became a widower at the age of
seventy-one, married again a fortnight after his wife's death.
His second wife was his mistress, an actress named Harriot
Mellon, thirty years his junior. Coutts's daughters were scan-
dalized and showed their displeasure by cold shouldering their

stepmother. They were still more annoyed when their father died in 1822, leaving Harriot the whole of his fortune. Harriot Coutts then married the Duke of St Albans and lived on her riches until 1837.

Angela was only a year old when her grandfather's second marriage rocked the family circle, so naturally she knew nothing about the scandal at the time. Her early training was in the hands of Hannah Meredith (later Mrs Brown), a governess of considerable character; and she spent three years in Europe with her mother, which gave her a taste for foreign travel and company. As a girl Angela Burdett was tall and plain, with a long face and a skin generally blotched with eczema. She was very kind-hearted; and formed a disinterested attachment for the step-grandmother who had been treated so unkindly by the family. When the Duchess of St Albans died there was another scandal; for she left the whole of her immense fortune (it brought in an income of about £80,000 a year) to Angela Burdett, who by that time was twenty-three.

Sir Francis Burdett, unreasonably furious that his wife had not been left the money, turned his daughter out of her home in St James's Place at an hour's notice. So Angela, with Hannah Meredith, walked across Piccadilly to her grandfather's former house in Stratton Street. The house now belonged to her; and with Hannah as her constant companion, in charge of all the household arrangements, she settled down very comfortably.

The vast inheritance did not turn Angela Burdett's head. She was intelligent and strong-minded and determined to use her money wisely. The three years she had spent on the Continent had broadened her mind; and now she set out to entertain all the distinguished foreign visitors to London and to make her friends among the foremost politicians, soldiers, scientists, churchmen, and the artists, writers and actors of the day. Almost every unmarried man she met proposed marriage; but Angela was not interested in marriage and terrified of fortune-hunters; and she had made up her mind to devote her wealth to philanthropic causes. Hannah Meredith was adroit at sensing the imminence of yet another proposal. She would retire to a room adjoining the drawing-room, leaving the connecting door ajar. When the proposal had duly been made and rejected Angela would recall her with a cough; and Hannah Meredith would return at once to change an awkward situation into general conversation.

The solitary exception to the list of Angela Burdett's rejected suitors was the Duke of Wellington. The two were close friends, and Angela had a deep veneration for the elderly hero. In 1847—when he was seventy-eight and she was thirty-three— she proposed marriage to him. 'My dearest!' he replied, having considered the matter overnight, 'You have before you the prospect of at least twenty years of enjoyment and Happiness in Life! I entreat you . . . not to throw yourself away upon a Man old enough to be your Grandfather! who however Strong, Hearty and Healthy at present! must and will certainly in time feel the consequences and infirmities of Age!'[12]

Baulked of her intention of marrying a man old enough to be her grandfather Angela Burdett proceeded to marry one young enough to be her grandson. At the age of sixty-seven she married her twenty-seven-year-old secretary, an American named William Ashmead Bartlett. When Queen Victoria heard of the impending marriage she called the bride a silly old woman. Angela Burdett had always dreaded the idea of giving up her independence; yet, when her family asked her why she did not simply let the young man live in her house without marrying him, she replied with some asperity, 'No woman is ever too old to be beyond the breath of scandal!'[13] The truth of the matter was probably that she loved him; and also that she had been desperately lonely for the past three years since the death of her devoted friend and companion Hannah Meredith. In any event, and despite the prognostications of evil, she was married in white and lived to celebrate her silver wedding; and the marriage was apparently happy.

During her lifetime Angela Burdett gave away immense sums of money to charity; and her benefactions ranged from the endowment of Colonial bishoprics to prizes for coster-mongers' donkeys; from the construction of model dwellings in the East End of London to the provision of drinking fountains for dogs. Her special concern for the welfare of women and girls was shown in the establishment and upkeep of schools and reformatories and in the provision of improved facilities for the training of girls in the National schools.

As a reward for innumerable good works the Queen over-looked her folly and raised Angela Burdett to the peerage in 1871 with the title of Baronness Burdett-Coutts; and the follow-ing year the Baroness became the first woman to receive the Freedom of the City of London. She retained her pre-eminence in death which occurred at the age of ninety-two, for the Dean of Westminster offered burial in the Abbey. Owing to lack of space, however, he made it a condition that the body should first be cremated. To this condition the widower agreed; but three days before the funeral he abruptly changed his mind and declared that as the Baroness would not have given the idea her approval the body would arrive uncremated. The Dean and Chapter now seriously considered rescinding their offer; but Mr Coutts (he had taken his wife's name) remained adamant, and in the end they gave way. After a sumptuous funeral the Baroness arrived at the Abbey to make history as the last corpse to be buried there uncremated!

Although less wealthy and—at any rate as far as the extent of her benefactions were concerned—less spectacular than the Baroness Burdett-Coutts was Lady Byron (1792–1860). In the midst of her stormy life Lady Byron took a keen interest in the charitable works of her contemporaries, Mary Carpenter among them, and was generous with her financial help. In 1834 she herself opened what must have been the first of a number of schools for pauper children; and although she complained that the children were little better than brutes, the softening in-fluence of the superintendent did wonders for their manners, and the school remained in being for nearly twenty years. 'We hear at present', wrote Harriet Martineau in 1855, 'much about the teaching of "common things"; but years before such a process was publicly discussed, Lady Byron's schools were turning the children of the poorest into agriculturists, artisans, sempstresses, and good poor men's wives. She spent her income . . . in fostering every sound educational scheme, and every germ of noble science and useful art, as well as in easing solitary hearts, and making many a desert place cheerful with the secret streams of her bounty.'[14]

While Harriet Martineau's admiration bordered on idolatry,

her approval of Lady Byron's close friend, Mrs Anna Brownell Jameson (1794–1860), who shared her interest in education but lacked the money to support it, was tepid, to say the least of it. Mrs Jameson was famous in her day as a critical writer on art and other subjects but Harriet Martineau thought her vastly over-rated and altogether inferior to her wealthy friend.

Anna Brownell Murphy was born in Dublin, the eldest daughter of a painter of miniatures, Brownell Murphy, and his English wife. When Anna was four years old the family settled in England, living first in Cumberland and eventually migrating to London. Anna, an independent child and the natural leader of her younger sisters, was intelligent and imaginative. She respected but heartily disliked the strict but efficient governess who ruled the Murphy schoolroom; but at sixteen she became a governess herself in order to help the family finances which were invariably low. Before she was seventeen she was introduced to a young barrister named Robert Jameson and fell in love with him. There was an engagement between them, but for some reason it was broken off; and Anna went off to Italy where she took another post as governess, and developed her latent interest in art, particularly church art. She did not stay away long but returned to England and four more years of teaching in a private family before Robert Jameson reappeared and the two were reconciled and married in 1825.

The Jamesons settled in London; but although they shared a taste for cultured society and for art and literature their childless marriage was unhappy almost from the start. Robert Jameson was cold and neglectful: his wife took refuge in writing, urged by her husband 'to make capital out of her talent.'[15] Anna Jameson's first book, which she published anonymously, was based on the journals she had kept while she was abroad. It was also well laced with fiction, and included an imaginary account of the death of the author and her burial in a monastery garden. The book, *The Diary of an Ennuyée*, appeared in 1826. But the author's identity was soon revealed (according to Harriet Martineau Brownell Murphy gave the game away at a dinner party); and Anna Jameson's friends were piqued at being hoodwinked into weeping at the death and burial of a woman who was still very much alive. The actress Fanny Kemble, who became one of Anna Jameson's closest friends, remarked after their first meeting that, having read the book, 'it was a little vexatious to behold her sitting on a sofa in a very becoming state of blooming *plumpitude*.'[16]

Anna Jameson's friends soon forgave her; for they were all devoted to the volatile red-haired charmer, with blue eyes, white skin and pretty, plump figure. The book had some success; and even the acidulated Harriet Martineau unbent sufficiently to remark with approval that she understood that it had been written 'to afford immediate pecuniary aid to Mr Jameson under some difficulty at the moment.'[17]

The closest of Mrs Jameson's friendships was with Lady Byron; and between these two highly emotional women, who had husband trouble in common, there were very strong bonds of affection. Yet, when Mrs Jameson was asked for her impression of Lady Byron after their first meeting in 1834 she replied without hesitation, 'implacability'.[18] In the end she suffered, as did so many others, from this implacability; for after nearly twenty years of friendship Lady Byron broke with her suddenly and violently. The reason given for the break by Mrs Jameson's niece and biographer Geraldine Macpherson was that Lady Byron had discovered after the death of her daughter Ada, Countess of Lovelace, that Ada had confided more deeply in Mrs Jameson than in her own mother. This may well have been so; but in any event Anna Jameson, whose emotional life after the failure of her marriage was centred on women rather than men, was utterly crushed by the parting. For some years she could not bear even to speak of it; and Geraldine Macpherson, her constant companion until her own marriage, who described them as 'almost one being', believed that the reason why she would never revisit Brighton after the breach 'was the fact of the many days passed there at intervals with that all-absorbing friend.'[19]

In comparison, Anna Jameson's parting from her husband was of very little emotional significance. In 1833, due partly to the efforts of his wife's influential friends, he was given an important legal post in Canada. At his request she joined him for a brief period; but the marriage had become impossible (apparently she told her mother and some of her friends that it was never consummated) and after 1836 they never met again. He agreed to make her an allowance of £300 a year but this was seldom if ever paid; and when he died in 1854 he left her nothing; and she was saved from penury only by the generosity of her friends who combined to give her an annuity of £100.

Both before and after her husband's death Anna Jameson wrote unceasingly. As the mainstay of her widowed mother and sisters and her niece Geraldine, whom she adopted and educated, she wrote a number of pot-boilers—'compilations of no great literary pretensions'[20]—but she also had her successes, including *Characteristics of Women* (1832), essays on Shakespeare's women characters; and her monumental *Sacred and Legendary Art*, a pictorial history of the Church from Roman times to the seventeenth century, which was published in four sections, the last remaining unfinished at her death. In her *Memoirs and Essays* (1846) she said some realistic things about the treatment of private governesses, but maintained that a governess's character was of more importance than her intellectual qualifications.

Hard work and adversity greatly changed her buxom appearance; and when in middle age she first met Carlyle he described her as 'a little hard, broad, red-haired, freckled, fierce-eyed, square-mouthed woman; shrewd, harsh, cockney-ish, irrational.'[21] But although initially he disliked her intensely he and his wife soon warmed towards her and she was a frequent visitor to Cheyne Row. Elizabeth Barrett, who was also somewhat daunted by her appearance, soon became her friend and so did Robert Browning. More than once they were on the point of confiding the secret of their engagement to her but refrained for fear that afterwards she would be blamed by the Barretts. When they reached Paris on their wedding journey Browning sent for Anna Jameson, and after a week of rest for Elizabeth Browning they all travelled together as far as Orleans.

Anna Jameson went abroad whenever she could, hunting material for her books—'a perpetual flitting from place to place'[22] was Harriet Martineau's sour comment; and it was typical of her industrious search for truth that her last illness should have been brought on by a chill which she caught in a snow storm as she ploughed her resolute way home from a day's work in the British Museum.

On her visits abroad she had inspected a number of sister-hoods and other nursing institutions. She was much impressed by them; and in 1855 she gave a drawing room lecture in London on *Sisters of Charity*. The following year she spoke on *Communion of Labour*, a plea for men and women to co-operate in a mighty effort to right the prevailing evils of society, and to women in particular to undertake prison and workhouse visiting and teaching in reformatory schools. It was once said of her that 'if she had been a mother, or, in the ordinary sense of the term, a wife, she would not have been found in the ranks of the "strong-minded".'[23] But among the strong-minded she was much admired, and rightly so, for she was competent, sensible and kind; and her lectures created a sensation in literary and philanthropic circles and were afterwards published and widely read.

In 1859 she attended the annual congress of the Social Science Association and joined in a discussion on the employ-ment of women. When she spoke, said one of her admirers, Bessie Rayner Parkes (later Mrs Louis Belloc—1828–1925), 'a deep silence fell upon the crowded assembly. It was quite singular to see the intense interest she excited. . . . Her singularly low and gentle voice fell like a hush upon the crowded room, and every eye bent eagerly upon her, every ear drank in her thoughtful and weighty words.'[24]

The success of the lectures had persuaded Bessie Rayner Parkes that something practical should be done to implement Anna Jameson's ideas. She and her friends were already involved in the struggle for married women's rights and the fight for girls' education. And so, early in 1858, with a mixture of daring and good sense, she bought a minor periodical which happened to be for sale and in *The English Woman's Journal* she produced a mouthpiece for the women's movement in all its aspects.

Chapter III

THE EDUCATIONISTS

The most remarkable of the women who rallied round their admired Mrs Jameson after her husband's death was Bessie Rayner Parkes's close friend Barbara Leigh Smith (later Madame Bodichon—1827–91). Barbara Leigh Smith, a golden looking and golden hearted girl who served as the model for George Eliot's *Romola*, was endowed with that 'plumpitude' which Fanny Kemble had noted in Anna Jameson and was, indeed, ample in every sense of the word. She wore her abundant red-gold hair in a thick plait about her head; her features were firm and expressive; her manner overwhelmingly enthusiastic; and her energy and determination were such that she influenced the women's movement at almost every point.

This ebullient young woman was the eldest of the five children of Benjamin Leigh Smith, a Unitarian and a Radical Member of Parliament for Norwich at the time of the repeal of the Corn Laws. The family was highly intelligent, original and broad-minded, and the children were encouraged to take an interest in politics and social questions. Among Barbara Leigh Smith's first cousins was Florence Nightingale; but, as her biographer pointed out, while 'Florence Nightingale's exhibition of Smith independence won for her the esteem of the entire nation, Barbara's earned for her little more than a reputation for oddity.'[1] And yet, eccentric or not, Barbara Leigh Smith was the gadfly which stung her companions into action and as often as not supported their work financially.

Mrs Leigh Smith had died young; and Benjamin Leigh Smith had decided to keep the family together instead of sending the children to boarding school. When the family was in London the girls attended the Westminster Infant School, the first of its kind in England. They shared the work and play of the poorest children of the neighbourhood and were encouraged to give what help they could to the Swedenborgian headmaster, James Buchanan. Buchanan was unconventional to a degree; but with the aid of Swedenborgian dicta quite incomprehensible to his pupils he contrived to give them a thorough grounding in reading and writing. In his spare time he gave the little Leigh Smiths private lessons at their home in Blandford Street, characteristically devoting himself to readings from the Bible, Swedenborg and the *Arabian Nights.*

The children's minds were also broadened by travel abroad; and Barbara was given every facility to develop a decided talent for water-colour painting. When she came of age her father gave her an allowance of £300 a year; for, unlike the vast majority of Victorian fathers, he believed in treating his sons and daughters equally. This income gave Barbara an almost unheard of degree of independence; she used it for the benefit of her friends and co-workers and devoted part to the establishment of a school in a poor district of London not far from her own home.

The Portman Hall School, as it was called, was as unconventional as even James Buchanan could have wished. It was undenominational, co-educational, and entirely without class distinction. It was attended by the sons and daughters of professional men, tradesmen and artisans; and the cost for each child was only sixpence a week.

Before embarking on the venture, Barbara Leigh Smith and a friend, Elizabeth Whitehead, who was to be responsible for the bulk of the teaching, made a special study of primary education and visited a number of schools in and near London. Barbara was herself one of the first students at Bedford College for Women which was founded in 1849. Although Bedford followed the college procedure of lectures and of work which was graded by class and not by marks, its standards were those of a school, and at the outset it had many defects. At Bedford Barbara pursued her passion for art. She became a competent artist and in the future she often exhibited; but throughout her life she was never able to reconcile completely her love of art with her dedication to the women's movement.

To the conduct of the Portman Hall School, however, she brought both her love of art and her dedication. The training was sound, varied and imaginative. The day always started with singing and the reading of some story which illumined the heroism of man. 'These readings,' wrote Elizabeth Whitehead later, 'struck the keynote of the day, and indeed the work of the school. They took the children out of their homes, and opened to them possibilities of life on higher moral planes. . . .'[2] The founders of the school aimed not simply to teach but to educate —and that was something very rare at the time. The children enjoyed their work and the school flourished for ten years; it was given up only because Elizabeth Whitehead was leaving to get married. By this time Barbara Leigh Smith was also married. Her husband, Eugène Bodichon, a French doctor who lived in Algiers, was as original and eccentric as Barbara herself. When asked once why she had chosen to marry him her reply was that he so closely resembled her idea of Caractacus. 'He is a native of Brittany,' she told Elizabeth Whitehead, 'in fact an ancient Briton.'[3] She found her raven-haired, raven-bearded Caractacus extremely handsome. Some of her friends thought him hideous and were far from enamoured of his habit of wandering in the woods about his wife's Sussex home clad in an Arab burnous or nothing at all. But, like his wife, Eugène Bodichon was a reformer. In Algiers, he was deeply concerned with the prevention as well as the cure of disease: he was keenly interested in anthropology and natural history, and he was one of the early champions of euthanasia. He had his interests; his wife had hers: and he was quite content for her to paint in Algiers or make periodic raids on England where she kept the temperature of women's movement at boiling point.

Barbara Bodichon's involvement in the educational side of the movement was the natural corollary of her experiences as student and teacher. At Bedford College she could not have failed to see how woefully inadequate was the grounding of most of the students, who had been trained by inefficient governesses or sent to equally inefficient boarding schools.

It was, in fact, the inefficiency of the private governess and her financial straits when old or out of work which caused a few enlightened people to take a searching look at the state of girls'

3. Elizabeth Garrett and
   J. S. Anderson

Josephine Butler

Sophia Jex-Blake

4. Emily Davis

Anne Jemina Clough

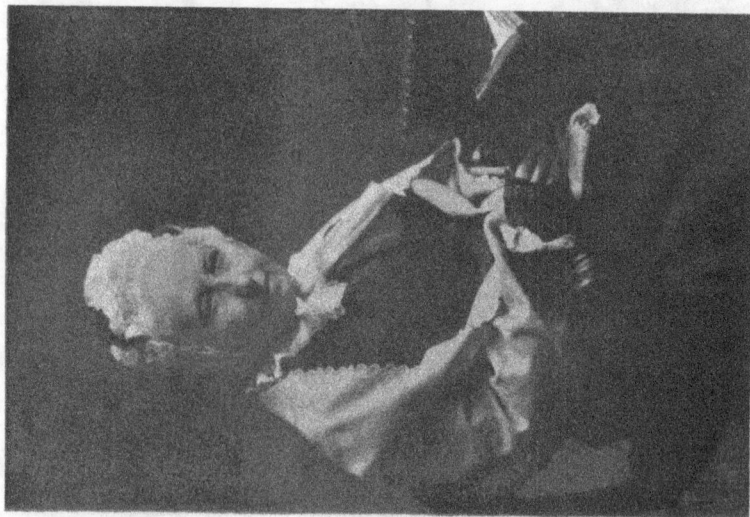

education among the large and prosperous middle classes, at a time when, paradoxically, their poorer sisters in the National schools were being educated in much the same way as the boys.

For years, apart from marriage, the career of governess had been the only one open to middle class women who had to earn a living. It was all very well for a kindly contributor to *Blackwood's Magazine* to suggest 'that it would be an excellent thing if all single women would get married as fast as they can, and the rest hold their tongues in a dignified manner';[4] but not every woman could hope to marry, and where was the dignity in suffering acute and unnecessary poverty in silence? The trouble was that most governesses were almost as ignorant as their pupils; and they were often grossly overworked and shockingly underpaid.

In 1841 a ladies' committee was formed with the object of 'affording assistance privately and delicately to ladies in temporary distress', and so the Governesses' Benevolent Institution came into being. The committee met fortnightly, 'and the amount of actual *destitution* among educated (sic) women, which thus came to their ears, is appalling to imagine'.[5] Scores of pathetic women now presented themselves to the committee for relief. They were in need of more than financial help, a fact abundantly clear to the Rev. Frederick Denison Maurice (1805–72), Professor of English Literature at King's College, London. Maurice, who had been interested in furthering women's education since his student days, was determined to see teaching raised to an honoured profession, with good pay and conditions; and so he and his friends in the Christian Socialist group, who had already been campaigning for improved pay and conditions for women workers in factories, mills and workshops, decided to institute an examination for a teaching diploma. The idea had to be abandoned, for the would-be candidates were far too ignorant to pass any examination however simple. Instead, Maurice and his friends (they included Charles Kingsley and Dean Trench, later Archbishop of Dublin) gave a series of lectures to governesses and other women who cared to attend. The lectures were so popular that with some financial assistance which was

D

providentially forthcoming at the moment they were used to form the nucleus of Queen's College for Women, which was opened in 1848 in a house in Harley Street next door to the Governesses' Benevolent Institution.

Queen's College, like Bedford, was more a school than a college. The various courses, though arranged primarily for governesses, were open to all girls of twelve years of age and over. They proved so successful that it soon became imperative to divide the students into seniors and juniors and to start a school in the house for younger pupils. Bedford College was not initially as successful as Queen's: the fact that it was undenominational had something to do with the suspicion with which the Victorians regarded it. Bedford was endowed by a generous widow, Mrs Elizabeth Reid, and opened some six months after Queen's in a house in Bedford Square; and, like Queen's, it took students of twelve years and upwards. The majority—but by no means all—of the students were already teaching or planning to teach. Among the exceptions at Queen's College were the poetess Adelaide Anne Procter (1825–64) an enthusiastic adherent of the women's movement; and Sophia Jex-Blake (1840–1912) who stormed the fortress of the medical profession for women; and foremost among the teachers were Frances Mary Buss (1827–94) and Dorothea Beale (1831–1906).

Frances Mary Buss was the daughter of a feckless artist and an intensely practical mother who supported the family by running a school. Frances Mary, after the most rudimentary education, had begun teaching at fourteen. At eighteen she was running a school of her own: at twenty-three she embarked on her life's work by founding the North London Collegiate School for girls—or ladies as they were then called. She was not free to attend lectures in the daytime, and so night after night she tramped to Harley Street and back from Camden Town, where she lived and where her school was situated, in order to attend the evening classes. For this reason she did not meet Dorothea Beale, who was there at the same time but attended during the day; but the two were to work closely together in the future in the Headmistresses' Association which they helped to found and in kindred bodies.

Dorothea Beale, three years Frances Mary Buss's junior, was the daughter of a scholarly doctor who was prepared to give his daughters the best education that money could buy. As a result, they had been taught by a series of incompetent governesses and sent to two boarding schools, one a finishing school in France and no better than its English counterpart.

Both these young women found at Queen's College precisely the sort of training they required; and both went on to provide for other girls what they themselves had lacked in their youth. Miss Buss returned to consolidate and build up her school. The North London was predominantly a day school, democratically run, without any class or religious distinctions. The fees were low, the standard of attainment high; and the girls were expected to work extremely hard. Later, Miss Buss established another school—the Camden—where the fees were even lower and which offered scholarships to take the brighter girls on to the North London. In 1871 she handed over her flourishing school to a board of governors and it became a public school, although she herself remained on as head mistress.

Dorothea Beale stayed on the staff of Queen's College for several years. Then, after a difference of opinion with the authorities and an unhappy experience as head mistress of the rigidly narrow Clergy Daughters' School at Casterton (the original of Charlotte Brontë's 'Lowood'), she found her niche. In 1858 she was appointed principal of the first proprietory girls' school in England, the Ladies' College at Cheltenham. The College was at a very low ebb at the time; but over the years Dorothea Beale transformed it into an exceedingly large and highly efficient day and boarding school, with its own branch for higher education, a kindergarten, and a teacher training department. Although Miss Beale could be practical when she chose she was by nature a mystic: one of her pet schemes (not surprisingly, it never came to fruition) was to found a dedicated order of teachers run on strictly monastic lines. She felt a strong affinity with the Anglo-Saxon scholar-saint, Hilda of Whitby, and named three of her additional works in her honour. These were St Hilda's, Cheltenham, a residential training college for secondary school teachers; St Hilda's College, Oxford; and St Hilda's in the East, a charitable settlement in the East End of London run by former pupils of the Ladies' College.

Miss Buss was also religious but she was no mystic. The accent in her schools was on sound and competitive work. To Miss Beale, however, competition was anathema; and she stood aside from some of the educational plans which were being formulated and put into action within the framework of the women's movement.

The chief protagonist (more accurately the ring-leader) of these plans was Emily Davies (1830–1921). Emily Davies was the dutiful daughter of a country parson. She had practically no formal education; but her father insisted that she should write weekly for his correction a piece of English composition. This task undoubtedly helped her to form a style of writing notable for its trenchant clarity.

Whenever she could escape from family and parochial duties at home Emily Davies came to London. Through one of her brothers, Lewelwyn, a London clergyman, and a firm believer in the ability of women to accept responsibility, she met Denison Maurice and was drawn into the educational circle. A chance meeting with Barbara Bodichon quickened her interest in the women's movement; and she was glad to do whatever work she could at the office of the *English Woman's Journal* in Cavendish Square.* When her father died she and her mother came to live in London, and her active work for the movement began.

Emily Davies, a dainty, demure looking little woman, was in reality a tough and doughty fighter. She soon made up her mind that what she wanted—and what she was going to get—was higher education for women. It infuriated her to see her friend Elizabeth Garrett's way to a medical degree cut off by London University's refusal to allow her to sit for the Matriculation examination; and so her first step was to form a committee of sympathisers (it included Barbara Bodichon) with herself as secretary, with the object of gaining the admission of girls to the university local examinations which had recently been opened for boys. After a certain amount of preliminary

* In December 1859 the offices were moved to a larger house in Langham Place.

skirmishing Cambridge University gave permission in the autumn of 1863 for a private and unofficial trial examination of girls to be held in London at junior and senior levels. 'Our breath was quite taken away,' wrote Emily Davies to a friend. She had fully expected a rebuff, and the favourable answer 'has thrown us into dreadful agitation. We have only six weeks to work up our candidates, and who can expect them to come up on such short notice? . . . We shall look unspeakably foolish if we have no candidates after all.'[6]

Emily Davies knew that she would never be able to find enough candidates in London alone: there were 25 from the North London Collegiate School; a number from Queen's and Bedford Colleges and several from other schools, including a school in Nottingham Place run by the social reformer Octavia Hill (1838–1912) and her family. But many more were needed if anything like a proper showing was to be made; and this meant bringing girls to London from the provinces, housing them and finding chaperones. Emily Davies could not hope for any candidates from Cheltenham, for Miss Beale was suspicious of public examinations which, she thought, could not fail to foster an undesirable spirit of competition. In the end she mustered 83 candidates. Not one of the girls had hysterics or collapsed with brain fever as her antagonists had confidently predicted. In fact, the girls acquitted themselves singularly well, except in the all-important subject of arithmetic in which there were 42 failures. To Miss Buss's fury ten of her 25 were among the casualties. She realized, as did the examiners, that this was the result of bad teaching; and so in future her pupils were relentlessly drilled in arithmetic and the mathematical machinery of her school was overhauled.

The next step was to get the examinations opened to girls on a permanent footing. Emily Davies set the stage at a special meeting of the Social Science Association held in April, 1864; and she sent a carefully worded invitation to the secretary of the London Centre of the Cambridge local examinations. 'We want you to come and testify (if you can conscientiously)', she wrote, 'that everybody behaved properly and nothing alarming or scandalous happened at the experimental examinations.' A number of Cambridge men were also being invited, she added, 'especially enemies, to give them a chance of being converted. I only hope the speakers on our side won't go off, as our enemies always do, with theories. It is dreadfully unsafe.'[7] She was astute enough to understand that her enemies would not be impressed by the sight of row upon row of plain and earnest-looking supporters of female education; and so she packed the front rows with young and good looking or elegant women. Among them was Elizabeth Garrett, who looked 'exactly like one of the girls whose instinct is to do what you tell them.'[8] 'Were you not delighted with the ladies?' she wrote afterwards to a friend. 'I gazed at them with serene satisfaction, feeling that their presence was doing as much good as other people's speeches.'[9]

The meeting had been surprisingly successful; but to Emily Davies' annoyance one of her own supporters had had the temerity to suggest that some of the examination subjects—Greek and mathematics—should be modified or omitted for girls. She herself was determined—and so was Frances Mary Buss—that girls should sit for the same examinations as boys and on precisely the same terms. In the end she got her way: after a three-year trial period Cambridge recognized the examinations for girls as a fixture and Oxford followed suit in 1870.

These concessions had been won in the teeth of fierce and prolonged criticism from certain quarters. The *Saturday Review*, for example, which never ceased to snipe at the women's movement, remarked that there was 'a strong and ineradicable male instinct, that a learned, or even an over-accomplished young woman is one of the most intolerable monsters in creation.'[10] And even among those who favoured an improvement in girls' education there were many to whom public examinations with the inevitable rivalry that accompanied them, were double suspect. 'Is this what the nation wishes?' asked Canon J. P. Norris at a meeting of the Social Science Association in September 1864. 'Are not the two sexes, in mental constitution as in all else, marvellously, beautifully, and distinctly supplemental one to the other? . . . Let men and women, by all means, if they wish it, study the same branches of knowledge with a most absolute liberty; but let them do it each in their own way, following each their own nature freely; and then, under nature's free unconscious guidance, each will develop their own congenital excellence, and the self-adjusting balance of humanity will not be disturbed.'

The *English Woman's Journal*, though naturally it differed in sentiment from the Canon, was not far behind him in rhetoric. 'Let woman put her shoulder to the slowly revolving wheel of progression', wrote one contributor, 'and she need not fear to be left behind, nor to be refused the countenance of her fellow-worker, man.'[11]

Emily Davies's shoulder was constantly at the wheel. She wrote a paper *On Secondary Instruction Relating to Girls* for the September 1864 meeting of the Social Science Association, in which she trounced official indifference to the subject and said some hard things about the men—and the women—who opposed it. 'On all sides', she declared, 'there is evidence that as regards intelligence and good sense, English women of the middle classes are held in small esteem. "A woman's reason" means, in popular phrase, no reason at all. A man who lets it be known that he consults his wife endangers his own reputation for sense. A habit of exaggeration, closely verging upon truthfulness, is a recognized feminine characteristic. Newspaper writers, expressing the prevailing sentiment, assume towards women an indulgent air which is far from flattering, giving them credit for good intentions, but very little capacity.' As for the women, they did little or nothing to refute the contention: they were seldom in good health or intellectually vital. 'It is rare to meet with a lady of any age, who does not suffer from headaches, languor, hysteria, or some ailment showing a want of stamina . . . Dullness is not healthy, and the lives of ladies are, it must be confessed, exceedingly dull . . . Busy people, and especially men, have a very faint and feeble conception of what dullness is . . . They think dullness is calm. If they had ever tried what it is to be a young lady, they would know better.' She was not asking for much, she maintained; merely the right for girls to be allowed to prove that their minds were not inferior to those of boys. 'In a word, let female education be *encouraged*—let it be understood that the public really *cares* whether the work is done well or ill—and the minor

practical questions will ere long find for themselves a satisfactory solution.' Emily Davies's sentiments might be extreme
yet she was enough of a Victorian to get a male supporter to
read her paper for her, and to sit listening in a nervous flutter
for fear that he would disown her more forceful remarks.

She had timed the reading of her paper well; for during the
summer of 1864 a Schools' Inquiry Commission had been set
up to examine middle-class education. An earlier Commission—
the Newcastle—had examined conditions in the primary
schools: another—the Clarendon—had dealt with the boys'
public schools. The new Commission (called the Taunton after
its Chairman Lord Taunton) was to deal with the schools
which lay between these two extremes; and so indifferent were
the authorities to the problem of girls' education that, while
girls' schools were not as much as mentioned in its terms of
reference, they were not expressly excluded.

Emily Davies soon put this little matter right. She gathered
from her preliminary soundings that there was a possibility that
the terms of reference could be interpreted as they stood to
include girls' schools, but there were also rumours to the
contrary. She therefore set to work with the help of one of her
co-workers—Miss Eliza Bostock—to draw up a memorial to the
commissioners and to persuade as many influential people as
possible to sign it.

To her intense relief the commissioners agreed to include
girls' schools, although it was pointed out to her that the
investigation would be narrower in the case of girls than in that
of boys. This was so because many girls were educated in private
schools and their head mistresses could refuse an inspection if
they wished; and also because the number of endowed girls'
schools in England which would automatically be open to
inspection was ridiculously small.

There was no need to remind Emily Davies of these obvious
facts. She was only too well aware that in the vast majority of
schools the education was superficial and frothy; and that while
there were endowments in plenty for boys' schools there were
practically none for girls'. She expressed her indignation on the
latter score in another paper for the Social Science Association
—*The Application of Funds to the Education of Girls*—in which she

pointed out that money intended for girls' schools was actually being diverted to schools for their brothers, and made an urgent plea for the foundation of scholarships and exhibitions for girls.

The findings of the Schools' Inquiry Commission revealed precisely the situation she had anticipated. While the excellence of schools such as the Ladies' College and the North London Collegiate was fully appreciated the Commission's Report told a very sorry tale of the state of girls' education as a whole, though it is only fair to say that in some cases the boys' schools were not very much better than the girls'. Miss Buss and Miss Beale, who both gave evidence to the Commission, complained most bitterly of the low standard of girls who entered their schools at twelve years of age and over; and Miss Beale produced examination papers to show how much better informed were girls in Cheltenham's National schools. Miss Buss in particular aroused the Commissioners' protective instincts by some womanly tears of nervous frustration. It was plain from her evidence—and also from Emily Davies's—that she was in favour of a similar form of education for boys and girls; but Miss Beale made it clear that she would prefer a more broadly based curriculum for girls and more freedom in the choice of examination subjects.

The paucity of endowments, the lack of scholarships, and above all the scarcity of good teachers were other important points which came to light. Trained teachers were essential, said the two head mistresses; but students from the training colleges were automatically drafted into the National schools where they were already proving their worth. Miss Beale solved this problem by establishing her own teacher training department: Miss Buss had to wait until the first of her pupils to go to Cambridge University returned to her as teachers; and she was herself instrumental in founding a teacher training college in Cambridge for students who would otherwise have started teaching without this additional preparation.

The findings of the Schools' Inquiry Commission were of great significance. They led to a most necessary overhaul of the endowment system; to the opening in towns all over the country of good, inexpensive day schools—the high schools— closely modelled on Frances Mary Buss's schools; and, to Emily

Davies's unconcealed glee, to approval for the establishment of
institutions of higher education for women.

It was in 1866 that the idea first came to her that the logical
answer to the work being carried on in the more advanced
schools was higher education; but although she gained many
adherents there was a cleavage between their ideas. Emily
Davies and Barbara Bodichon called for a genuine academic
education in a college which, though independent, should be
connected for purposes of teaching and examination with an
existing university. There were others, however, who wanted
a more broadly based system with a wider choice of subjects and
in some cases—Greek and mathematics for example—a lower
standard of attainment. These people argued that since the prevailing system for men was not wholly satisfactory it should not
be imposed on women. Emily Davies did her best to win over
the other side but she was unable to do so and was powerless to
prevent some of her own supporters from deserting. The two
categories could not therefore present a united front to their
enemies, who were many and furious and prepared to fight to
the last ditch for the right to keep women in intellectual subjection. They were still convinced that men were superior;
and that any attempt at university education would either unsex
the women or drive them into a nervous and physical breakdown. To these arguments the *Scotsman*, a champion also of
medical education for women, replied that 'the difference
between men and women is not dependent on difference of
training; but . . . as tenderness does not make a man effeminate,
but nearer to the highest ideal of manliness, so courage,
dignity, and wisdom would make woman not masculine, but
more intensely womanly'.[12]

Womanliness and equality were the keynotes of Emily
Davies's educational saga; and in 1862 and again in 1866 she
tried to persuade the University of London that in the interests
of justice women should be allowed to matriculate.* She was
intensely annoyed to learn that, instead, a special examination
for women over seventeen was being contemplated, which
would offer a wider choice of subjects than the matriculation.
This examination, which came into force in 1869, drew from

* cf. Chapter 4.

her a typical retort. 'I am afraid', she wrote to a friend on the University Senate, 'the people who are interested in improving the education of women are a thankless crew . . . We are really obliged to Convocation for their kind intentions in offering us a serpent when we asked for a fish, tho' we cannot pretend to believe that serpents are better for us.'[13]

She was of course considered thankless; and she made no secret of her opposition to the special examination. Since, however, it was all that London would offer she accepted the compromise, and the special examination remained in force until 1878 when the University opened all its examinations and degrees to women.

There were to be no special examinations in her dream college, which was to offer advanced tuition and examinations of the Pass Degree and Honours standards of Oxford or Cambridge. Cambridge, the first university to open its local examinations to girls, was naturally her choice of the university to which her college might be affiliated; and her Cambridge friends encouraged her in the idea. Early in 1867 she was writing to Barbara Bodichon in Algiers: 'Now that the scheme is about to be brought down from the clouds, it seems necessary to make some sort of statement about it . . . The best plan seems to be to have a rather large general committee of distinguished people to guarantee our SANITY, and an executive to do the work.' She had been advised, she continued, that at least £30,000 would be needed to establish the college and maintain it until it could pay its way. 'It is not a large sum, considering that there is to be but one college of this sort for Great Britain, Ireland, and the Colonies, and considering how easy it is to raise immense sums for boys' schools. But considering how few people really wish women to be educated, it is a good deal.'[14]

Emily Davies herself subscribed £100, Barbara Bodichon, who was well off and generous, £1,000;* and within a year the contributions amounted to £2,000. Despite her generosity and her enthusiasm Barbara Bodichon was not initially invited to become a member of the general committee, which was both influential and undenominational (it included a devout Church

* She left the college £10,000 in her will.

woman, a Unitarian and a Jewess). Emily Davies, a stickler for etiquette, was suspicious of women who 'jumped like kangaroos';[15] and Barbara Bodichon, a flamboyant character, was too closely associated with the suffrage fight to be generally acceptable. Emily Davies had temporarily relinquished her own suffrage work in order to devote herself to education; but in 1869 she relented, and Barbara Bodichon, whose advice had already been freely sought and taken, was invited to join the committee.

The committee was faced with two main problems. The first was money, which was not coming in as quickly as had been hoped: the second was the examination syllabus. A number of supporters of the college were opposed to the suggestion that students must work for the Cambridge Ordinary (or Poll) degree, which they considered unworthy of a university, or the Tripos, which they considered too specialized. Led by Henry Sidgwick, Fellow of Trinity College, these malcontents decided to present a memorial to the University asking for the creation of special advanced examinations for women.

A special examination, however advanced, was a 'serpent' to Emily Davies; but to Anne Jemima Clough (1820–92), an educationist of a much milder kind, it was a perfectly edible 'fish'. Anne Clough, a sister of the poet and much influenced by him, was born in Liverpool, the daughter of a cotton merchant, but spent her childhood in South Carolina where her father had business interests. The Clough boys went to English schools and universities, but Anne's education was as haphazard as Emily Davies's. She was sixteen when the family returned home, a self-conscious, gauche girl, her mind resolutely set on doing good. She started teaching; and after her father's death in 1840 she and her mother migrated to Ambleside in the Lake District where she opened a school of her own. Over the years her educational interests widened; and in 1866 she organized a Liverpool branch of the Schoolmistresses' Association, founded earlier in the year by Emily Davies for the benefit of teachers and governesses. With the help of Josephine Butler and her husband, who was Principal of Liverpool College, Anne Clough arranged for a series of lectures to be given to women and girls in several northern towns. From these lectures sprang the North of England Council for Promoting the Higher Education of Women, with Josephine Butler as President and Anne Clough as Honorary Secretary. The Council's immediate goal was the establishment for women of an examination higher than the university locals. This brought Anne Clough in touch with Henry Sidgwick and his friends, who presented their memorial to Cambridge University in 1868, and were rewarded the following year with the establishment of the higher local examination for women over eighteen.

Emily Davies was furious. 'I have heard', she wrote to a friend, 'that [Miss Clough] is pressing the scheme on the ground that it will be specially adapted to women's needs. I have known this all through, but it has not hitherto been necessary to dispute about it. Now, however, the question is being put: Do practical, thoughtful, and working women want degrees and a common standard, or is it only the clamour of a few fanatics and women's rights people? . . . You see it won't do to blow the trumpet with an uncertain sound. It only leads to misunderstandings, and the misunderstandings reappear at Cambridge . . .'[16] She stuck to her guns, even though the majority of her own committee thought she was being unreasonable. 'We do not want certificates of proficiency given to half-hearted women',[17] she roundly declared.

She was feeling sore not only because of the success of Sidgwick's memorial but also because for lack of adequate funds her dream of a full-sized college was fading. Barbara Bodichon had seen the red light first. 'I know you thought I was damped', she wrote after a particularly trying meeting, 'but that is not true, but I should have shut my eyes and closed my reason to all evidence if I had not seen up and down the world this last two months that there is a frightful coolness about the College.'[18]

To Emily Davies, there was only one way to stop the rot: to open a college, even a small one, without further delay. In the circumstances a small house with a few students seemed best. Barbara Bodichon and others on the committee were in favour of a house in Cambridge; but Emily Davies turned down this suggestion out of hand. It would be most injudicious, she argued, to let the young women loose in a university town, where the 'smallest indiscretion on the part of any student would be disastrous'.[19] She therefore went ahead on her own and took a small house in Hitchin, Hertfordshire, which was far enough from Cambridge to avoid the danger of indiscretion but not too far for the Cambridge lecturers and tutors who had promised to visit the college. In October, 1869, the first five students, chosen from twenty-one aspirants, arrived. They were welcomed at the door by Emily Davies, who could scarcely contain her pride and excitement in the new adventure.

Emily Davies was not prepared to take any office and so allow her freedom to barter for further concessions to be hampered; but while she refused to become Mistress of the College (except once in an emergency) she was constantly around. Her duty, as she saw it, was to produce good examination fodder, no easy task since the students were most inadequately grounded. She would not yield an inch, however, and gave them only three years and one term—the same period as the men—to take their Tripos examinations. The Tripos was the goal for them all, for the authorities would not give permission for women to take a Pass degree. They had to do an immense amount of preliminary work: some took as long as two years to get through the Cambridge Previous examination, with its compulsory mathematics and classics, leaving themselves barely four terms to complete their degree course.

Their tyrant also saw to it that work was interspersed with health-giving country walks and games of cricket and fives in the garden. She took them swimming in the Hitchin public baths; and even learnt to play fives herself; but she would not countenance football, which by no stretch of the imagination could be called ladylike. Never for a moment did she relax her hold on the proprieties; and there was a nasty moment for the students when they dressed up as men to act scenes from *Twelfth Night*. Emily Davies told them that their outrageous behaviour would bring the college into disrepute; they replied that she was violating their rights as individuals; and it took all Barbara Bodichon's tact and persuasiveness to smooth things over.

Barbara Bodichon, a constant visitor, thought the accent on plain living and high thinking too pronounced. A diet of boiled beef and mutton might be nourishing, for example, but it was certainly dull; and the walls of the rooms were drab until she brightened them with a selection of her own sketches. She invited the students to stay in her Sussex home during the vacation, and in this and other ways did her best to soften the impact of Emily Davies's insistence that the sole reason for their continued existence was the good of the college. And for one term she took it in turns with another enthusiast, Lady Stanley of Alderley (1807–95) to act as Mistress.

The students were allowed to take their examinations only unofficially and by courtesy of the examiners. They were not members of the University and they could not be awarded degrees; but there was great rejoicing when in 1873 two of them passed the Tripos examinations in classics and one in mathematics. Nobody could deny any longer that a woman's brain was as good as a man's

In 1873 the lease of the Hitchin house expired, and Hitchin was incorporated as Girton College. In 1874, despite Emily Davies's misgivings, the College moved to Girton on the outskirts of Cambridge.

By this time a series of lectures had been organized in Cambridge leading to the higher local examination; and the success of the lectures underlined the need for a residential hostel for women students. Emily Davies, when approached, refused to ally her college with any other; and so in 1871 Anne Clough had been invited to take charge of Merton Hall, a house which had been acquired for the purpose. Merton Hall was moved to Newnham in 1875 and was incorporated as Newnham College five years later. The serious, conscientious but undynamic Anne Clough was Principal of Newnham for twenty-one years. Her system was the antithesis of Emily Davies's. Not for Newnham students the desperate race for the Tripos. Initially, they were encouraged to work only for the higher local examination and they could take their time about it. By 1885, however, four-fifths of the students were in fact working for the Tripos; and after a series of impressive Girton successes the first woman to be placed above the Senior Wrangler was a Newnham student. Most appropriately, she was Philippa Fawcett, the daughter of Elizabeth Garrett

Anderson's younger sister, the suffrage leader Millicent Garrett Fawcett. Yet even this culminating success would not drive the authorities into admitting women formally to examinations and degress and so to membership of the University.

Chapter IV

THE DOCTORS

One of the most outstanding figures in the women's movement was Elizabeth Garrett (later Mrs Garrett Anderson—1836–1917) who joined the circle of women workers in 1859 at about the same time as her close friend Emily Davies. The new house in Langham Place was large enough for rooms to be used as a club and was known as the 'Ladies' Institute'. There was a luncheon room and a reading room well stocked with papers and journals; and the women who thronged the Institute could scheme and plan to their hearts' content.

Elizabeth Garrett, six years Emily Davies's junior and greatly influenced by her, looked just as demure and accommodating and in reality was equally pertinacious. She was the second daughter of a self-made business man, Newson Garrett of Aldeburgh in Suffolk, who was as adventurous and original in thought as Benjamin Leigh Smith. At thirteen Elizabeth with her elder sister Louisa was sent for two years to the Academy for the Daughters of Gentlemen at Blackheath, run by the Misses Browning, step-aunts of the poet. If their education was not very advanced, at least the girls left school with a fair knowledge of French and a determination to continue their studies. At home they were expected to take some part in household activities; but Elizabeth continued to read and to tackle Latin and mathematics with some help from her brothers' tutor. She also kept in touch with her schoolfriends and it was through some of them that she first met Emily Davies, at the time still immersed in domestic duties and social work in her father's parish.

Louisa Garrett, gentlest but most inspiring of sisters, married in 1857 and went to live in London; and Elizabeth Garrett and

E

Emily Davies met often in London when the former was staying
with her sister, the latter with her clergyman brother; and they
gravitated naturally to the busy hive of women's righters in
Langham Place, where the *English Woman's Journal* and other
activities were being carried on. The campaign for higher
education waged by Emily Davies and the campaign to open
the medical profession to women waged by Elizabeth Garrett
were carried on simultaneously; but of the two the fight for
medical education was the harder. At first, Elizabeth Garrett
had no idea of studying medicine, but in 1859 she attended
some lectures on the subject given by Dr Elizabeth Blackwell
(1821–1910).

Elizabeth Blackwell was born in England but had been
brought up, and lived, in America. In 1849, after graduating
with the highest honours at the Geneva Medical College in New
York she became the first woman to gain an American medical
degree. She then went to Paris to continue her studies but was
refused admission to every hospital and clinic except the
Maternité, an institution for the training of midwives. While
working at the *Maternité* she caught an ophthalmic infection
which destroyed the sight of one eye and also her ambition of
becoming a surgeon. In 1850, having recovered her health and
spirits, she came to London; and there she was given permission to attend lectures by the authorities at St Bartholo-
mew's Hospital, the Professor of Midwifery alone refusing to
countenance her presence. She made very little contact with
the students, however, and was feeling lonely and rather lost
when Bessie Rayner Parkes and Barbara Leigh Smith sought
her out, eager to be friends with a woman who had made
medical history. They introduced her, among others in their
circle, to Florence Nightingale, who spoke freely to her of her
hopes and ambitions; to Lady Byron and to Mrs Jameson.
Elizabeth Blackwell basked for a while in this soothing atmosphere of admiration and then decided to return to America to
practise medicine in New York. Although her credentials were
impeccable she could not obtain a post. She therefore set up in
private practice, and by hard work and undeniable competence
broke down the prejudice against her as a woman doctor. In
1852 she gave a series of lectures on the physical education of

girls which showed that she had a serious contribution to make to the subject; and these lectures were reprinted in book form and well received. By 1857 she was sufficiently established to realize one of her dearest hopes; and on May 12th New York's first Infirmary for Women and Children was opened and staffed entirely by women.

Medical training for women was by now carried on in several cities besides New York; and in 1858 Elizabeth Blackwell was persuaded by her friends in London to pay them another visit and help them to begin an assault on the British medical profession. While she was in England the British Medical Council agreed to put her name on the Register. Had she arrived a year later this would not have been possible; for under a new charter the Medical Council closed this loophole to the profession by refusing to admit to the Register the holders of foreign degrees. In future, only candidates trained in recognized British schools would be eligible.

Encouraged by the success of Anna Jameson's lectures, while she was in England Elizabeth Blackwell gave a series of lectures on *Medicine as a Profession for Ladies*. She spoke with quiet authority and deeply impressed her audience with her sincerity and appeal to reason rather than emotion. To one member of the audience Elizabeth Blackwell made an especial appeal, 'the bright intelligent young lady whose interest in the study of medicine was then aroused—Miss Elizabeth Garrett'.[1]

When, by arrangement, Dr Blackwell and Elizabeth Garrett met the older woman had assumed that the younger had already decided to try for a medical career. In fact, Elizabeth Garrett was far from sure if this was what she wanted; but she was too polite to say so, and in the course of their talk her mind was made up. 'I remember feeling very much confounded', she wrote in after-life, 'and as if I had been suddenly thrust into work which was too big for me.'[2] But the decision once made (and the masterful Emily Davies had a good deal to do with it) there was no going back, although the twenty-three-year-old girl made her plans with understandable caution. She could not hope for day-to-day advice from Dr Blackwell, who returned to America in the autumn of 1859 with the object of training students for the British field; but she had the solid—though not always uncritical—support of Emily Davies who was in no doubt at all about the wisdom of her choice, and her sister Louisa, now Mrs Smith, whose London house became her home.

It was not until the following summer that Elizabeth Garrett broke the news of her determination to her parents. Newson Garrett was astounded and, initially, disgusted. But Elizabeth was not deterred. 'He will soon be reconciled if I succeed', she wrote confidently to Emily Davies.[3] Mrs Garrett was a different proposition: for two days she stayed weeping in her bedroom, moaning that Elizabeth would disgrace the family if she left home to earn a living. Elizabeth remained obdurate; and she ignored the warning of family friends who told her that she would be the death of her mother if she persisted in her insane ambition. Instead, she relied on her father's love of justice and freedom to bring him to her side. In this she was not disappointed. Newson Garrett not only withdrew his opposition but took her on a round of visits to Harley Street specialists to get advice on the best means of starting a medical career. This advice, given in some cases with rudeness and contempt, was entirely negative; but with each refusal Newson Garrett's determination to help his daughter by every means in his power was strengthened.

Elizabeth's next move was to call on Mrs Russell Gurney, wife of the Recorder of London, who was himself an advocate of higher education for women. Mrs Gurney was a member of a committee which had been set up as a result of Dr Blackwell's lectures to encourage the idea of medical training for women. She gave Elizabeth Garrett an introduction to William Hawes, a governor of the Middlesex Hospital, who arranged for her to be admitted if she showed that her intention was really serious. Elizabeth Garrett therefore suggested that she should work as a nurse for six months. Her offer was accepted; and she was attached to a surgical ward, which in those pre-Listerian days was very far from being a place for the fainthearted.

Almost from the start, however, Elizabeth was treated more as a student than a nurse. She was allowed in all the wards in attendance on the doctors; and by May, 1861, she was also attending lectures and demonstrations, working in the dissecting room and receiving private coaching. This last concession gave her some anxious moments. Emily Davies, ever mindful of the proprieties, had advised her that she should not receive private tuition from a man; but on this occasion Elizabeth took the contrary advice of others and nothing untoward happened. Another problem was the question of dress. Elizabeth, a feminine young woman, disliked the working-clothes adopted by a friend with whom she was studying chemistry. 'I do wish she dressed better', Elizabeth wrote to Emily Davies. 'She looks awfully strong-minded. She has short petticoats and a close round hat and several other dreadfully ugly arrangements.'[4]

Elizabeth herself, with her pleasant looks and manner, was concerned only that the students should accept her as one of themselves; and although at the outset they were disposed to be friendly she soon destroyed their confidence by her undeniable ability. In the examinations which followed the lecture course she won a certificate of honour in each subject. 'May I entreat you,' wrote the examiner, 'to use every precaution in keeping this a secret from the students.'[5] Elizabeth breathed not a word of her success; but a little later she was tactless enough to answer correctly a question which had baffled the class of students. This was too much for their dignity: they drew up a memorial against her official admittance, which she had confidently hoped would be confirmed for the new academic year. The students argued that the presence of a woman inhibited the lecturers in the frank discussion of medical matters, undermined the respect due from rightminded men to members of the opposite sex, and held them up to the ridicule and contempt of their fellow students in other hospitals. As a result Elizabeth was informed that she would not be permitted to attend lectures after the end of the current session.

Fortunately, she was immensely resilient. She wasted no time in futile regrets but, having taken counsel with her friends, she started all over again. The main obstacle was the refusal of examining bodies to award degrees to women. This meant that no medical school would accept women students, on the grounds that if they practised at the end of their course they would be doing so illegally. A foreign degree would not help Elizabeth Garrett as it had helped Elizabeth Blackwell; for this way to the Register had by now been closed. It was therefore necessary to find some body to which the examination rule did not apply: and Elizabeth Garrett found it in the Society of Apothecaries, which stipulated under the terms of its Charter that it would examine 'all persons' who satisfied its requirements. She decided in 1862 to work for this examination, which would give her a licence to practise, and at the same time to ask permission to matriculate at the University of London, since matriculation was the first step to a full MA degree. A memorial was drawn up by Emily Davies, signed by Newson Garrett on his daughter's behalf, and supported by a number of influential people including William Ewart Gladstone, Richard Cobden, the Russell Gurneys and Frederick Denison Maurice. London University refused: it had no intention at that time of opening examinations or granting degrees to women.

Elizabeth Garrett remained serenely optimistic. Voting in the Senate had been close—ten votes for a motion to extend matriculation to women and ten against—and the motion was lost only when the Chancellor, Lord Granville, gave his casting vote against it. 'It is a most cheering sign of the turn of public opinion that we should have been so near winning,' wrote Elizabeth to her father: and to Elizabeth Blackwell: 'When they are having another Charter eight or ten years hence, we may try again and succeed.'[6]

She continued to study and to insinuate herself for brief periods into hospital wards and attend demonstrations. And in 1865, after a frustrating delay during which she received many rebuffs and was accepted—and promptly rejected—by St Andrew's University, she took the only course open to her and applied for permission to take the examination of the Society of Apothecaries. Despite the terms of its Charter the Society had never contemplated the possibility that a woman would apply and replied that this was impossible. Newson Garrett threatened legal action: and the Society, advised that he had a strong case, gave way. Elizabeth passed the examination with ease. As she wrote later to Emily Davies, two of the examiners had remarked to a mutual friend 'that it was a mercy they did not put the names in order of merit, as in this case they *must* have put me first'.[7]

The Medical Council was now obliged to put her name on the Register. The Society of Apothecaries then made sure that no other woman should slip in by the back door by passing a resolution to the effect that in future only candidates from recognized medical schools should be granted a diploma; and for the next twelve years Elizabeth Blackwell's and Elizabeth Garrett's remained the only women's names on the Register.

Now that she was a qualified practitioner Elizabeth Garrett opened a small dispensary for women and children in Marylebone, London. Within a few weeks between sixty and ninety patients appeared on each consulting day; and Elizabeth was visiting them in their homes and also acting as midwife. She loved the work; and was much relieved to find that doctors were not discriminating against her. This was a tribute to her personality and competence; for opinion in the medical profession, in the Press and among the general public was, for the most part, actively hostile to the medical education of women. Even if women possessed the necessary intellectual qualifications, which he sincerely doubted, wrote 'A Physician of Twenty-one Years Standing', for example, 'can we deny that the general delicacy of females is a serious bar to an occupation which necessitates exposure at all hours and in all weather? Are there not physical qualifications which are insurmountable . . .? And supposing it were proposed to limit the practice of medicine to ladies who had passed the grand climacteric, what a rare combination of faculties and opportunities would be necessary to insure a continuance of those studies which had necessarily commenced at an earlier period of life, when the energies of mind and body rendered the acquisition of such various knowledge possible . . .'[8]

Another objection came from patients who valued the doctor's bedside manner. In cases of prolonged chronic illness, wrote one of them, 'where a single lady in middle life is necessarily much isolated, the relation between her and her physician becomes a most valuable one; he is often the only tie between her and the outer world from which she is excluded, her only gentleman friend, adviser, and assistant in matters for which a

gentleman is needful, and he could not be *replaced* at all by a
Lady Physician'.[9]

Elizabeth Garrett was impervious to these and other objections. She was showing in her own work that there was a need
for women doctors; and she meant to underline this need by
improving her own qualifications. To this end, in 1869 she
decided to take advantage of the opening of medical degrees to
women by the University of Paris. Through influential friends
she got permission to take her degree without residence in
Paris; and in 1870, after performing two operations and answering the written and oral examinations in French, she was
awarded her MD diploma with credit. On this occasion the
medical Press condescended to give her some belated encouragement and praise. 'Her friends,' declared the *Lancet*,
'must have been highly gratified to hear how her judges congratulated her on her success, and to see what sympathy and
respect were shown by all present.'[10]

In the same year she accepted an invitation from the
husbands of her dispensary patients to stand for Marylebone at
the first elections to be held for the London School Board, to
which women as well as men were eligible. She came out at the
top of the poll, high above the other candidates. Emily Davies
also won a seat on the London School Board, and so did Lydia
Becker, the prominent advocate of women's suffrage. Their
election was gratifying, declared the *Englishwomen's Review*,
which had succeeded the *English Woman's Journal* in 1866, 'as
it removes in some degree the stigma of inferiority hitherto
attached to women'.[11]

Emily Davies, Elizabeth's mentor, was delighted by her
success in both fields; but she found a certain levity in her
friend's conduct which, to her, was most reprehensible. On
more than one occasion in the past she had lectured her on this
point; and in 1870 she complained that 'it is true your jokes
are many and reckless. They do more harm that you know.'[12]
Yet this tendency to joke and be witty was part of Elizabeth's
charm: without it her devastating efficiency, sense of duty, and
a certain brusqueness of manner might well have made her
seem inhuman.

In 1871, the year of her double triumph, Elizabeth married.

Her husband, with whom she was deeply in love, was J. G. Anderson of the Orient Steamship Line, a man who supported her in all her endeavours yet never hesitated to criticize her if he thought she was being overbearing or unreasonable. As Dr Garrett Anderson, Elizabeth combined family and professional life with conspicuous success. She worked as hard and with as much thoroughness as ever, and it was through her initiative that the New Hospital for Women was opened in 1872 above the old dispensary and staffed entirely by women. Elizabeth was senior physician and the only doctor to undertake major surgery: the other doctors, of course, had no British qualifications. The hospital was soon bursting at the seams with patients and before long it was moved to larger quarters.

Leadership of the campaign to open the British medical profession to women was by now in the hands of a forceful and pugnacious young woman, Sophia Jex-Blake (1840–1912). Sophia, the youngest by six years of the children of a conscientious, conventional ex-lawyer who lived in Hastings with his delicate, fretful wife, was to all intents and purposes an only child. Headstrong and unruly, passionate and emotional, she was outwardly devoted to both parents but had a powerful maternal love for her mother. Yet although she longed to please and was overcome with remorse when she failed, she was incapable of behaving like a typical Victorian girl and lacked Elizabeth Garrett's tact and charm. Her parents sent her to a succession of repressive boarding schools in a futile attempt to cure her 'wildness'. 'You behaved so ill,' wrote her mother on one occasion, 'that I doubt if I could have borne another day without being laid on a bed of sickness, and I might never have recovered.'[13]

Sophia could repent but she could not amend. At school, she always excelled in mathematics and Latin though not in religious knowledge or deportment, and one school refused to keep her. By the standards of the day she was very well taught, but she finished her education without any promise of a career to canalize her energies and undoubted ability or to provide relief from the storms of her unhappy, tormented nature. Her parents expected her to marry; but since she was not allowed to go to theatres or parties she did not mix with her contemporaries who, in any event, would have found her a difficult proposition. At eighteen, however, she learned of the existence of Queen's College, and decided on the spot that to Queen's she must go. Elizabeth Garrett would have waited for a propitious moment to sound her father: Sophia Jex-Blake was too impatient to wait a single day. 'Tried to speak to Daddy last night,' she wrote in her diary. 'He very impracticable, I after a while very undutiful. At last I went into hysterics, which frightened him dreadfully, poor old man. I shall certainly go.'[14]

She did; and within a year she was offered the post of tutor in mathematics on the staff. By now, Mrs Jex-Blake was too cowed by her unpredictable daughter's demands to make any protest; but Mr Jex-Blake was made of sterner stuff. Wage-earning was unladylike, he told his daughter, and if she must teach she should do so in a voluntary capacity. Why should it be wrong for her to teach, demanded Sophia, and right for her brother Tom?* The exasperated Mr Jex-Blake insisted; and for once in her life Sophia gave way. But, having taught for a year unpaid at Queen's College, she took herself to Germany to teach; and, on her return home, informed her parents that she wished to study the American system of education, since teaching was to be her life's work. Germany had seemed bad enough; America was far worse; but this time her parents both bowed to the storm and let her go without too many protests.

In Boston Sophia met one of Elizabeth Blackwell's protégés, Dr Lucy Sewell, Resident Physician to the New England Hospital for Women and Children; and the course of her life was changed. In Lucy Sewell, a strong-minded but attractively feminine young woman three years her senior, Sophia found inspiration and also the friend for whom her emotional nature craved. She was fascinated by the importance of the work already being carried on by women doctors and so medicine began to supplant education as her goal. Since Lucy Sewell was the epitome of charm and as ladylike as even the exacting Mr Jex-Blake could wish Sophia brought her on a visit to England. The Jex-Blakes capitulated and put up no defence when Sophia told them that she wanted to study medicine in Boston.

* Later Principal of Cheltenham College and Headmaster of Rugby.

She returned to America and with high hopes entered the Boston Medical School. But in the autumn of 1868 Mr Jex-Blake died very suddenly; and Sophia, who could never do anything by halves, impulsively threw up her work and went home to mother her mother. The situation was quite impossible: Mrs Jex-Blake and her daughter were incompatible; and there was no room in the house for two martyrs. Sophia stayed at home until the end of the year, studying in her spare time, and then decided to try for a medical degree at a British university. Her affection for Lucy Sewell was unchanged; but she probably felt it her duty to remain within reach of her mother.

As she knew, there was no point in approaching London University which had turned down Elizabeth Garrett's application, and a tentative approach to Cambridge was met with a blank refusal. But an introduction to Edinburgh University from Josephine Butler, a recent acquaintance, sounded more hopeful; and in March 1869 Sophia presented herself with some trepidation before the Dean of the Medical Faculty, Professor Balfour, and Dr Christison, Professor of Medical Jurisprudence, its senior member. Professor Balfour proved a good friend and ally, and among Sophia's other friends in the University were Sir James Simpson, the gynaecologist, and David Masson, Professor of Rhetorick and English Literature, and a keen supporter of higher education for women. In Dr Christison, however, she had met a relentless, implacable enemy.

The request she made was modest enough; she merely asked permission to attend the medical students' lectures. The Medical Faculty granted her request; but in the complex structure of the University's constitution it was only one of four bodies concerned in the affair. The other bodies were the Senatus, composed of the Principal and professors of all the faculties; the General Council, which comprised all the graduates registered as members; and the University Court, a representative body which included the most influential members of the administration. The Senatus confirmed the Medical Faculty's decision; but it was promptly reversed by the University Court on the grounds that to grant special privileges to a single woman was simply not worth while.

This was only a temporary setback. Immediately the decision

was announced two new candidates appeared, Isabel Thorne and Edith Pechey. Isabel Thorne, a married woman, had spent some years in China where her child had died as a result, she was sure, of negligence and a lack of understanding on the part of the doctors. She had returned to England convinced that women and children would be better cared for by women doctors than by men and with a strong desire to qualify herself. Having learnt what she could at Bedford College of chemistry, anatomy, hygiene and midwifery she had applied for admission to the Society of Apothecaries and been rejected. Edith Pechey, a girl of twenty-four, was sure that if women were to succeed as doctors they must prove themselves not just as good as their male colleagues but better. She was modest and gay and possessed a sense of humour, an asset not possessed by Sophia Jex-Blake; but she was deadly serious in her ambition to study medicine and had only hesitated to come forward before because she doubted her ability to make good.

Two more women candidates appeared at about the same time; and Sophia, as their spokesman, requested that they should have a class of their own, and undertook to pay whatever fees were required. She also asked for permission for them to matriculate and then to proceed to a medical degree. After due consideration by the various bodies concerned the necessary permission was given; and the five women students, who had settled down to work straight away, all passed their matriculation. They were to be charged double the normal fees for the privilege of their separate class; but Sophia, who was generous as well as richer than the others, was ready to make good the deficiency.

Everything now seemed set fair; but the women had reckoned without Dr Christison and his supporters who were quietly biding their time, certain that the women could not possibly stay the course. When the class lists for the winter session of 1869–70 were published, however, they found to their dismay that all the women had passed their examinations, four of them with honours. This was a rude awakening; but worse was to follow. The hesitant Edith Pechy had come top in the chemistry examination for which a scholarship was annually awarded. The money would have been useful to Edith Pechey, apart from the prestige; but in the event the scholarship went to the man who came next to her in order of merit, and she was fobbed off with one of the bronze medals presented each year to the five best students. The authorities, pressed for their reason, excused themselves by saying that as Edith Pechey was not a member of the regular class she was not entitled to the scholarship. And yet a motion put forward by Professor Masson and seconded by Professor Balfour in the General University Council which would have admitted women to the regular classes was defeated by 58 votes to 47. Several members of the Medical Faculty, notably Drs Christison and Lacock, were positively vituperative: and Christison, who was physician to the Queen in Scotland, went so far as to make use of her name. He had, he declared, received 'a communication, not a formal message, but still a message to the effect that Her Majesty concurred with his opinion on the subject'.[15] Christison probably spoke without the Queen's authority; but he must have been well aware of her sentiments. The Queen considered the bare possibility 'of allowing *young girls* & young men to enter the dissecting room together' to be 'an *awful* idea'.[16]

Christison and Lacock, who had previously told Sophia that he could not conceive of any decent woman—let alone one who called herself a lady—wishing to study medicine, were now singled out for a sharp rebuke in *The Times* of April 25, 1870: 'We cannot sufficiently express the indignation with which we read such language, and we must say that it is the strongest argument against the admission of young ladies to the Edinburgh medical classes, that they would attend the lectures of Professors capable of talking in this strain.'

The *Lancet* was equally sharp. 'It has been reserved for Dr Lacock, professor in the most famous university of Edinburgh,' it declared, 'to set an example which we trust, even the least courteous or gentlemanly of first year's students will hesitate to follow. . . . If used [by a student] we should simply have . . . concluded that the delinquent would be at once expelled with ignominy from his school. Unfortunately there are no such punishments for highly-placed men like Dr Lacock. . . .'[17]

The women rather enjoyed the publicity they received; but,

as David Masson warned Sophia, Christison and his clique were determined to get rid of them. If Sophia had been like Elizabeth Garrett she would have tried, as Masson suggested, to wriggle on; but tact and finesse were not her strong points. She had browbeaten her father into submission; and now in Christison she saw a father-figure who could be forced to yield in the same way. Unfortunately, Christison, a respected and influential figure in university circles, was far stronger than she knew; and the male students were only too ready to follow his lead.

With the completion of the women's first full year and the arrival of new women students fresh problems arose. If the original five were to continue they must now attend an anatomy class and also receive clinical instruction in the wards of the Royal Infirmary. The first problem was solved by admitting the women to the Extra-Mural School conducted by fully qualified and authorized lecturers who were not University professors. The second proved far more troublesome. The Infirmary was governed by a Committee of Managers elected by the subscribers; and Christison, who was himself a Manager, contrived to override a preliminary decision to admit the women to the wards. The students then took a hand and organized a petition to keep them out; and, with tacit encouragement from Christison and his friends—one of whom generously remarked that it was greatly to their credit that they had not 'pelted the ladies away from the classes'[18]—they made a concerted attempt to drive them out of the Extra-Mural School. The anatomy class had been running without any trouble for about a month, but full term had not yet begun. It opened with an influx of trouble-makers, who began their campaign with knowing winks and whispers and outbursts of ribald laughter.

The women students took no notice, and the trouble-makers had to think again. November 18, 1870, was the date of the anatomy examination, and the women, nervously convinced that they would indeed be pelted, went to Surgeon's Hall in a body, shepherded by an anxious Sophia. A dense crowd had gathered outside the Hall. It consisted, wrote Sophia later, 'of the lowest class of our fellow-students . . . with many more of the same class from the University, a certain number of street rowdies and some hundreds of gaping spectators who took no particular part in the matter. Not a single policeman was visible, though the crowd was sufficient to stop all traffic for about an hour.' The women, continued Sophia, 'walked straight up to the gates.' (She does not say how they circumnavigated the crowd: maybe it gave way or else it was not quite so dense as she supposed!) The gates 'were slammed in our faces by a number of young men who stood within, smoking and passing about bottles of whisky, while they abused us in the foulest possible language, which I am thankful to say I have never heard equalled before or since.' At this moment a friendly fellow-student emerged from the hall, wrenched open the gate 'in spite of the howls and efforts of our half-tipsy opponents,' and escorted the women into the building and the anatomical classroom, 'where the usual examination was conducted in spite of the yells and howls resounding outside, and the forcible intrusion of a luckless sheep, that was pushed in by the rioters.' Dr Handyside, the lecturer in anatomy, gave the animal a quizzical look. ' "Let it remain," ' he snapped, ' "it has more sense than those who sent it here." ' When the examination was over Dr Handyside offered to let the women out by a side door. Sophia refused; and added provocatively that she assumed there were enough gentlemen present to ensure a safe conduct. Twenty-four students gallantly responded. They 'formed themselves into a regular bodyguard . . . , and encompassed by them, we passed through the still howling crowd at the gate, and reached home with no other injuries than those inflicted on our dresses by the mud hurled at us by our chivalrous foes.'[19]

It was clear that the riot was not a spontaneous outburst but an organized affair; and hints were made in the Press and in an anonymous letter received by Edith Pechey that certain professors had been behind it. During the next few weeks the women were followed in the streets by students, shouting abuse, sometimes 'using medical terms to make the disgusting purport of their language more intelligible.'[20]

The next move made on the women's behalf was a fresh attempt to get them admitted to the Infirmary. At an election

meeting of Managers a favourable panel was defeated by a very
small majority; and a little later when a motion to admit them
was introduced it was supported by a petition signed by 956
Edinburgh women. At this meeting Sophia Jex-Blake, who had
taken the precaution of becoming a subscriber to the Infirmary,
made a speech on behalf of her fellow-students. This was a
tactical blunder which Elizabeth Garrett would never have
committed; but Sophia, who had been sorely tried, had no
objection to being a martyr. 'I will not say that the rioters were
acting under orders,' she declared; but 'this I do know, that the
riot was not wholly or mainly due to the students at Surgeon's
Hall. I know that Dr Christison's class assistant was one of the
leading rioters, and the foul language he used could only be
excused on the supposition I heard, that he was intoxicated. I
do not say that Dr Christison knew of or sanctioned his presence,
but I do say that I think he would not have been there had he
thought the doctor would have strongly objected to his
presence.'

Dr Christison rose to protest against Sophia's language 'in
regard to an absentee'. Sophia was asked to withdraw the word
'intoxicated', to which she replied amid laughter that 'if Dr
Christison prefers that I should say he used the language when
sober, I will withdraw the other supposition.'[21]

Sophia's comments may well have been justified but they did
her cause no good. The petition was defeated, and the women
were denied entry to the Infirmary. And the unfortunate
Sophia found herself with an action for slander on her hands,
brought by Mr Craig, Dr Christison's assistant.

Fresh help was, however, on the way. At the instigation of
the Lord Provost an influential and representative 'Committee
for Securing Complete Medical Education to Women in
Edinburgh' was set up. The Committee, which undertook to
finance a continuance of the fight, stood by Sophia in her law
suit. Technically she had no grounds to stand on and pleaded
guilty. The jury showed its sympathy by awarding Mr Craig
a farthing's damages; but the judge countered this by ordering
her to pay the costs which amounted to £915 11s 1d. The
Committee wrote a letter to the Press inviting contributions
towards the costs: the response exceeded all expectations and

the fund was over-subscribed by £112.

Led by the *Scotsman*, the lay and medical Press were now strongly on the women's side. 'The difficulties which are put in the way of women obtaining the higher education are discreditable to the enlightenment of the age,' declared one paper—the *Daily News*—on October 27, 1871. 'The University of Edinburgh two years ago threw its Medical Faculty open. To allow those [women] who took advantage of this wise and liberal policy to be annoyed, checked, thwarted in their course, to cut them off from advantages for which they have been invited to work, and honours which they have fairly won, is not only a great injustice to them, but would be altogether dishonourable and discreditable.'[22]

The women might bask in this atmosphere of sympathy but it was getting them nowhere with the University. By the opening of the 1871–2 session the original five had taken all the extra-mural courses and could go no further without clinical instruction in the Infirmary. At the same time three new candidates whose fees had already been accepted were refused permission to matriculate; and they were only allowed to take the examination when Sophia's legal advisers informed the authorities that their action was illegal.

For the next few months the fight continued as before. Sometimes it even looked as though the women would win, but the Senatus always contrived to evade the issue. In the end a legal ruling had to be sought. The University Court had come up with the proposal that if only the women would relinquish their demand for graduation they could finish their medical education and qualify for certificates of proficiency. But certificates of proficiency were worthless, for no one could practise without a degree; and so the women's case was presented before Lord Clifford, the Lord in Ordinary, in July 1872. Lord Clifford's judgment upheld the women's claims; and five months later, after further delaying tactics, a favourable panel of Infirmary Managers was elected, and the women, now working for their finals, were at last admitted to the wards.

But the Senatus still held a trump card. It appealed against Lord Clifford's judgment; and in June, 1873, the judgment was reversed in the Inner Court by a majority of seven votes to

F

five. The University was then informed that it had no responsibility towards the women whatsoever.

An appeal on the women's behalf could still have been made to the House of Lords; but the Lord Provost's Committee, which had paid the costs of both actions, reluctantly decided against it. The decision was taken not on financial grounds alone; but also because of the endless delays which would have been involved and of the continuing hostility of the Medical Faculty. Sophia accepted the decision with a degree of courage, which was all the more remarkable because it came at a moment of bitter personal humiliation. In the midst of the legal battle, in which she had played a prominent part—canvassing, preparing arguments, and interviewing her lawyers—she had sat for her final examinations and failed. Her friends were aghast; her enemies triumphant; and she herself maintained that her papers had not been impartially judged. Fortunately, she was resilient as well as brave. She had found many friends and supporters in Edinburgh, and although the University was now closed she and her fellow-students were determined to try somewhere else.

This was easier said than done. Appeals were made to a number of medical schools but not one of them responded. Several of the women were by now so disheartened that they decided to qualify abroad and practise later in England, even though their names would not be placed on the Medical Register. This was a course which appealed to Elizabeth Garrett Anderson, who had been annoyed and embarrassed by the publicity surrounding the fight. In a letter to *The Times* on August 5, 1873, she made the point that a hundred unregistered women doctors practising medicine efficiently would draw attention and sympathy to their cause. More than one provincial hospital had already appointed unregistered women doctors to its staff, and the women were working on equal terms with the men.

This argument infuriated Sophia Jex-Blake. As she knew, Elizabeth Garrett had won her unique place by a judicious blending of hard work, ability, patience and tact; but she also knew that Elizabeth had never lacked money or the help of influential people. Sophia herself was not short of money; but few of the other women could afford to study abroad, and there was nobody to ensure that they could do as Elizabeth Garrett had done and work for a Paris degree in England. And so Sophia wrote an angry reply to *The Times* sneering at women who were content with foreign degrees and urging potential women doctors to join her in the front line of attack. She was convinced that in spite of the Edinburgh defeat the women now had enough support to continue the fight at home; and she said as much in language which was anything but restrained.

The question had already been ventilated in Parliament. It was raised again in 1874, and although the issue was postponed it was clear that there was considerable sympathy for the women's case in the House of Commons.

Sophia, who had as usual been working overtime in the background, was still hunting for an alternative route to her goal. In the process she had found two important allies, Dr A. T. Norton of St Mary's Hospital, and Dr Anstie, who had been vainly trying to persuade the Westminster Hospital to accept women students. Norton now came up with an admirable idea: that a medical school for women should be opened with lectures given by lecturers from the recognized medical schools. A provisional committee was set up; and at the first meeting it was agreed that Dr Anstie should be dean of the school and that the committee should be composed of registered practitioners. Sophia supported this decision, which automatically excluded her from membership of the committee, and agreed to act as secretary. She was determined that Elizabeth Garrett Anderson should join the committee if only because the omission of her name would do harm to the cause. Dr Garrett Anderson was very much against the idea of a women's school and so was Dr Blackwell whom she consulted; but for the sake of unity they both agreed to serve. In due course the provisional committee was replaced by an executive council made up of influential members of the public as well as doctors.

Elizabeth Garrett Anderson and Sophia Jex-Blake appreciated one another's good qualities, but they were entirely antipathetic. Sophia hated Elizabeth's caution and concern for personal dignity: Elizabeth was terrified of what the impetuous

Sophia would do next. It was unfortunate but inevitable that the two had to work in harness.

Sophia Jex-Blake was tireless in her work as secretary of the committee. Within a month of the first meeting she and Isabel Thorne had collected £1,400 from their friends to form a working capital; and she had found and gained possession of a house in Henrietta Street (later Handel Street), St Pancras. On October 12, 1874, the London School of Medicine for Women was opened, with Sophia as Organizing Secretary and 14 students, and the number increased to 23 during the first session. Unfortunately, Dr Anstie had died suddenly just before the lease of the house was signed; but Dr Norton stepped into his place as dean; and the lectures were all given by highly qualified men.

By the end of the second year of the three-year course enough money had been raised to meet most of the running costs of the School. The main difficulties still to be met, however were the refusal of the 19 examining boards to recognize the School; and the continued refusal of the hospitals to admit women for clinical instruction. There was growing support among the general public; but unless the difficulties could be overcome the School could not continue.

There was growing support also in the House of Commons, with Sophia the dominant figure behind the scenes, supplying arguments and facts and, at the request of W. F. Cowper-Temple (afterwards Baron Mount-Temple), the text of a draft Bill. In 1874 and again in 1875 Cowper-Temple introduced an Enabling Bill 'To remove doubts as to the powers of the Universities of Scotland to admit women as students and to grant degrees to women'; and although the Bill was defeated the debates had blown the issue wide open.

Since every other route was still blocked Sophia, Isabel Thorne and Edith Pechey applied to the Royal College of Surgeons in 1876 for permission to take the diploma of midwife; but the examiners, who sensed that the women would use their licence to practise as a springboard to obtain further concessions, resigned in a body rather than examine them. In the same year the Lord President of the Privy Council invited the General Medical Council to state its views on the admission of women to the profession. After a debate lasting three days the Council passed a resolution which, in essence, neither accepted nor rejected the idea.

In the circumstances the best course was to introduce another Enabling Bill. Russell Gurney steered the Bill through Parliament and on August 12, 1876, it became law. The new Act enabled all medical corporations to examine women, despite any restrictions their Charters might contain. The Edinburgh students naturally decided to approach the University, which no longer had legal grounds for refusing to examine them. Once again the Senatus was too clever; and their application was refused on the grounds that the extra-mural courses they had taken did not constitute an official part of the degree course.*

Elsewhere, however, the authorities were more amenable; and in 1877 Sophia Jex-Blake and Edith Pechey, who had by this time taken the M.D. of Berne University, took their degrees at the Irish College of Physicians, the first examining body to make use of the new powers. In the same year their names were at last placed on the Medical Register, together with the names of three other Edinburgh students. This was a triumph; but the students at the School of Medicine still lacked the all-important clinical experience. In 1876, at Elizabeth Garrett Anderson's instigation, the London Hospital was approached; but on the advice of the staff the authorities refused to countenance the idea that one or two of the teaching wards in the vast hospital should be set aside for the clinical instruction of women students. The Honorary Treasurer of the School, J. B. (afterwards Sir James) Stansfeld, M.P., then set to work to persuade the authorities of the nearby Royal Free Hospital in Gray's Inn Road to admit the women; and by the spring of 1877 he had succeeded. The following year, after a friendly interview between Elizabeth Garrett Anderson and Lord Granville, London University opened its matriculation and its other examinations and degrees to women.

The bitter fight was over; and Sophia Jex-Blake, who had been consulted by Stansfeld at every turn during the negotiations with the Royal Free Hospital, had had a very great deal

* Edinburgh did not admit women to graduation until 1894.

to do with the victory. 'Defeated at Edinburgh,' he wrote, 'she carried her appeal to . . . the High Court of Parliament, representing the Nation itself. The result we see at last.'[23]

For Sophia there had been another bitter struggle. In her capacity as Organizing Secretary of the School she had been energetic, competent and utterly loyal, though tactless and often over-bearing. But she was not always in London: she had been to Berne and Dublin, for instance, and she sometimes stayed with her mother, who had become very dependent on her. And because she was authoritative she had steadfastly refused to delegate responsibility, and so had made a number of enemies. With the opening of the Royal Free Hospital to women the status of the School was enhanced and administrative changes became necessary. At a meeting of the Executive Council held while Sophia was in Dublin receiving her degree both her name and Elizabeth Garrett Anderson's were proposed for the post of Organizing Secretary. Elizabeth, who had joined the provisional committee originally only to avoid an open breach, had no desire to become secretary and was well aware that her appointment would be a crushing blow to Sophia, who had served the School so long and so well. She therefore contrived to get the decision postponed; and before the next meeting of the Council a compromise candidate had been found in Isabel Thorne, whose appointment satisfied both factions. Isabel Thorne, Sophia's friend since their Edinburgh days, would have preferred to take her M.D. and practise medicine; and she only accepted the appointment when it became clear that Sophia would not be elected. 'About the best possible,' Sophia wrote in her diary with a really noble disregard of her own disappointment, 'with her perfect temper and excellent sense, so much better than I.'[24]

Although she remained a Trustee of the School and a Council member, Sophia could not bear to stay on in London, but went to Edinburgh where she established herself in private and dispensary practice. When in 1883 Dr Norton resigned as Dean of the School, Dr Garrett Anderson was the obvious choice as his successor. Only Sophia Jex-Blake was in disagreement: she had never forgiven Elizabeth for resisting the establishment of the School in the first place or conquered her personal animosity, which caused her to believe that but for Elizabeth's intervention she herself would have still been Organizing Secretary. For the first time since she left London, Sophia attended a Council meeting, and proposed a nominee of her own as Dean—Edith Pechey. No one seconded the proposal; Elizabeth Garrett Anderson was appointed; and Sophia, angry and humiliated, returned to Edinburgh. In 1885 she founded an Edinburgh hospital for women; and the following year, in a burst of defiance, a women's school of medicine. She never again attended a Council meeting in London; but, in her capacity of Trustee, wrote letters of protest whenever she considered that too much money was being spent on the expansion of the Medical School. On one such issue she resigned in 1897. Two years later, her own school having failed, she retired from active work and, outwardly calm at any rate, she spent the last thirteen years of her life in Sussex.

Sophia had wilfully put an end to her association with the Medical School which was indeed the child of her brain. Under Elizabeth Garrett Anderson's wise direction (she was Dean for twenty years, from 1883–1903) the School grew and prospered: and its relations with the Royal Free Hospital were cemented in 1897 when the School became known officially as the London (Royal Free Hospital) School of Medicine for Women.

For nearly thirty years—from 1866–1892—Elizabeth Garrett Anderson was senior physician to the New Hospital for Women which had developed from her small dispensary for women and children, and which, following its initial move was reopened in 1890 in new buildings in Euston Road, and after her death was renamed the Elizabeth Garrett Anderson Hospital.

When in 1902 Dr Garrett Anderson retired from the Medical School the Council showed its appreciation of her truly magnificent services by appointing her to the specially created post of President. She had already provided a successor in her brilliant protégé Dr Mary Scharlieb, who had originally been moved to train as a doctor by the sufferings of the Indian women in purdah; and to the end of her life she retained her affection for the School. The tradition of service to the School remained in her family; for her daughter Louisa, who organized the first hospital managed by women at the Front in the 1914–18 War, was one of the students; her son was Treasurer; and in the succeeding generation the connection was retained.

Chapter V

THE LADIES' CIRCLE

Barbara Bodichon, who was hand in glove with Emily Davies in her plans for higher education, was even more deeply involved in other social reforms. Her indignation at the straits to which Caroline Norton had been reduced led her to study the law as it affected married women; and in 1855, having mastered the details, she proceeded with advice from a family friend, Matthew Davenport Hill, Recorder of Birmingham, to draw up and print *A Brief Summary in Plain Language of the Most Important Laws Concerning Women.* Very sensibly, she made no comment of her own on the laws: there was no need since they spoke for themselves. Her unvarnished statement of fact was widely circulated and created an absolute sensation. Caroline Norton had learned the meaning of the laws by bitter experience, but the majority of women had little or no idea of their implications. When, for example, Mrs Grote, the historian's wife, appeared in court to give evidence that she had been robbed of her purse and her watch, she was electrified to hear these objects described as the property of her husband; and the legal explanation subsequently provided stung her into joining the ranks of the reformers.

Barbara Bodichon's pamphlet was placed by Davenport Hill before the Law Amendment Society; and the Society, after considering the laws, framed proposals which would grant property rights and the power to making wills to married women and would give them the same privileges as their unmarried sisters. The women's movement really went into action in 1855 when Barbara Bodichon held a drawing-room meeting in her father's house and, as a result, formed a committee of women to collect signatures for petitions in support of the Married Women's Property Bill which was to be introduced into the House of Commons by the Law Amendment Society. Public meetings were also held, resolutions were passed, and petitions were drawn up. Twenty-six thousand signatures were collected in the course of a year, and Barbara Bodichon was herself responsible for three thousand of them. She also drew up her own petition. This did not go forward in her name but in the names of two older, more celebrated women, Mrs Jameson and Mrs Howitt, a popular writer of stories and verses, who is remembered today—if she is remembered at all—by the verses commencing: ' "Will you walk into my parlour?" said the Spider to the Fly.'

The Married Women's Property Bill was a succulent fly in the spider's web of the *Saturday Review*. 'There is a perfect rage for Acts of Parliament to redress all the little social and domestic miseries of human life,' it declared. 'So long as the petticoat rebellion was confined to a mistaken petition of a few literary ladies whose peculiar talents had placed them in a rather anomalous position, we really had not the heart to say anything about it;' but the proposals of the Law Amendment Society 'set at defiance the experience of every country in Christendom and the common sense of mankind. . . . There is besides, a smack of selfish independence about it which rather jars with poetical notions of wedlock.'[1]

The disabilities of Caroline Norton and Anna Jameson were well known to the committee; but in their hunt for signatures they uncovered scores of equally distressing cases. The petitions, which were presented in both Houses of Parliament, made an impressive showing, especially when by mistake they unrolled themselves in the House of Lords and the women's petition alone stretched the whole length of the Chamber.

The Married Women's Property Bill was introduced in the House of Commons in May, 1857, and passed its Second Reading. But about the same time another Bill, also concerned with the tribulations of married life, was introduced. This was the Marriage and Divorce Bill, which proposed that divorce should become possible without an Act of Parliament, and made suggestions for certain reliefs to married women separated from their husbands. This was the Bill which reflected Caroline

Norton's trials and became law in 1857. It gave the opponents of reform the chance which they were quick to seize of blocking the Married Women's Property Bill on the grounds that enough had already been done to redress the wrongs of married women.

This was a cruel blow to Barbara Leigh Smith and had more than a little to do with a subsequent breakdown in health. There must have been plenty of people to sneer at the intrepid reformer who could not stand up to adversity; and Mr Leigh Smith packed his daughter off to Algiers, where she met and became engaged to her future husband.

The committee which had worked so hard was now dis-banded and its members turned to other aspects of reform.* But in the *English Woman's Journal* they had a forum on which the marriage laws and all the other known wrongs of women could be debated. As Barbara Bodichon was in Algiers Bessie Rayner Parkes bore the chief burden, and she struggled man-fully to produce a journal which should be accurate, telling and unemotional, and would give her enemies no chance to criticize or sneer. The *Journal* printed articles on the problems of employment, of education, medical education and similar subjects; and wherever possible the situation in Britain was compared with conditions in countries overseas. There were also articles on great women pioneers—Florence Nightingale, Elizabeth Blackwell and Rosa Bonheur among them; and in a lighter vein there were book reviews, stories and verses. The editor's insistence that contributions should be impartial and restrained produced a crop of dull and lifeless articles and stories and verses of an ultra-moral, banal kind. Even so, for its day and age, the *Journal* was a most praiseworthy produc-tion; and the problems it discussed were real and important.

The lack of suitable employment prospects for women came high on the list of priorities which the *Journal* debated. Accord-ing to the *Saturday Review*, 'the great majority of women who can be profitably employed are employed . . ., and brace-making, bugle-trimming, and blonde-stitching, etc., absorb,

* The Married Women's Property Acts of 1870 and 1874 pro-vided some form of relief; and the process of reform was completed by the Acts of 1882 and 1893.

in such a place as London, all profitable labour . . .' Employment, added the *Review*, was a fixed quantity and any poaching by women on men's preserves could only result in lowering the men's wages. 'Well,' commented the *English Woman's Journal* with more enthusiasm than sense, 'is even this a result which ought to alarm a philanthropist?'[2] In fact, as Harriet Martineau pointed out in an article on *Female Industry* in the *Edinburgh Review* in April, 1859, apart from employment in agriculture and in mills and factories, 'women who must earn their bread are compelled to do it by one of two methods—by the needle or by becoming educators'. She might have added a third—prostitution, a method in which the intensity of the competition had depressed women's earnings to a miserable level. Sempstresses might earn as little as a shilling for a twenty hour day; and Harriet Martineau quoted from the annual report of the Governesses' Benevolent Institution to show how pitiful were the rewards of the educators. 'The tale is plain enough,' she said. 'So far from our country-women being all maintained as a matter of course by us, "the bread winners," three millions out of six of adult Englishwomen work for subsistence, and two out of the three in independence.'[3] The great need was to extend the scope of employment openings to women and, as a corollary, to educate the women to meet their new responsibilities. There was a further need—to break down existing prejudice against the employment of women; and Harriet Martineau instanced the case of a shop-owner who tried the experiment of employing women in the drapery department, only to find that women shoppers refused to be served by members of their own sex.

While Barbara Bodichon was in Algiers she tried to ease the employment situation by writing a pamphlet, *Women and Work*, a plea to men to receive women in the professions and to women to be prepared to assume new and arduous duties. She described the idle, pampered woman who took everything and contributed nothing to the common good as an encumbrance on the earth, and she pointed to the totally inadequate rewards paid to women who worked, especially to those of the middle classes. *Women and Work* was far more discursive than Barbara Bodichon's admirable Summary of the property laws; it was badly arranged and badly written, and clearly lacked the guiding hand of Davenport Hill, for whom Eugene Bodichon was not an adequate substitute. The Press gave it a rough passage, the *Saturday Review* remarking unctuously that 'women are fatally deficient in the power of close consecutive thought . . .Men have too much experience of the sex's charming ways', it added, 'ever to trust them with government or politics, economy or moral philosophy.'[4]

Publication of *Women and Work* coincided with the publication of a second edition of a book by Bessie Rayner Parkes, *Remarks on the Education of Girls*, in which she claimed that women could make a special contribution to learning; and that their education would be valueless if it did not include a knowledge of the facts of life and freedom to read as widely as they chose.

The mere suggestion that women should be given such literary licence threw the *Saturday Review* into transports of horror. 'Is there a plague of Egypt worse than the strong-minded woman?' it cried. 'However, we do not fear that this species of vermin will ever infest English drawing-rooms . . .'[5]

'Vermin' was really the last ephithet to describe Bessie—or Elizabeth—Rayner Parkes, although it was true that her background, like that of Barbara Bodichon, was liberal, unconventional and Unitarian. She was a descendant of the Unitarian Dr Joseph Priestly, who had been forced by the weight of popular opinion to live in America; and her mother was American.

Bessie and Barbara had been friends from childhood; and one of Bessie's earliest recollections of this friendship was watching Benjamin Leigh Smith kneel down to fasten his young daughter's shoe lace. The memory of this service—so eccentric by Victorian standards—remained with Bessie throughout her life. By nature, she was more thoughtful and pliant, less impulsive and ebullient than Barbara. As she grew older she turned more and more to religion, and in middle life became a Roman Catholic, leaving Barbara to a more humanitarian way of thinking. Both girls were artistic; but while Barbara found her outlet in painting, Bessie chose poetry and produced some poems of a higher standard than the mawkish, sentimental verses which many of her contemporaries were turning out by the yard. The two friends loved foreign travel; and in 1850, when Barbara was twenty-three and Bessie twenty-one, they were allowed to go to Europe alone and unchaperoned except by one another. Barbara insisted on wearing blue-tinted spectacles, a habit which would of course have passed unnoticed today but gave rise to some jeers and cat-calls in Germany; and Bessie, furious at her friend for making herself a figure of fun, stumped around in heavy boots. Apart from the slight altercation which ensued the tour was an unqualified success; and if Bessie protested at Barbara's spectacles the girls were at one in their hatred of the fashionable habit of tight-lacing and corsets, both electing to wear loose, comfortable and shapeless garments.

Bessie was the only one of Barbara's friends who did not protest at the apparent folly of her marriage to Eugène Bodichon. But when at the age of thirty-eight Bessie fell in love with Louis Belloc, a Frenchman and an invalid, and insisted on marrying him despite his poor expectation of life, Barbara Bodichon was most censorious. However, once the marriage had taken place she ceased to carp; and when, after five years of happy married life Bessie was left a widow, Barbara became the most stalwart of helpers to her and to her two brilliant children, Hilaire and Marie (later Mrs Belloc Lowndes).

As colleagues Barbara and Bessie worked well in harness; and they found among the young women who flocked to help them a number of extremely competent workers. The mainspring of the employment side of the work was Jessie Boucherett (1825–1905), the youngest daughter of a Lincolnshire landowner, a country lover, and a fearless rider to hounds. Jessie Boucherett, who was also widely read, was interested in social problems. In 1859 she was much impressed by Harriet Martineau's article on 'Female Industry' in the *Edinburgh Review*; and the discovery at about the same time of an issue of the *English Woman's Journal* sent her scurrying down to London with offers of help. She had expected to find the editor of the *English Woman's Journal* a frumpy, elderly woman: instead, when she entered the Langham Place offices she found thirty-year-old Bessie Rayner Parkes, 'a handsome young woman dressed in admirable taste', and Barbara Bodichon, 'beautifully dressed, of radiant beauty with masses of golden hair'.[6] Jessie Boucherett (she must also have belonged to the no-corset, shapeless-garment brigade) was quickly drawn into their circle; and with the co-operation of Barbara Bodichon and the poetess Adelaide Anne Procter, a former student at Queen's College, she founded the Society for Promoting the Employment of Women.

Adelaide Anne, who was far better known as a poetess than Bessie, was the eldest child of a minor poet, Bryan Procter. He hailed her birth with a sonnet beginning, 'Child of my heart! My sweet beloved Firstborn!'; and referred to her in another poem as his 'golden-tressed Adelaide'. She managed to live down her father's verses and to become a highly successful minor poet and a keen and efficient worker in the cause.

Delicate in health (she died of tuberculosis before she was forty) Adelaide Anne Procter was unfailingly cheerful and lively, and modest despite her fame. She must have made an odd contrast to the tough, energetic Jessie Boucherett, who lived till she was eighty, an ardent Tory, a founder member of the Freedom of Labour Defence League, and an eager advocate of poultry and pig-farming as careers for educated women. Among the other occupations which Jessie Boucherett advocated were nursing for those with 'strong nerves and superior intelligence as well as good health', telegraphy, the tinting of photographs (tinted photographs were all the rage), the copying of law papers and of documents in private businesses, wood engraving, house decorating, ivory carving, shoe making, clerical work and cookery. Educated women could be trained for all these occupations; and for women who were too old for technical training and not strong enough to nurse she suggested a cookery course and domestic service either in England or in the colonies. 'I fear they will consider this a degradation,' she wrote in her forthright manner, 'but I do not see what else there is for them to turn to, and it is less degrading to live by honest work than to depend on charity'.[7]

An additional worker in the Society for Promoting the Employment of Women was Jane* Lewin, a niece of Grote the

---

* Some sources refer to Jane and some to Sarah Lewin: presumably she was one and the same person.

historian. The desperate need for a society of this kind was emphasized by the crowds of out-of-work governesses and other
timid, untrained and helplessly 'genteel' women who came to
the offices for help and advice. One of the chief barriers to the
large-scale employment of women, especially as shop assistants,
clerks and cashiers, was their ignorance of figures. Jessie
Boucherett therefore opened an arithmetic and book-keeping
class which in time became a regular day school. It was unfortunately impossible to find suitable work for many of the
applicants; but with the expansion of trade and industry employment openings increased, especially when it became clear
that the guileless women were prepared to work for far lower
wages than men. Four great occupations were opened to
women between 1860 and 1870, for by this time there was
beginning to be a demand for women shop-assistants, clerks,
telegraphists and, or course, for nurses. The expansion of trade
and industry accounted for the first two openings; there was
never any lack of employment for nurses; and, as women
telegraphists started work almost as soon as the invention of
telegraphy had been perfected, there had been no opportunity
for anybody to think up a reason to keep them out.

'*Why* do women not print?' demanded Bessie Rayner Parkes
in 1860. 'I am sure that the true answer is that they have not
yet shown the energy which is required to have and to practise a
new trade.'[8] She realized that printing had always been
regarded as man's preserve, partly through prejudice but also
because of the long hours of standing and the lifting of heavy
weights which were involved. Nevertheless, the Society started
its own printing business—the Victoria Printing Press—under
the direction of a most capable enthusiast, Emily Faithfull
(1835–95). The daughter of a Surrey clergyman, Emily
Faithfull had early chafed against the restrictions of vicarage
life; and in later years had some success as a lecturer in the
United States.

The main assignment undertaken by the Victoria Press was
the printing of the *English Woman's Journal*, but it undertook
other jobs as well. Emily Faithfull solved the problem of fatigue
by introducing three-legged stools for the female compositors
and employed men for the heavy work of moving the chases.

Sub-editing and proof-correcting held no difficulties for women and in 1860 Emily Faithfull could write with pardonable satisfaction that 'there seems to be no kind of printing for which women are not well adapted . . . The Victoria Press is no longer an experiment, but an accomplished success'.[9] One of her prize exhibits was a vast handbill mounted on cardboard, showing the various types of employment now open to women.

The employment of women in commercial printing firms was facilitated by strikes among the male employees. In Scotland they were first employed by an Edinburgh printer in December 1871; and three years later Jane Lewin reported that about eighty women were working as printers in Edinburgh. 'There can be no doubt,' she wrote, 'that in this, as in other trades where women will generally work for a lower rate of wages than men, masters would be willing to employ them, and it is equally natural that the work-people already employed should resent an influx of cheaper labour.'[10] According to the Census of 1871, there were 741 women printers in England; and in 1876 a Women's Printing Society was established to provide apprenticeship opportunities for girls and to find jobs for qualified women printers. But the continued employment of women at low rates of pay inevitably led to strikes by the men; and, as the women were so badly paid, the quality of their work suffered accordingly. The final result was inevitable: printing proved to be one of the trades in which women were never to be allowed to do work normally undertaken by men.

By 1876, however, progress was recorded in a number of occupations which have remained open to women. The General Post Office was employing a growing number of women clerks; and among other occupations women were employed as upholstery workers, dispensers, shop assistants and art decorators. They were even beginning to break into the hair-dressing trade, hitherto a strictly male preserve. In the early days of the movement Louisa Garrett, the eldest of the remarkable band of Garrett sisters, had caused girlish laughter in the office when she recounted a conversation she had just had with the man who had washed her hair. She had asked him if he did not agree that hairdressing was a suitable occupation for women and he cried out in horror: 'Impossible, madam! Why it took ME a fortnight

G

to learn it.'[11] By 1876 the wind of change was blowing through the hairdressing trade. According to the annual report of the Society for the Employment of Women, 'Miss Minnie Moore has started on her own responsibility, and is working up a business connection satisfactorily. She has at present only a small room . . ., but it is nicely fitted up, is very clean indeed, and contains all that is essential to the comfort of ladies, for either shampooing, cutting, or dressing of hair. She understands the arrangement of artificial hair, and the Committee take this opportunity of recommending her to ladies residing in the neighbourhood of Kensington.'[12] Miss Minnie Moore was a pioneer employer; but the 1871 Census showed that over the past decade the number of women hairdressers and wig makers had increased from 501 to 1,240, a healthy sign of what was to come.

From the 1860s onwards there had been advocates of separate trade societies for women; and in 1874 a Women's Protective and Provident League was founded to help working women form their own unions. The founder was a remarkably able young woman, Mrs Emma Paterson (1848–86). She was born in London, the daughter of the headmaster of a group of parish schools, and showed an early interest in the political and industrial status of women. For five years she worked as assistant secretary of a working men's club, and in 1872 became secretary of a women's suffrage committee. She resigned the following year when she married Thomas Paterson, a cabinet-maker and wood-carver who was much interested in the Trade Union movement for men.

The Patersons spent a year's honeymoon in America, and Emma was particularly impressed with the working of the Female Umbrella Makers' Union of New York. On her return to England she adapted this idea and formed the Women's Protective and Provident League, composed mainly of middle class men and women who were willing to instruct women in trade union principles and provide the money to launch some women's societies. With Emma Paterson's guidance a number of small unions were formed, among them bookbinders, printers, upholstresses, shirtmakers, dressmakers and tailoresses. The trouble was not so much to launch a union as to keep it alive; and this was extremely difficult in face of overcrowding, the low wages paid to women, their unskilled status and resultant tendency to move from one occupation to another. Emma Paterson's main interest was the printing society. Having mastered the craft herself she worked for a time with Emily Faithfull on the Victoria Press and in 1876 founded the Women's Printing Society in Westminster which proved a modest success and to which she devoted all her spare time for the rest of her life. Her great contribution, however, was not in the establishment of these ephemeral women's societies but in her fight for the rights of women workers in existing trade unions: it was a fight directed not against the employers but against the working men who were determined to keep the women out. In 1875 she was the first woman delegate ever to attend the Trade Union Congress; and thereafter year by year she strove with patience and tact to overcome the obstinate prejudice of the working men's delegates and to secure the appointment of women factory inspectors. By the end of the nineteenth century, although the small women's unions were dying off, women were being generally admitted on reasonable terms to the men's trade unions. Two women who also did a great deal to improve the life of women in industry and ensure their recognition by the Trade Union movement were the women's suffrage worker Esther Roper and her close friend Eva Gore-Booth, younger sister of Countess Markievicz who was to become in 1918 the first woman elected to Parliament.

An employment opening which emanated directly from the activities of the Society for the Employment of Women was a new emigration scheme. The innovator was Maria Susan Rye (1829–1903) who was also one of the organizers of the Victoria Press. Maria Rye, a solicitor's daughter, had decided at the age of sixteen to devote herself to good works in Chelsea where she lived with her parents and eight brothers and sisters. As she went about the parish she became aware of very limited employment openings for women and also of the iniquities of the law concerning married women. As she had some journalistic ability she wrote an article on married women's property and sent it to the *English Woman's Journal*. Bessie Rayner Parkes was so impressed that she promptly invited Maria Rye to join the coterie of workers in the Society for Promoting the Employment of Women.

Aside from her work on the Victoria Press Maria Rye opened a law engrossing office in Portugal Street, Lincoln's Inn; and there, 'law papers of all kinds were carefully and skilfully copied, deeds were engrossed, sermons and petitions were copied, and circular letters were written at eighteenpence the dozen, and envelopes at five shillings a thousand'.[13] The law engrossing office made a modest profit; but the number of applicants for work was so far in excess of the posts available that Maria Rye decided to try and implement a plan which had been in her mind for some time. She firmly believed that the only hope of suitable employment for a large number of middle class women was in the colonies, and she was anxious to do something to help them to emigrate. As she pointed out in 1860, however, there was 'no free and assisted passage offered to any one colony, for any description of women except household servants';[14] and whatever Jessie Boucherett might think, middle class women resisted any idea of going into domestic service. But Maria Rye was convinced that in the colonies, particularly in New Zealand, there would be openings for educated women, especially as school teachers and governesses, and that if it could be made known that women were willing to emigrate money would be forthcoming to help them. She set to work with a will; money was raised by public subscription; and in 1862 the Female Middle Class Emigration Society was established with Maria Rye and Jane Lewin as joint secretaries. The Society was instrumental in sending emigrants not only to New Zealand, but also to Canada and Australia; and Maria Rye kept her eye on the working as well as the middle class emigrants.

On her first visit to New Zealand she accompanied a party of working class girls. The voyage took four months and to Maria Rye it was no holiday. Having nursed all the girls through bouts of sea-sickness she herself succumbed; but, as she wrote to a friend, 'my malady was . . ., I fully believe, brought on from imbibing sherry and soda-water as a preventative'. As soon as the girls had gained their sea legs they provided fresh cause for anxiety by their amorous behaviour with members of the crew. The captain locked the ringleaders in their cabin for the night, an act which so incensed the crew that they went in a body to demand the girls' release. The captain ordered the men below: they refused to budge, whereupon he called for arms, and, grumbling, the men withdrew. Later in the evening, however, they reappeared and the situation looked really ugly. 'I think this fright was worse than the first,' wrote Maria Rye, 'for the pistols were had out a second time, and one unfortunately going off, was construed into the first fire, and commencement of the battle. The mate fortunately had presence of mind enough to call for a light and ask for names; this, with the pistols, had its desired effect, and all slunk back and retired.'

This incident put an end to the trouble; and the fearless and energetic Maria Rye was now free to organize a school for the girls, the best of whom 'were very ignorant and very frivolous and self-opinionated',[15] and to preach Sunday sermons to the crew who, to her pleased surprise, turned up in force to hear her.

Conditions in the emigrant ships were often shockingly bad; and on a visit to Brisbane Maria Rye discovered that the death rate among emigrants travelling by a certain shipping line was alarmingly high and that the survivors arrived at their destination more dead than alive. In the port hospital she found thirty orphans whose parents had died on the voyage out herded together with the physically and mentally sick. The pathetic waifs roused all her fighting instincts; and, having bullied the government into lending her an empty building, she begged or borrowed furniture and equipment, installed the thirty orphans and gave each one of them a thorough wash. As soon as the orphans had settled down she started raising money to support them, and formed a committee to run the home, which was later enlarged to accommodate a hundred children. She also instigated the appointment of three colonial commissions to enquire into the state of the emigrant ships; and, as a result, conditions began to improve.

From 1868 onwards Maria Rye devoted all her efforts to the emigration and welfare of destitute children—or 'gutter children' as she felicitously called them. With the help of two of her sisters she opened a home for waifs and strays in Peckham.

The waifs—all girls ranging in age from three to sixteen—were given some general and religious education and when they were old enough were trained in domestic economy. They were then drafted to a sister home which Maria Rye had founded in Canada and, after some additional training, were sent as domestic servants to suitable homes. The watchful Maria personally escorted each batch of girls to Canada and kept in touch with them afterwards; and by 1895 it was reckoned that she had found homes for 500 girls whose start in life had been wretched in the extreme. In that year the two homes were transferred to the Church of England Waifs and Strays Society; and Maria Rye retired from active life. She had long since cut adrift from the Women's Employment Society because its members were becoming increasingly embroiled in the fight for women's suffrage, a fight with which she was not at all in sympathy. Her work with the Middle Class Emigration Society had been carried on by Jane Lewin until 1886; and the Society was later merged with similar bodies in the British Women's Emigration Association.

Among other early recruits to the women's movement was Isa Craig (later Mrs Knox—1831–1903), who added lustre to the movement when she was appointed assistant-secretary to the Social Science Association. Isa Craig, the only child of an Edinburgh hosier and glover, lost both her parents in childhood and was reared by a grandmother. Although she left school before she was ten her love of English literature helped her to develop a natural gift for writing; and after contributing verses to the *Scotsman* for several years she was given a post on the paper. In 1857 she came to London to take up the appointment she had just been offered with the Social Science Association. The appointment of a woman was a revolutionary step not lost on the *Saturday Review*, which had already said some harsh words about the President, Lord Brougham, and about the presence of women at the Association's meetings. 'There are decided advantages in this Universal Palaver Association,' wrote the *Review*. 'It must be remembered to Lord Brougham's credit that he is the first person who has dealt upon this plan with the problem of female loquacity . . . It is a great idea to tire out the hitherto unflagging vigour of their tongues by encouraging a taste for stump-oratory among them . . . Lord Brougham's little *corps* of lady orators, preaching strong-mindedness, gives a new aspect to the Association's presence . . . We heartily wish the strong-minded ladies happiness and success in their new alliance; and do not doubt that they will remember to practise the precept of one of their debaters "not to mind being thought unladylike". It is always better not to mind that which is inevitable.'[16]

The 'lady orators' were naturally encouraged by the appointment of a woman to the staff of the Association. But Isa Craig only held her appointment for a year, resigning in 1858 when she married her cousin John Knox, a London iron merchant. She continued to support the movement, however; and she struck another cultural blow for her sex when she won a £50 prize offered for a centenary poem on Burns, her ode being chosen out of 621 contributions.

Isa Craig was also on the committee of the Ladies' Sanitary Association, founded in 1859 to instigate necessary reforms in the home. 'It is for man's comprehensive mind to devise schemes for draining and cleansing our towns,' wrote a contributor to the *English Woman's Journal*, 'and for placing the necessaries of life within the reach of all; and it is for his strong hand to execute these schemes . . . It is for woman, in her functions as mother, housewife and teacher, to effect these urgently needed changes in infant management, domestic economy, education, and the general habits of her own sex, without which humanity could never attain to its destined state of bodily perfection . . . It is for her to teach and apply the laws of health in her own provinces, where man cannot act.' In simple language, district visiting would provide an excellent opportunity to ferret out sanitary shortcomings and suggest possible remedies. District visitors were well placed to carry out this work 'without being obtrusive, or violating any of the laws of courtesy which should be held sacred alike in intercourse with peasant or peeress'.[17] In 1860 Lord Palmerston interpreted the functions of the Ladies' Sanitary Association in terms which were probably not meant to be as patronizing as they sounded. The ladies, he said, could 'facilitate the attaining of such articles as whitewash brushes and ventilators, as well as the mending of broken windows. They may also enforce . . . a careful attention to the many details which conduce so much to health and domestic comfort . . . and render home attractive rather than repulsive to husbands and sons. They can also be instrumental in promoting habits of temperance . . .'[18]

Since epidemics of typhoid and other infectious fevers were rife at the time it is clear that, if they achieved nothing else, members of the Association could do something to persuade the ignorant housewife of the value of fresh air and personal and household hygiene. The Association, which was affiliated to the Social Science Association, published a number of propaganda pamphlets with such weighty titles as, *The Cheap Doctor: A Word about Fresh Air*; *On the Evils of Rising too Early after Childbirth*; and *The Black Hole in your Own Bedrooms*. It also printed and sold vast numbers of verses to prove that cleanliness indeed came next to Godliness.

In the early years of its existence the Langham Place circle, or the Ladies' Institute as the house in Langham Place was called, was both a club and an employment agency, the focal point of all the women reformers. Each fresh challenge was met with alacrity and almost childlike enthusiasm; and apart from the major campaigns there were a number of minor but lively skirmishes with authority. Every one was delighted, for example, when the South Kensington Art School accepted its first woman student; and only temporarily discouraged when she was expelled for whistling, because this gave them the idea of forming their own Society of Female Artists.

There was a pleasing triumph over the manager of the Marylebone swimming baths who had refused to admit women because, so he said, they did not wish to use the baths. The women then persuaded him to agree to admit them if thirty applied; and thereafter a contingent from Langham Place presented itself every Wednesday afternoon. Within a few minutes 'the fair visitors', 'clad in appropriate garb', would emerge from the dressing cubicles, 'descend a short flight of steps, seize one end of the rope attached and plunge at once into the refreshing element'.[19]

If at first the fair visitors could not swim they soon learned, and within a few years women had proceeded from graceful exhibitions of 'ornamental swimming' to long-distance swims. In 1875, for example, 'Miss Emily Parker started from London Bridge at 5.3 to swim to North Woolwich, a distance of ten miles. The tide was moderately good, but the wind was dead against the swimmer, making the water at times very rough and lumpy, and the constant breaking up of the waves distressed her considerably. She, however, arrived at Woolwich at 7.26, and was carried into North Woolwich Gardens, where Mr Holland afterwards presented her with a gold medal value ten guineas.'[20] It was not such a far cry from intrepid Emily Parker to the women Channel swimmers of a later period.

Chapter VI

THE OUTSIDERS

Two women whose work complemented but exceeded the work of the others were the great social reformers Octavia Hill (1838–1912) and Josephine Butler (1828–1906).

Octavia Hill, the pioneer of housing reform, was the eighth daughter of the eleven children of James Hill, a corn merchant and banker of Wisbech in Cambridgeshire. James Hill was well known in the locality for his interest in penal and municipal reform, and is said to have ridden fifty miles to secure the freedom of the last man to be sentenced to death for sheep stealing. Mrs Hill was the daughter of Dr Thomas Southwood Smith, an authority on sanitation and fever epidemics; and Octavia first learnt about slum conditions from her grandfather. The younger Hill girls were educated by their mother, a woman of strong character and unaffected piety. They all had to earn their living, for James Hill failed in business and had a breakdown in health from which he never recovered.

Octavia, the artistic member of the family, was sturdy but small in stature, with a wide and pleasant face. She was sent to London in her teens to work at the Ladies' Guild, a co-operative venture started by the Christian Socialists and managed for a time by her mother. Her job was to teach toy-making to the children from a ragged school; and the work gave her an insight into the lives of the very poor. She was naturally much influenced by Denison Maurice and she hero-worshipped John Ruskin, who took an interest in her art and gave her copying work to do.

The Ladies' Guild did not last long. It was split by sectarian differences, and Maurice, the formative religious influence in Octavia's life, was too much of a heretic for the orthodox

Christians. The Guild was closed down in 1856; and Octavia, who continued her toy-making teaching, was made secretary of another of Maurice's ventures, some classes for working women which were attached to his Working Men's College in Great Ormond Street. In this job she had to work closely with the voluntary teachers, of whom she had a poor opinion. 'As I am thrown among "ladies",' she snorted, 'I hope I may discover good in them.'[1] Rightly or wrongly she thought the 'ladies' looked down on her because she was young and also because she was obliged to accept a salary of £25 a year instead of working voluntarily as she would have preferred. And she was irritated when they behaved like many other voluntary workers and cut lectures for social engagements, calmly expecting her to give their lectures for them. But if she disliked the teachers, she had to learn to work with them; and she became very fond of the working women pupils.

Two of Octavia's sisters were already teaching, and Mrs Hill was trying to make a living as a journalist; but potentially Octavia was the family breadwinner. Quixotically she had saddled herself with her father's debts, although since he was a discharged bankrupt she was not legally responsible. For two years she struggled to keep the family together, at some cost to her health and nervous stability; and then Sophia Jex-Blake swept into her life. Octavia, who was eighteen at the time, was engaged to give twenty-year-old Sophia book-keeping lessons; and between the two girls, neither of whom had yet found her sense of direction, there sprang up one of those intense and passionate friendships which seem to have been common among the ranks of the "strong-minded' and which, though highly emotional, appear in a number of cases to have been physically innocent. Sophia and Octavia were too much alike for a peaceful friendship. They were ardent but obstinate, undeviating, and determined never to be put in the wrong. Both were affectionate; but while Sophia was ruthless towards her parents Octavia was devoted to her entire family.

From the start Octavia, who was the more sensitive and restrained of the two, suffered from her friend's sudden explosions of rage; yet when Sophia, who had been appointed mathematical tutor at Queen's College, suggested that she should share a house with the Hills, Octavia agreed. Sophia, generous as always, was ready to pay more than her share of the expenses; and a large house was bought in Nottingham Place, near Harley Street, with room for them all and some additional rooms which they proposed to let. The decision brought forth an angry outburst from Mr Jex-Blake. 'You cannot really mean to take a house and let lodgings,' he wrote to Sophia, 'in direct opposition to your dear mother and me. It would be quite disgraceful, and we can never consent to it. . . .'[2]

Naturally Sophia went ahead; and early in 1862 she and the Hills had moved into the house. Life was anything but smooth, for by May Octavia was threatened with one of those break-downs in health to which in moments of crisis so many of her long-lived contemporaries were prone, and went to stay with an older, less demanding friend. During her absence Sophia, with her usual disregard for other people's feelings, behaved as though she were the head of the house and clashed with Mrs Hill, who was anything but a cypher. After a series of battles both sides appealed to Octavia, who quailed before the storm she had unwittingly provoked. But because she put her family and her peace of mind first—and there could have been no peace in a continuing relationship with Sophia—she told her that she must go, and thus brought the friendship to an end. Sophia was pathetically eager to resume it; but Octavia, who in her quiet way could be equally ruthless, was firm in her refusal; and the two young women went their separate ways to fame.

When Sophia had gone the Hills turned the house into a school for the daughters of tradesmen and artisans. Miranda, Octavia's elder sister, had been teaching since the age of thirteen. Emily, a younger sister, had been to Queen's College; and Octavia put in some hard work and herself gained a certificate from Queen's. The school, part day and part boarding, took pupils from 12 to 18. Boarding conditions were cheerless, but the Hills were accustomed to discomfort and the boarders lived as family. The girls were trained, wrote Octavia, in 'habits of neatness, punctuality, self-reliance and such practical power and forethought as will make them useful in their homes'; but, she added, hopefully 'I think they may be taught to delight in them.'³ Although her intentions were excellent Octavia was not such a good or understanding teacher as Miranda. 'You know I've a damping, cool sort of way with [children]', she said, 'that just stabs all their enjoyment. I don't think I've any child nature left in me.'⁴

The Nottingham Place school in its way was as unconventional as Barbara Bodichon's Portman Hall, where Octavia held a drawing class; but the girls were well grounded in academic as well as practical subjects. Several of them sat for the original Cambridge University trial examinations in December 1863; and when the local examinations were put on a permanent footing there were always candidates from Nottingham Place.

But already Octavia's interests had veered away from teaching and her first love, art, towards the problem of rehousing some of the poorest people in the London slums around her. She was able to interest Ruskin in her ideas; and in the spring of 1865 he advanced the money to buy three houses in a court near Nottingham Place, asking only a very low rate of interest.

The houses were full of tenants; and each house had a resident landlord who had to be got rid of before anything practical could be done. Living conditions were squalid: the roofs leaked; plaster dropped from the walls; the bannisters on the unlit staircases had been burnt as firewood by the tenants; there were no washing facilities; and the drainage was indescribable. It was only natural that the tenants should match their living conditions: they were filthy, drink-sodden and quarrelsome and their children were in a pitiful state.

As soon as the landlords had moved out Octavia got down to the essential business of providing wash-houses; scrubbing and white-washing the passages and yards; replacing the bannisters; and reglazing windows. She hoped that this cleansing of the Augean stables would persuade the tenants to keep their own rooms clean. It did nothing of the sort; and within weeks the new windows had been broken, the bannisters burnt and the rest of the repair work ruined. Octavia's friends had warned her that this sort of thing would happen; and she felt that the situation could only be retrieved if the tenants got to know and trust her. She therefore decided to collect the rents herself every week. At first she met with a good deal of hostility, especially when the tenants realized that they must pay regularly or risk being turned out of their rooms. More than once a defaulting tenant would lock the door while she was in his room, and tell her he would open it only when she had agreed to let him off. On these occasions she would stand motionless and silent while the tenant bullied and abused her; and when he had talked himself to a standstill she would calmly repeat her demand. In the end she generally won her point; and although she hated evicting tenants she was convinced that only by the prompt payment of rent could she persuade them that tenants as well as landlords had responsibilities. Her implacability, her courage in going about alone with her money-bag in alleyways which the police only patrolled in pairs, and above all the underlying friendliness of her approach overcame the tenants' animosity and gained their co-operation.

Once she had won their confidence Octavia Hill was able to show them how much they stood to gain. An agreed sum had been set aside for repairs and innovations; and if the property was well kept money would be saved which could be spent on improvements of the tenants' own choice. This was a popular move; and so was the organization of a band of older girls who undertook for a small weekly payment to keep the yards, stairs and passages clean. Not so popular was her ban on lodgers, which had meant that as many as eighteen people sometimes lived in a single room. Instead, she would offer to let a large family have an additional room at a minimal rent, and without bringing obvious pressure to bear she generally persuaded them to take it. When tenants were out of work she tried to find employment for them; and she encouraged those in work to save. Her reforms were sensible; her methods businesslike; and she succeeded in placing the project on such a sound footing that in the spring of 1866 she was able to buy six additional houses.

The new property had an open space which Octavia converted into a playground for the children and a place where their elders could sit and rest. Among her other communal schemes was play-acting, an activity which appealed to her close friend and helper Emma Cons, who in after years took over the management of a music hall, ran it as a place of popular entertainment where drinking was strictly forbidden, and passed it on to her niece Lilian Baylis to be transformed into the Old Vic. Emma Cons, tough and outspoken, was a more robust character than Octavia Hill and criticized her efforts to prettify the courts with the artistic touches beloved of Ruskin. Octavia gave her friend control of some additional courts which she had acquired near Drury Lane; and Emma Cons made an admirable manager, although she was more concerned with stamping out drink than with bringing beauty into the lives of the tenants.

Octavia attracted a great many helpers, so many in fact that her sister Miranda nicknamed her St Ursula. It was most fortunate that she was willing and eager to delegate authority. Her health alone made this desirable, for she suffered from a variety of complaints—mostly nervous in origin—and had to take frequent holidays. A long and particularly serious breakdown in health occurred in 1878. The ostensible cause was prolonged overwork, but there were two contributory causes. The first was Octavia's decision to break off an engagement to one of her helpers, the weak-willed son of a jealous and over-maternal widow, who would have made her an impossible husband. The second was a breach with Ruskin, who lambasted her when he was told that in private conversation she had expressed doubts of his 'ability to conduct any practical enterprise successfully',[5] and published his letters and her rather halting replies in his *Fors Clavigera*.

But Octavia's willingness to delegate was independent of the state of her health and made it possible for her work to spread far more quickly and effectively than would otherwise have been possible. She herself was now freed from the need to earn a living, for her friends had raised a fund in 1874 which enabled her to give up her teaching and copying and devote her life to housing reform. Outsiders flocked to her for training; and she encouraged them to be independent, giving to each the responsibility for a different sector of the property. 'Take the initiative yourselves,' she told them, 'manage the details yourselves, think over your problems yourselves, for you alone can; when you have made yourselves tolerably independent of us then you or we may extend the work but not till then.'[6]

The result of this imaginative and practical approach was the introduction of Octavia Hill's system of housing reform in English towns, on the Continent and in America. Her additional work sprang naturally from it. She was closely connected with the activities of the Charity Organization Society, which was established to prevent indiscriminate and wasteful giving and to canalize the work of existing benevolent societies and individuals. Her appreciation of the need of town-dwellers for open spaces led her, in conjunction with others, to found the National Trust in 1895; and it was largely through her efforts that Parliament Hill Fields in London and many other open spaces were preserved for the public. She was often asked to advise on legislation to promote social reform; but, apart from the Charity Organization Society, she was not anxious to take part in organized political effort, preferring to rely on voluntary means. For this reason she refused to join the Royal Commission on Housing in 1889; but in 1905 she agreed, though with some misgivings, to serve on the Royal Commission on the Poor Laws which made a three-year survey of conditions in London and the provinces. She brought to this work the energy of a much younger woman and a wide knowledge of people. She was doubtful about her own contribution, but its value was appreciated by her colleagues. 'At critical moments of discussion and controversy,' said one of them, 'she would intervene with a few words of undeniable common sense and insight and solve the problem we were considering.'[7]

The report of the Commission was published in 1912, shortly before Octavia's death at the age of seventy-four. Appreciation of her work was shown in the offer of a funeral in Westminster Abbey; but the family refused, knowing that she would prefer to be buried beside her favourite sister Miranda, who had predeceased her by two years.

Octavia Hill's achievement, though outside the main stream of the women's movement, flowed naturally from it. Not so Josephine Butler's, which split the movement from end to end. Josephine Butler was certainly the most interesting, and

5. Mrs Drummond opposite the terrace of the House of Commons addressing MPs, inviting them to the Hyde Park demonstration

Arrest of Mrs Pankhurst, Miss Pankhurst and Mrs Drummond. Mr Jarvis reading the warrant at Clement's Inn, October 13, 1908

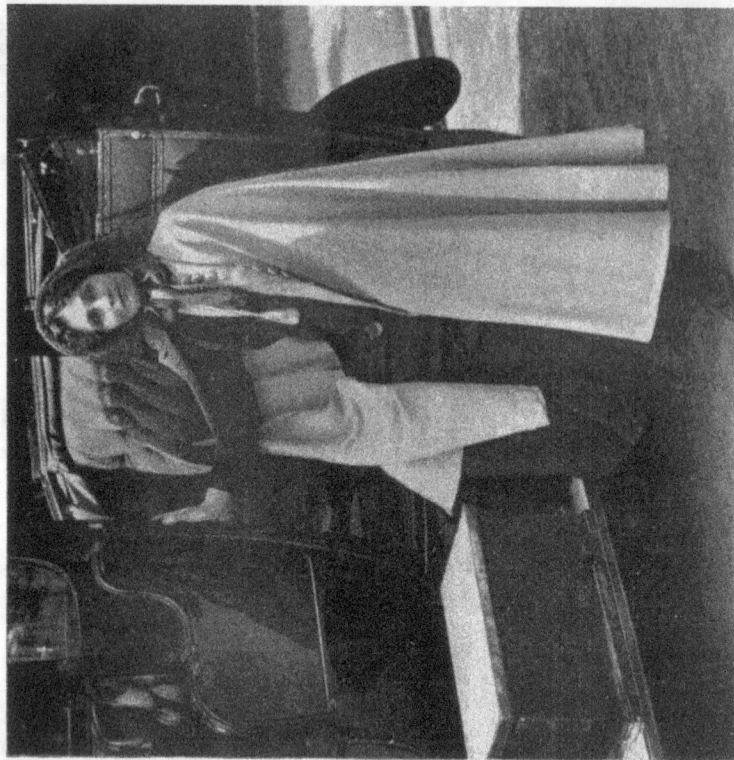

Emmeline Pankhurst

6. Mr and Mrs Pethick Lawrence and Miss Christabel Pankhurst going to Bow Street, October 14, 1908

probably the greatest of the pioneers. She saw the women's question not simply in its various facets but as a whole; and, as her biographer states, she 'constantly reiterated the necessity for building a society in which men and women should play an equal part.'[8] Her spiritual fervour, her mental and physical courage, and her persuasive oratory brought thousands to her cause; and had she not centralized her energies she might have become the presiding genius of the entire movement. Her leadership would have been securely underpinned—as was her own work—by her marriage. Barbara Bodichon's marriage, though happy enough, had an element of the bizarre: there was something maternal in Bessie Rayner Parkes' love for her invalid husband Louis Belloc: but George Butler, scholar, schoolmaster and clergyman, was the ideal husband for a crusading wife; his sympathy and support were always available to her; and theirs was indeed a marriage between equals.

Josephine Butler was the seventh child of John Grey of Dilston, Northumberland. She had a very happy childhood, and although she and her sisters had little formal schooling they learned much from their father who discussed agriculture, politics and world affairs with his family, imbuing his children with the spirit of service to the community. Josephine grew into a really beautiful young woman, tall and slim, with the fine features and facial bones which ensured the continuance of her beauty into old age. She was twenty-two when she met George Butler, a splendid looking young man of exceptional ability, son of a headmaster of Harrow. George Butler was as strong and as wholesome as he looked; but Josephine was considered delicate. 'If I can help you by my strength of physique,' he wrote to her shortly before their marriage in 1852, 'depend upon it I will do so. In other matters I think you are more capable of giving me aid than of borrowing it.'[9]

The Butlers went to live in Oxford where George Butler was Examiner to the University and where he was ordained a clergyman in 1854. His influence in the University was increasing; but in 1856 when his wife was threatened with tuberculosis and warned that the climate of Oxford might be fatal to her lungs he threw up his job and migrated to Cheltenham and the post of Vice-Principal of the College. At

H

Cheltenham their four children—a girl and three boys—were born, and there the great personal tragedy of their lives occurred. Their daughter, aged five, rushing to meet her parents who were returning to the house from a visit, fell over the bannisters of the staircase and was killed in their presence. The shock and the grief were overwhelming. Husband and wife, upheld by their Christian faith, clung to one another; but on Josephine the tragedy left a permanent scar. From childhood onwards she had been deeply religious, with that streak of mysticism which assured her that one day she would be 'called' to the service of the Almighty. After her daughter's death she went out of her way to find people who had suffered even more than she had done. She found them in the slums of Liverpool, to which the family moved in 1866 when George Butler was appointed Principal of Liverpool College; they were the dregs of society, the inhabitants of workhouses and prisons, the down-and-outs and the prostitutes. With her husband's full approval and support she visited prisons, work-houses and hospital wards and opened her own home to the sick and dying. When the Butlers' house grew too small for the patients they opened a hostel for them, and because Josephine Butler genuinely loved her outcasts they responded to her.

At this time she was also involved in the problems of higher education. In 1866 Anne Clough came to her and her husband for advice and Josephine Butler became President of the North of England Council for Promoting the Higher Education of Women. In 1868 she went to Cambridge to present a petition signed by 500 teachers and 300 other women urging the University to make provision for a special examination for women, and this led in 1869 to the establishment of the Cambridge higher local. On her way home she went to London to discuss with Jessie Boucherett the importance of education and technical training in the opening of fresh avenues of employment. In London she met Emily Davies, to whom, of course, she appeared in the guise of yet another serpent bent on denying women their full educational rights; but, as a supporter of women's suffrage, she was far more welcome.

If she had been sufficiently interested Josephine Butler might at this stage have taken on the leadership of the women's movement, even though educationally she would never have won Emily Davies to her side. But it was in 1869 that she received her long-awaited 'call' to take up the cause of the prostitutes, who were being hounded by government regulations, and those women who might or might not be 'respectable' but were being victimized as prostitutes.

There is no question that Josephine Butler believed that her call came directly from God; but it is interesting to speculate on the motive underlying her choice of a vocation which could not fail to make her notorious at a time when discussion of sex was taboo. Did she in fact receive a call? Was she driven to abase herself by a sense of guilt for the death of her child which could only be expiated by the horror and disgust of her contemporaries? Or was it simply an all-embracing love? In any event, she could not possibly have chosen a harder, less popular task; but whatever her underlying motive she brought to it courage of the very highest order.

Like Octavia Hill and other Victorians—Florence Nightingale included—she had to do constant battle with psycho-somatic illness; for her mental attitude towards her health, the cause of anxiety throughout her long life, was closely bound up with her attitude towards her work. She had an inherent dislike of doctors, who either professed themselves baffled by her symptoms or suspected that some at any rate were self-induced. 'I have consulted nine doctors now on this very matter of my heart,' she wrote to a friend in 1868, shortly before she received her 'call'. 'They all said that I would *never* be strong. . . . Not one attempted any *medicine* except slight palliatives and soothing things with which I am now surrounded and know how to use. Every doctor has told me that God is my only physician (which I know) and that all my ailments were so complicated with the spiritual and intellectual being that it would be an impertinence in them to think they could manage me. . . .' Elizabeth Garrett, as a woman doctor, was the most acceptable, 'for she entered much more into my mental state and way of life . . . , *because* I was able to *tell* her so much more than I ever could or would tell to any *man*. She, too, said she could never promise me I should be well.'[10] The cause and nature of Josephine Butler's illnesses—like those of Octavia

Hill—are obscure; but it seems possible that sub-consciously she used ill-health as one of a series of obstacles to be beaten down in the path to her goal. This would in no sense detract from the magnitude of her achievement; but it would help to explain her gluttony for punishment.

The 'call' when it came was too insistent to be denied; and in 1870 Josephine Butler gave up the presidency of the North of England Council for the Higher Education of Women in order to devote herself to a campaign to overthrow the State regulation of prostitution. Under this system, which had been initiated by Napoleon and adopted throughout Europe, women living in garrison towns could be termed by the police 'common prostitutes' and as such they were obliged, on pain of repeated terms of imprisonment, to undergo periodical medical examination. The authorities maintained that the examination (it was not applied to men but only to women) checked the spread of venereal disease and guarded from infection soldiers and sailors who could not be expected to remain continent when separated from their wives.

The first Contagious Diseases Act was passed in England in 1864, at a time when Josephine Butler was too lost in personal grief to realize what it involved. Others, however, had already spoken out against State regulation. In 1860 Florence Nightingale had resisted a scheme for the provision of brothels for the Army in India: in 1863, that most respectable of spinsters, Harriet Martineau, had inveighed against State intervention. In a series of articles in the *Daily News* she demanded proof that the regulations had diminished contagious diseases in other countries; and argued that the recognition of prostitution as a necessity could only vitiate the morals of the armed forces.

By 1866, when Josephine Butler first became aware of the problem, the Contagious Diseases Act had been re-enacted and its scope extended to fresh districts. By 1869 she knew that her mission was to get the Acts abolished. There were, of course, a great many people who sincerely believed that the Acts were beneficial, since the expressed aim—to guard the health of the forces and protect their families from disease—was unexceptionable. The medical profession, with few exceptions, was solidly behind them; and to Elizabeth Garrett and the women doctors who had been fighting for their professional existence (though not to Elizabeth Blackwell) they were an unpleasant necessity.

The state of public opinion was largely unknown, for by tacit consent the subject was considered too disgusting for open discussion. Among adherents of the women's movement, however, it produced a deep and painful cleavage. Denison Maurice and Emily Davies, for example, approved of the Acts; but it was generally agreed that the educational workers would be wise to stand aside from the struggle, and most of them obeyed. One who took no notice of this advice was Elizabeth Wolstenholme (later Mrs Wolstenholme-Elmy—1834–1918). As headmistress of a Manchester girls' school, Elizabeth Wolstenholme had given evidence before the Schools' Inquiry Commission; she was active in the Married Women's Property Bill agitation; she was prominent in the suffrage movement. Now she took up the banner of abolition in the North of England and recruited a number of helpers, most of them from the Society of Friends.

The split in the women's movement was most painful among the suffrage workers, whose own cause was unpopular enough in all conscience. Some came out boldly for abolition: others were in sympathy but withheld their support because they feared it would damage the suffrage cause: others found the matter too distressing and improper to mention at all.

The decision was ultimately taken that the suffrage movement as a whole must play no part in the crusade; and this led to bitter argument, votes of censure and private indignation meetings by the score; and culminated in the formation of separate suffrage organizations.

'The principle upon which we have taken our stand,' declared the organization formed by those who would not support the crusade, 'is of careful avoidance of even apparent mingling with any other agitation. . . . We hold it to be important that no person conspicuously engaged either as officer or lecturer in some other agitation now proceeding, to which we will not further allude, should hold any conspicuous place in the movement for women's suffrage.'[11]

On this side was the suffragist leader Millicent Garrett Fawcett (1847–1929), Elizabeth Garrett's younger sister. Millicent Fawcett agreed wholeheartedly with Josephine Butler that the Acts were iniquitous and should be repealed; but she steadfastly refused to take any part in the crusade and to the end of her life remained convinced that she had done the right thing.

The denial of support by suffragists—and women doctors— was a serious blow to the abolitionists. To Josephine Butler the fight for abolition and the fight for the suffrage were simply different aspects of the crusade to release women from subjection. 'If I were not working for Repeal,' she said in 1873, 'I would throw my whole force into getting the suffrage.' And again: 'I feel more keenly than I ever did the great importance of our having votes *as a means* of self-preservation. We cannot *always* depend on the self-sacrificing efforts of noble men . . . to right our wrongs, and now that the labourers are going to be enfranchized, our case becomes the *worse*; we shall be utterly swamped and lost, if we have no representation, if we become (though more than half the nation) the one unrepresented section under a Government which will become more and more extended, more popular, more democratic and yet *wholly masculine*. Woe is me! That people cannot see it!'[12]

And so, despite her other commitment, Josephine Butler continued to support the suffrage cause. Her efforts did it no harm; and it is hard to believe that support for abolition by all those suffrage workers who were personally in sympathy with it could possibly have rendered the suffrage battle more bitter than it was. The hostility of the women doctors was even harder to endure, for their support would have counted for a very great deal. In fact, the cause did not lack supporters but as yet they were quite unorganized. Nevertheless, by 1869 the work of such men as the Rev. Dr Hooppell, principal of a nautical college, Daniel Cooper of the London Rescue Society, and Dr Bell-Taylor of Nottingham had led to the formation of the National Association for the Abolition of the Acts; and it was this Association which Josephine Butler agreed to lead in a nation-wide campaign. Her acceptance is a tribute not to her courage alone but to her husband, who risked his career and his reputation to go with her every step of the way.

The Association could not have made a better choice. Josephine Butler, who was quite without self-consciousness, was endowed with beauty of voice as well as of person, with utter sincerity and an uncompromising attitude towards the evil she attacked; and was, as a result, an inspired, and inspiring, speaker. Among the first of her influential supporters was Professor James Stuart, a close family friend, who had lectured for the North of England Council for the Higher Education of Women; Henry Wilson of Sheffield, a business man who took charge of the organization of the campaign, and several Members of Parliament, among them Jacob Bright. She made her first speech to a small gathering of women at Leeds, and her quality was instantly apparent to Mrs Jacob Bright and Miss Wolstenholme who were in the audience. Her first major speech was to an audience of working men at Crewe: it was a triumph and was followed by a series of working men's meetings in other Northern towns.

Josephine Butler returned to Liverpool at the conclusion of this first tour to found a Ladies' National Association for Abolition and to draw up a manifesto to be signed by women of distinction. Among the 124 signatures she obtained were those of Florence Nightingale, Harriet Martineau, 'the sisters and other relatives of the late Mr John Bright, all the leading ladies of the Society of Friends, and many well-known in the literary and philanthropic world.' On the draft manifesto Josephine Butler appended a note in her own writing: 'There are more who would like to sign, but they are afraid of their names being known—dear gooses!'[13]

Press comment on the manifesto was damning. The signatories were accused of seeking notoriety at any price and of indulging in a 'hobby too nasty to mention'. After this initial outburst of abuse the Press clamped down on the subject; and a newspaper had to be founded by the Association to report meetings, resolutions, and progress.

At the start progress was more marked in the North of England than the South; but in 1870 the abolitionists decided to raise the issue at a by-election at Colchester. The Liberal Government candidate was General Sir Henry Storks, formerly

Commanding Officer at Malta, who had himself administered the Acts, and whose only regret, he said, was that he had not been empowered to extend them to the wives of serving men. Colchester, as a military centre, was one of the towns in which the Acts were in force; and it was therefore an obvious seat for an abolitionist candidate. In a three-cornered fight there was no prospect of his winning; but the abolitionists hoped that he would split the vote and so damage Government prestige.

The campaign was violent and bloody. Josephine Butler, who was billed to speak at a women's meeting, was persuaded to stay away from the adoption meeting, from which the candidate and his supporters emerged covered with bruises, mud and filth. Josephine, who had been doing some discreet canvassing in a working class district, returned to her hotel for a night's rest, only to be told by the landlord that he had found her a room in a working-class house because a gang of toughs had threatened to burn down the hotel if he allowed her to stay. Next day she was escorted by a devious route to her meeting. Since the women had no votes all she could do was to try and persuade them to influence their husbands to vote for the abolitionist candidate; and after the meeting she was delighted to overhear a tiny woman threaten a powerful-looking man that, 'if you don't vote like she says, I'll KILL you.'[14]

Many of the voters had only recently been enfranchised and they took the campaign very seriously. Sir Henry Storks' views on the desirability of extending the Acts to servicemen's wives did him no good at all, especially with the new voters. He was soundly beaten at the poll, losing to the Conservatives what had been considered a safe Liberal seat. 'Bird shot dead,' [15] James Stuart telegraphed Josephine Butler, who had already gone home. Storks' defeat was a triumph for the abolitionists and it proved to be a turning-point in the history of the campaign.

A few months later a Royal Commission was appointed to examine the working of the Acts, and their extension was stopped pending publication of a report. Josephine Butler had no time for a Commission whose members had been carefully chosen to represent both sides of the issue. To her, the Acts were evil and should be abolished: it was pointless to enquire into their administration. She was called to give evidence in

March, 1871, a testing ordeal from which she did not emerge unscathed. Those members who favoured retention of the Acts looked on the abolitionists as religious cranks who were in no way representative of public opinion and on Josephine Butler as a latterday Joan of Arc whose visions were pernicious; and it was only natural that she should have been asked to back up her arguments with positive proof. In some instances she was quite unable to do this; and although her statements could not be disproved she weakened her case considerably. In the circumstances it seems strange that she was not better prepared; but it may have been that she was flustered as well as distressed by the intensity of the hostility she encountered, as she described it: 'the hard, harsh view which some of these men take of poor women, and the lives of the poor generally. . . . I felt very weak and lonely. But,' she added, 'there was One who stood by me. I almost felt as if I heard Christ's voice bidding me not to fear.'[16]

She may have been ill prepared, but there was no mistaking her honesty and spiritual power. 'I am not accustomed to religious phraseology,' wrote one of the Commissioners afterwards, 'but I cannot give you any idea of the effect produced except by saying that the influence of the Spirit of God was there.'[17] Several Commissioners who had hitherto supported the Acts now became abolitionists, among them Denison Maurice, and Charles Buxton, MP, Vice-President of the Pro-Act Association, who resigned on the grounds that the Acts were a complete failure.

The Commission reported in 1871 in favour of discontinuing compulsory medical examination and of raising the age of consent from twelve to fourteen. In 1872 a Bill was introduced in the House of Commons by the Home Secretary designed to raise the age of consent, take other measures to protect young girls, and repeal the Contagious Diseases Acts. In their place, however, regulations were proposed to apply throughout the country which would permit the police to arrest women on suspicion. The Home Secretary made no secret of his own feelings. 'I believe we shall have powers, with regard to the whole country, such as we never had before,' he announced gleefully. 'The mesh may be somewhat larger, but the net will have a far larger sweep; and although many who are now taken will escape, many more will be taken than is now the case under the existing law.'[18]

Since the Bill had its good points the National Association for the Abolition of the Acts, which included all the abolitionist Members of Parliament, believed that if it passed its second reading amendments could be introduced in committee. A resolution that the second reading should not be opposed was carried at a meeting of the Association, despite the opposition of Josephine Butler and members of the Ladies' National Association, who condemned the Bill out of hand. While the Bill was before the House the Press reopened its columns and, as before, the abolitionists—particularly the women—were subjected to abuse and derision. Meanwhile, the Bill, which satisfied neither side, was dropped.

The struggle continued unabated for the next twelve years, with the abolitionists making almost imperceptible progress. They gained a number of important recruits, the most influential being J. B. Stansfeld, MP, who had served in Gladstone's Government as President of the Poor Law Board and, as Honorary Treasurer of the London School of Medicine for Women, was largely responsible for the admission of women students to the wards of the Royal Free Hospital in 1877. Stansfeld jeopardized his political future by joining the abolitionists; and *The Times* expressed mournful regret 'to find a statesman of [his] eminence identifying himself with this hysterical crusade.'[19]

While the fight went on in England, in December 1874 Josephine Butler paid the first of a number of fact-finding visits to the Continent and braved the rigours of Continental disapproval which was expressed with a degree of violence equal to anything she had encountered in her own country. On her first visit she prepared the ground for the establishment of the British and Continental Federation for the Abolition of Government Regulation of Prostitution, with Stansfeld as President and herself and Henry Wilson as joint Secretaries; and she also began a personal enquiry into the workings of the White Slave Traffic.

At about the same time the first breach was made in the

ranks of the medical profession which, with very few exceptions, had been solidly pro-Act. A Liverpool doctor, Dr Nevins, with a hospital appointment which obliged him to give instruction on venereal disease, made a scientific study of the Regulations which proved conclusively to him that they had done nothing to check the spread of infection. He therefore founded a medical association to support abolition; and when the medical Press refused to publish his findings or accept any articles or letters on the subject he started a journal to provide the necessary forum.

The gradual conversion of the medical profession was of inestimable value to the abolitionists. Public opinion, roused by the abolitionist crusaders, was also beginning to crystalize; and when a poignant appeal for help from a woman who was not a prostitute but had been arrested and third-degreed by the police was printed in the *Daily Telegraph* it whipped up public indignation, the more so because the unfortunate woman had committed suicide and the letter was published after her death.

Progress inside Parliament was also becoming apparent; for although the Acts were still in force they had not been extended. In 1879 a Select Committee was appointed to inquire into the working of the Acts and to recommend whether they should be retained, extended or abolished. The Committee was far more favourable towards abolition than the Royal Commission of 1871; and Josephine Butler, who was again called to give evidence, was treated with helpful courtesy and spoke with impressive clarity. All the same, the Committee opted for retention of the Acts, although a minority report drawn up by Stansfeld and published in 1882 recommended that they should be abolished.

The minority report was, however, the prelude to decisive action. In 1883 Stansfeld decided that the time was ripe to force the issue in Parliament; and at the opening session he arranged for a motion to be introduced in the House of Commons in the Debate on the Address which condemned compulsory medical examination under the Acts. To mark the occasion the Society of Friends organized a two-day convention at which prayers were offered for Divine help. A number of similar prayer meetings were held; and Josephine Butler hired a room at an hotel near the Houses of Parliament and arranged for continuous prayer to be offered for the duration of the debate. Clergymen of different denominations came in turn to take the services; the room was packed with women and there was also a sprinkling of men. As Josephine Butler wrote afterwards to one of her sons, there were 'well-dressed ladies, some even of high rank, kneeling together (almost side by side) with the poorest, and some of the outcast women of the purlieus of Westminster'. From time to time Josephine left the prayer meeting to go to the Lobby of the House, where she was informed that some Members were acutely embarrassed at the thought of 'all those women' praying for them. The Debate on the Address went on so long (probably with design) that no time was left for the abolitionist motion; but it was introduced later on, and when the division was called it was plain that the abolitionists had triumphed. 'I thought of the words: "Say unto Jerusalem her warfare is accomplished," ' wrote Josephine, who had been awaiting the decision in the Ladies' Gallery. 'It was a victory of righteousness over gross selfishness, injustice and deceit and for the moment we were all elevated by it. When the figures were given out a long-continued cheer arose,which sounded like a psalm of praise. Then we ran quickly down from the gallery and met a number of our friends coming out from Westminster Hall. It was half-past one in the morning, and the stars were shining in a clear sky. I felt at that silent hour in the morning the spirit of the Psalmist, who said: "When the Lord turned again the captivity of Zion, we were like unto them that dream." It almost seemed like a dream.'[20]

Victory was not complete. The Acts were promptly suspended and were repealed three years later. Yet the age of consent had not been raised and the law was powerless to prevent the pro- curing of young girls. A Bill to amend the law and so eliminate the White Slave Traffic had been introduced several times, but although it had passed the House of Lords it had made no headway in the Commons.

In the summer of 1885 the abolitionists resolved to try the effect of disclosure of the White Slave Traffic in the Press. Josephine Butler and Benjamin Scott, Chamberlain of the City of London, approached the journalist W. T. Stead, who agreed to make his own inquiry into the facts and publish the result. He was horrified at what he discovered; and in order to show how simple it was to buy and sell young girls he asked Josephine to help him to buy a child. Josephine agreed, and got in touch with a former brothel-keeper who had been converted by Mrs Booth of the Salvation Army and was now going straight. With the woman's unwilling connivance (for she had no wish to be involved in undesirable publicity) a thirteen-year-old girl was bought from her mother for £5 and handed over to Stead. He took her to a brothel, left her there for the night under special protection, and next day, after having her medically examined to make sure she was still a virgin, he sent her to Paris in the care of a woman Salvationist. The child came to no harm; but Stead was able to show in a series of powerful articles in the *Pall Mall Gazette* that it was the simplest thing in the world to procure a young girl, use her, and then sell her to White Slave traffickers.

Stead's sensational indictment aroused tremendous excitement and indignation; and as a result the Criminal Law Amendment Bill was rushed through Parliament, becoming law in August, 1885. This was another great victory for the abolitionists. But Stead and the ex-brothel keeper had to stand trial, accused of abducting the child without her father's knowledge, since in law she was the property of her father and not her mother. By a stroke of irony it was later found that the child was illegitimate and the father had no legal claims on her. Meanwhile, Stead was convicted and sentenced to three months' imprisonment, the woman to a year. The sentence bore particularly hardly on the woman, who had played her part only with the utmost reluctance and had had to submit under cross-examination to the revelation of the sordid story of her past. It can have been small comfort to her to know that Josephine Butler had published a pamphlet in which she praised her for having repudiated her former sins.

A good many people thought Stead had undertaken the assignment purely for the sake of publicity. Elizabeth Garrett Anderson, for one, thought it entirely unnecessary 'to flood the world with sensational articles—disgusting and untrue'.[21] Her sister Millicent, though not officially an abolitionist, sent a letter to him in prison: 'I cannot find words to say how I honour and reverence you for what you have done for the weakest and most helpless among women [and] if gratitude and honour from myself and many hundreds and thousands of your countrymen can help you at this stress, I want you to have that help.'[22] And, to Josephine Butler, Stead combined 'the deepest tenderness of a compassionate woman with the manly indignation of a . . . father . . .'[23] Whatever Stead's motives, he certainly helped the abolitionists to gain a victory which might have taken months or years more to reach by less drastic methods.

With the passage of the Criminal Law Amendment Bill Josephine Butler was free to devote more time to the international problem. It was largely through her efforts that the condition of the State brothels—the main channel for the White Slave Traffic and riddled with venereal disease—was brought to light; but it was not until 1927 that the system was finally stamped out under the auspices of the League of Nations.

Josephine Butler, who had been saddened by the death of her husband and helper in 1890, lived on for another sixteen years. In 1901 she resigned from active work; but people continued to flock to her for advice, and to the end of her life she remained the central figure in a crusade which still had its problems to solve.

Chapter VII

THE CONSTITUTIONALISTS

On November 21, 1865, a serious discussion on woman's right to participate in public affairs was held by the Kensington Society, which met at the house of a Mrs Manning to debate topics of the day as they related to women. Emily Davies was present and so were Jessie Boucherett, Elizabeth Garrett, Sophia Jex-Blake, Frances Mary Buss, Dorothea Beale and Elizabeth Wolstenholme. Barbara Bodichon read a paper on the suffrage which was received with such enthusiasm that she wanted there and then to found a women's suffrage committee. The timing seemed right to her, for earlier in the year Emily Davies with Bessie Rayner Parkes and Isa Craig had driven about Westminster in a hired carriage covered with placards asking for votes for John Stuart Mill, who had been invited by the citizens of Westminster to stand for Parliament. Mill, who was a keen supporter of women's suffrage, had accepted only on condition that he would not be required to canvass or take any interest in local affairs and, rather surprisingly, his conditions had been accepted. It was only natural that the Langham Place circle should rush to his side even though their help was suspect. 'We called it giving Mr Mill our moral support,' wrote Emily Davies, 'but there was some suspicion that we might rather be doing him harm, as one of our friends told us he had heard him described as "the man who wants to have girls in Parliament".'[1]

To his female supporters' delight Mill was elected; but Barbara Bodichon's suggestion of a suffrage committee was vetoed by the cautious Emily Davies who was afraid that a campaign to emancipate women would attract the kind of wild extremists best calculated to harm the cause of higher education. Outwardly submissive, Barbara Bodichon consulted Mill. A Reform Bill was to be brought before the House in April, 1866; and Mill was of the opinion that if she could get a hundred signatures to a petition for the enfranchisement of women he would be in a position to present it. Barbara returned in triumph to Emily Davies, who withdrew her objection. And so in 1866 the first women's suffrage committee was set up in London, with the help of Barbara Bodichon, Emily Davies, Elizabeth Garrett, Jessie Boucherett and Octavia Hill's sister Rosamond.*

Those women who had been active in the Married Women's Property agitation ten years earlier were familiar with the technique of collecting names for petitions; but this time a difficulty at once arose (it was to become much more serious later) as to whether the petitioners should ask for the vote for all women householders or only for single women and widows. Emily Davies was sure that the inclusion of married women would only provoke an unnecessary storm; but Mill insisted on all or nothing. A form of words had therefore to be devised which was capable of being interpreted either way. Among the signatures collected—nearly 1,500—were those of Harriet Martineau, Josephine Butler, and the scientific writer Mary Somerville, who was later to give her name to Somerville College, Oxford. Millicent Garrett, not yet twenty-one, was too young to sign; and Florence Nightingale, whose name would have meant so much, had refused to join the committee for, to her, getting the vote was the least of women's problems.

Mill had asked for something which he could 'brandish with effect'[3] and he had certainly got it. The petition was to have been carried to Westminster Hall by Barbara Bodichon and

---

* Octavia Hill was never a supporter of the enfranchisement of women. 'I feel I must say how profoundly sorry I shall be if women's suffrage in any form is introduced into England,' she wrote at the height of the militant movement in a letter to *The Times* in July 1910. She considered that 'political power would militate against [women's] usefulness in the large field of public work in which so many are now doing noble and helpful service. This service is, to my mind, far more valuable now than any voting power could possibly be. . . .'[2]

7. Millicent Garrett Fawcett, about 1892

Millicent Garrett Fawcett

The first Suffrage Caravan Tour through Leicestershire and Northamptonshire, 1909

8. Charlotte Despard

Eleanor Rathbone addressing a NUWSS meeting in Edinburgh, *c.* 1928

Emily Davies, but Barbara was ill on the great day—June 7, 1866—and so Elizabeth Garrett took her place. 'I should like to see the faces of Members when the question is brought up for the first time in the House of Commons,' said Emily Davies to Mill's step-daughter Helen Taylor. 'I think there must be truth in your theory as to the peculiar fitness of women for fighting.'[4]

Westminster Hall was crowded with men but there was not a female in sight except for an old woman selling apples. Fortunately Elizabeth spotted a familiar face in the crowd, the blind MP Henry Fawcett who was in love with her sister Millicent. Henry Fawcett sent his secretary in search of Mill; and the two young women, embarrassed by the size of their package, carried it over to the apple seller who obligingly hid it under her stall. She enquired what was in it and, when they told her, insisted on taking it out, unrolling it and adding her signature.

Mill duly presented the petition; and the mere fact of its existence created quite a stir. 'The vote, we are told, is a solemn trust, and involves high responsibilities,' argued the *Saturday Review*. 'If so, then we should be cautious on whom we confer the trust, and whom we should burden with the responsibilities.'[5] And *Blackwood's Magazine* published an anonymous tirade from a woman who claimed, on what grounds she did not say, to speak for the vast majority of her sex. 'If Mr Mill perseveres in his foolish delusion—if he drags our names, which are spotless, and not for vulgar mouthing, into schedules and statistics— if his uncalled championship continues to expose us to the smartness of newspaper articles, and the gibes of honourable members . . . —not even certain sacred words of true love and reverence which he has uttered in his lifetime . . . will deliver him from our indignation and resentment . . .'[6]

Nothing came of the petition; but Mill had stated his readiness to introduce an amendment on woman's suffrage to the Reform Bill. According to Henry Fawcett, certain Members anticipated 'such fun in the debate that they gave up dinner-parties to be present at it.'[7] Mill was no orator; but his uncompromising honesty made its own effect. He quickly demolished the argument that women had no need of the vote because they were already sufficiently represented by the influence they exerted over their husbands. 'Sir,' he declared,

I

'we do not live in Arcadia . . . and workmen need other protection than that of their employers, and women other protection than that of their men. I should like to have a return
before this House of the number of women who are annually
beaten to death, kicked to death, or trampled to death by their
male protectors; and in the opposite column, the amount of the
sentences passed, in those cases where the dastardly criminals
did not get off altogether. I should also like to have, in a third
column, the amount of property the unlawful taking of which
was, at the same sessions or assizes by the same judge, thought
worthy of the same amount of punishment. We should then
have an arithmetical estimate of the value set by a male
legislature and male tribunals on the murder of a woman . . .
which, if there is any shame in us, would make us hang our
heads.'[8]

Some Members did indeed hang their heads; for among the
seventy-three who supported Mill's amendment was John
Bright, who was agitating for the vote for working class men
but had hitherto rejected the idea that women also had a claim.
But Disraeli, who had previously supported the idea, was
against it now that he was in office; and Gladstone also voted
against the amendment. But it was a great consolation to the
women to know that so many Members had voted for the
amendment and that Mill had been listened to with respect.

In the interval which had elapsed between the presentation
of the women's petition and the debate on the Reform Bill in
May, 1867, a number of small suffrage committees had come
into being; the petition committee had established itself as a
provisional committee of thirteen with Emily Davies as secretary; and Barbara Bodichon had read a paper on *Women's
Suffrage* at the Social Science Congress. Her paper was well
received but created little or no interest outside the ranks of
the converted. 'You will go up and vote upon crutches,' she
wrote to Emily Davies, 'and I shall come out of my grave and
vote in my winding-sheet.'[9] There is no record of Barbara's
appearance in 1918 when women over the age of thirty first
went to the poll: she had been dead for nearly thirty years;
but Emily Davies, at the age of eighty-eight, walked to the
polling station unaided. In the intervening years, although

constant in her support of women's right to vote, Emily Davies's activities in the early stages of the fight were concentrated exclusively on higher education. She resigned from the provisional committee to make way for the eldest of the Garrett sisters, Louisa Smith; and when to the distress of her family and friends Mrs Smith died of appendicitis in 1867 the secretaryship devolved on the willing Barbara Bodichon.

To one woman who had listened to Barbara Bodichon's paper the subject had been both new and exciting. She was Lydia Becker (1827–90), daughter of a German father and a Lancashire mother, and a young woman of keen insight and thoroughness of purpose. Lydia Becker, who was distressingly plain and wore ugly steel-rimmed spectacles, had hitherto devoted her considerable powers of intelligence to the collection of scientific and botanical information. But botany and science seemed dry as dust in comparison with the enthralling cause which she now proceeded to adopt with all her Germanic emotion and efficiency. By January, 1867, she had formed the Manchester Women's Suffrage Committee, with Jacob Bright, MP for Manchester and John Bright's younger brother, and Elizabeth Wolstenholme among its members. In June, the London committee was reformed on a more representative basis as the London National Society for Women's Suffrage; and one of its chief objects was to keep in touch with the Manchester committee and others which were being formed, in Edinburgh, Bristol, Birmingham, and elsewhere.

For the next two years prospects seemed bright: petitions were organized; the suffrage societies flourished. It was even thought possible—since the word 'person' was used in existing franchise laws—that women were already legally enfranchised. Lydia Becker collected the names of 5,346 Manchester women householders who wished to claim the privilege of voting; and a test case was heard before the Court of Common Pleas in November, 1868, the women being represented by Sir John Coleridge (afterwards Lord Chief Justice) assisted by a brilliant young barrister and Doctor of Laws, Richard Marsden Pankhurst. The test case failed; but the suffragists were not downhearted. A little more concerted action, they thought, and the fight would be over; and so they hurried to establish additional local societies, to address meetings, distribute pamphlets, and send deputations to Members of Parliament.

The first large public meeting was held in London in 1869. There was a formidable list of speakers, including Mill, Charles Kingsley, James Stansfeld, John Morley, Henry Fawcett, and Millicent Garrett, now his wife. The audience was attentive; the meeting went well; and the speakers congratulated one another on making an excellent start, although there was some sniping in the Press at women speakers appearing on the same platform as men.

Millicent Garrett Fawcett, who was making her first public speech, was twenty-two years of age. Her interest in women's suffrage was already of long standing. Indeed, there is a story (it may be apochryphal) that as a small child she had sat listening while her elder sister Elizabeth mulled over the great causes of the day with Emily Davies. 'Well, Elizabeth,' said the dictatorial Emily, 'it's quite clear what has to be done. I must devote myself to securing higher education, while you open the medical profession to women. After these things are done, we must see about getting the vote. You are younger than we are, Millie, so you must attend to that.'[10]

This is precisely what Millie set out to do. She was a good little girl and she grew into a good and noble-hearted woman, with her elder sister's pleasing serenity of expression and her dedicated but dignified approach to problems. She was under twenty when she fell in love with Henry Fawcett, a Fellow of Trinity College, Cambridge, Professor of Political Economy, and Radical MP for Brighton. Fawcett, who had been blind for nearly ten years as the result of a shooting accident, was a man of considerable resolution and charm. His blindness was a challenge to Millicent, who was eager to help him in the political work which she, too, found congenial, and which involved him in continuous support for the emancipation of women. Her parents, however, insisted on a period of separation before the engagement was announced, thinking—so they said—that he might change his mind. Elizabeth took her parents' side. 'I had a most awful letter from Lizzie,' wrote Millicent to her sister Louisa Smith, 'and whenever I was a moment alone with Mother, she would say, "Dear, I am tormented by the idea that very likely, now he has had a little quiet time to think of what he has done, Mr Fawcett may heartily regret what has passed" '. Elizabeth, she added, had suggested that she should ask Barbara Bodichon's opinion of Henry Fawcett, but Millicent would have none of that. 'I don't know Mme Bodichon,' she added tartly, 'but, judging from Dr Bodichon's appearance, I should say that it was improbable that we should agree in the choice of husbands. Dr Bodichon is more like a he-hag than anyone else I can recall just at present . . .'[11]

Elizabeth's fierce antagonism is not at all easy to explain. Her biographer* relates how several years earlier she herself had refused to marry Henry Fawcett—as she had refused to marry several other men—because she was too deeply committed to her chosen career. She had, however, been very much attached to him, but had turned him down after asking her sister Louisa's advice. She was invariably over-protective towards young girls and it must have irked her to find that Louisa was now on Millicent's side. It is probable that Millicent never knew that Henry Fawcett had wanted to marry Elizabeth: but stubbornness was one of her chief characteristics; and on this occasion, as so often in the future, she was obdurate. Family objections gave way; Elizabeth was sisterly both to husband and wife; and after her marriage Millicent became her husband's secretary and guide, while he became her mainstay in the suffrage cause. In 1868 their only child, Philippa, was born, destined to play a unique part in the women's movement as the first Cambridge woman student to be placed above the Senior Wrangler in the Mathematical Tripos.

In 1870 the first separate Women's Suffrage Bill was drafted by Richard Pankhurst and introduced in the House of Commons by Jacob Bright (Mill had lost his seat in 1868). It passed its second reading by a majority of 33; but a week later Gladstone threw his weight against it in committee and it was rejected by 126 votes.

So began a long series of hopes and disappointments. The previous year the municipal franchise had been extended to women

* Jo Manton, *Elizabeth Garrett Anderson* (Methuen, 1965), pp. 156–7 and 180–2.

ratepayers without any particular difficulty; but those women who imagined that they would get the parliamentary vote in the same way were gravely mistaken. There were one or two compensations. In 1870 women became eligible to serve on the school boards established under the new Education Act, and as already stated, Lydia Becker, Elizabeth Garrett and Emily Davies were among those elected. In the same year the Married Women's Property Act, for which so many women had slaved, at length became law. And also in 1870 the Local Government Board was established, and two years later the first woman Poor Law Inspector was appointed. When Gladstone declared that if women really wanted the vote they must first prove by public service their ability to accept so grave a responsibility, they hastened to do as he suggested; politically this got them absolutely nowhere.

After the failure of the 1870 Women's Suffrage Bill it was decided to try and form a society in every borough and county constituency, and speakers were sent from London to address meetings all over the country. Public speaking was something to which the majority of the women were completely unaccustomed; and, apart from the nervous strain, they did not even know if their voices would carry in a large hall or the open air. Millicent Fawcett's first appearance was a triumph; but she had been helped by her youth and charm as well as the illustrious company in which she made her debut. Lydia Becker, plain and austere-looking, was not so fortunate. Her first appearance was in Manchester in 1868 at a meeting addressed among others by Jacob Bright and Richard Pankhurst: it was followed by the canard that there were now three sexes—masculine, feminine and Miss Becker. The *Saturday Review*, as ever, had some caustic comments to make on the undesirability of women stepping into the limelight: an article which it printed by the popular novelist Eliza Lynn Linton entitled *The Shrieking Sisterhood* is typical of its attitude.

Nevertheless, recruits came bravely forward. Among them were Mill's step-daughter Helen Taylor; Harriet Grote (she amused Millicent Fawcett by referring to her husband invariably as 'the historian'); and Agnes and Rhoda Garrett, sister and cousin respectively of Millicent, who had embarked on an unconventional business as house-decorators. A more influential recruit was Lady Amberley (1842–74), daughter of the second Lord Stanley of Alderley and daughter-in-law of the former Prime Minister Lord Russell. After a certain amount of natural hesitation Lady Amberley agreed to read a paper on female suffrage at the Mechanics Institute in Stroud. She spoke extremely well, yet, as she wrote afterwards to Helen Taylor, 'I had no sympathy with me at all . . . Amberley was the only supporter I really had, and people expressed surprise to me afterwards to see that a woman could lecture and still look like a lady! . . .'[12] Lady Amberley had underestimated herself; for within a fortnight she had formed a small suffrage committee, much to the annoyance of Queen Victoria who came to hear of it. 'The Queen,' she wrote to Theodore Martin, who was engaged at the time on his biography of the Prince Consort, 'is most anxious to enlist everyone who can speak or write to join in checking this mad, wicked folly of "Woman's Rights" with all its attendant horrors, on which her poor feeble sex is bent, forgetting every sense of womanly feeling and propriety. Lady Amberley ought to get a *good whipping*.'[13]

The Queen's letter was not, of course, made public; but she was not alone in her condemnation. The general feeling was summed up by an MP (a Mr Scourfield) in 1872 when the second reading of another Women's Suffrage Bill was defeated by 79 votes. Scourfield expressed deep fears that if women were ever given the vote 'their husbands would find only dry metaphysical lectures awaiting them instead of their dinners, and advised English women to rely upon their natural attractions and their domestic virtues, and upon the proud intellectual position which some of their sex had attained'.[14]

Despite the really heroic efforts of Lydia Becker and the others the cause was not making headway. For twenty years—from 1870 till 1890—Lydia Becker did everything she possibly could to advance it, supervising the parliamentary campaign behind the scenes, founding and editing the *Women's Suffrage Journal*, and organizing and speaking at countless meetings. She was sensible, patient and undeviatingly sanguine, and despite a certain rigidity of mind and manner she received a response which was always respectful and sometimes warm. There were moments when her starved emotional nature betrayed her into a wave of hysteria. 'How they listened—how they cheered,' she wrote to a friend after a meeting of working-class women in Manchester. 'If my eyes had been shut I should have fancied it was men who were cheering and clapping . . . I can't tell you how my heart went out to these women: and to see them look at me—oh, it was really sacred—awful: it was if I received a baptism. It has been a new life to me to know and feel the strength there is in those women . . .'[15]

This sort of response is more reminiscent of the latter-day militants than of the stubborn, sturdy tacticians who set the pace at the beginning and kept it up to the end. Millicent Fawcett would never have allowed herself to think—much less to write—in this way. She was an admirable speaker, with a fine voice, a trenchant style, an excellent sense of timing, and a sane and humorous outlook. She was tirelessly energetic, absolutely honest and entirely unpretentious; and she possessed a rock-like determination which nothing could move. Throughout the dramatic and passionate scenes to come she remained exactly the same, leading, guiding, exhorting, standing steadfastly aside from violence, and for fifty years keeping her personal dignity intact. Because she neither ranted nor raved, chained herself to railings, or went to prison for her beliefs the strength of her leadership and the importance of her contribution to the outcome are all too often forgotten.

Millicent Fawcett, who had found fulfilment in a happy marriage, had many of the personal graces which Lydia Becker lacked. But the suffrage movement owes much to the older woman's patience and enthusiasm and to the work of her loyal deputy Helen Blackburn (1842–1903), another plain but dedicated woman, who, as secretary to the London Suffrage Committee, was responsible for much of the parliamentary work.

During the years of Lydia Becker's leadership the breach caused by Josephine Butler's crusade was healed by Leonard Courtney, who had succeeded Jacob Bright as spokesman in the House of Commons and in 1879 managed to draw the two suffrage factions together again. The suffrage cause was regularly debated in Parliament, but in 1884 it received a knock-out blow with the passage of the Reform Bill which gave every male householder the vote. Despite a memorial begging for the inclusion of women and signed by 79 Liberal Members Gladstone, who did not oppose women's suffrage on principle but always contrived to oppose it in practice, evaded the issue by insisting that the Bill as it stood was quite controversial enough.

To the suffragists this was a bitter betrayal; and from that time onwards Millicent Fawcett, who had never really trusted Gladstone, lost no chance of pointing out his failings. She was not, as she said of herself, 'a forgiving person'. She could not forget an injury: indeed, 'the black mark which might be acquired in her judgment was not at all easy to wipe out, and . . . no one who held the old-fashioned view of women could ever stand well in her eyes.'[16]

The year 1884 was personally as well as politically a dark one for Millicent Fawcett: in that year her husband died and she had to soldier on without his wise support. Next year an additional political problem cropped up with the creation of the Primrose League, which followed the Conservative Party lead uncritically; and the Primrose League was followed in 1886 by the Women's Liberal Federation, started by Mrs Gladstone 'to help our husbands'.[17] The Women's Liberal Federation was more sympathetic towards women's suffrage than the Primrose League; but both organizations used women as helpers and canvassers and so gave many people the impression that women already had as much political influence as was good for them.

This led to a second split in the ranks of the London suffragists. The majority maintained that the only thing to do was to work for the vote within the framework of the Liberal Party; but a minority faction led by Millicent Fawcett, who had no faith in the intentions of Gladstone or his Party, wanted to keep the suffrage issue free from party entanglements. In 1888 the minority faction walked out, after a stormy session, to form a suffrage society of its own.

The two factions coalesced temporarily in 1889 to face a blow from an unexpected quarter. This was a protest published in the *Nineteenth Century Magazine* and signed by a number of prominent supporters of the women's movement, among them the

novelist Mrs Humphrey Ward. 'We believe,' they declared
with immense gravity, 'that the emancipating process has now
reached the limits fixed by the physical constitution of women.'[18]
The suffragists might rage that this was nonsense; but the harm
was done, and their opponents now had every excuse for saying
that women themselves did not want the vote. In due course
Mrs Humphrey Ward became the leader of the Women's
National Anti-Suffrage League; and in this capacity she and
Millicent Fawcett were to cross swords on many occasion.

In 1890 the suffrage cause lost the faithful Lydia Becker; and
with her death the *Women's Suffrage Journal* ceased publication,
and for a time the parliamentary work suffered. But although
the 1890s had opened badly and many workers seemed to be
losing heart, the two opposing factions were reunited once
more. As the London Society for Women's Suffrage they were
linked in 1897 under the presidency of Millicent Fawcett with
eighteen provincial societies under the title of the National
Union of Women's Suffrage Societies. The National Union was
a thoroughly democratic concern. Policy was hammered out at
the annual meetings of the Council attended by representatives of all the constituent societies. Between meetings the work
was carried on by an Executive Committee elected at the
annual Council meeting, its membership including people
distinguished in other fields besides politics. As Millicent
Fawcett saw it, the chief objective of the National Union was
the conversion of public opinion, for, to her, conversion was just
as important as actually winning the vote. If progress was
inevitably slow, she lost no opportunity of keeping the cause
alive both inside and outside Parliament. It is not always
realized that between 1866, when Mill's suffrage amendment
was lost, and 1903, when the militant suffrage movement was
born, nearly 1,400 public meetings and demonstrations were
held; a great many petitions were organized and presented; and
innumerable leaflets and articles were printed. The usual
electoral procedure was to support any candidate who was
pledged to uphold women's suffrage; but on three occasions
later in the campaign independent Women's Suffrage Candidates were put up, each time however with very poor results.

The National Union made many converts; and recruits

learned their political duty under Millicent Fawcett's watchful eye. If their enthusiasm rose to dangerous heights she reminded them that they must never breatk the law: if they made claims which they could not substantiate she put them gently but firmly in their place: and when they were depressed by reverses she infected them with her own steady belief that in the end the cause would triumph. She herself was so much in demand as a speaker that at one time she curtailed her appearances. Speaking was never a pleasure; but she would not shirk it and urged her supporters to follow her example. 'No one knows whether they can speak or not till they try,' she declared. 'I believe any one *can* speak who has anything to say. Of course they don't like it, but no more do I.'[19]

Several times during the 1890s there was a glimmer of hope. In 1894 a petition signed by a quarter of a million women was exhibited in Westminster Hall; and in 1897, the year of the Queen's Golden Jubilee, for the first time since 1886, a suffrage bill passed its second reading, by a majority of 71. By now however, Gladstone's continuing intransigence had effectively destroyed all hope of decisive Liberal intervention. After 1897, as Millicent Fawcett recorded, 'the anti-suffragists in Parliament used every possible trick and stratagem to prevent the subject being discussed and divided on in the House.' One of the most resourceful of the 'antis' was the well-known journalist Henry Labouchère, Liberal Member for Northampton, 'to whom it was a congenial task to shelve the women's suffrage question'. On one occasion Labouchère and his friends successfully prevented a suffrage bill from coming before the House with a protracted debate on the previous bill, which dealt with 'verminous persons'.[20]

Despite all the hard work of Millicent Fawcett and Lydia Becker's other heirs the cause was losing rather than gaining ground, and Press coverage was dwindling accordingly. Then, in 1899, came the outbreak of the Boer War. Feeling in the country was sharply divided; and among the 'pro-Boers' who blamed the Government for the outbreak, were many members of the women's suffrage societies. Millicent Fawcett, who supported the Government, was attacked by some as a bloodthirsty Jingo, 'with a mind quite closed to reason or argument.'[21]

With her usual imperturbability she took no outward notice of
the abuse but clung to the moderate views which were natural
to her, looking forward to a just peace and equal political
privileges for all South Africa's white peoples. During the war,
which unleashed so much bitter feeling, the Press clamped down
entirely on the women's suffrage issue; and it was in this climate
of frustration that militancy was bred.

Chapter VIII

THE MILITANTS

The militant suffrage movement is, of course, inextricably bound up with the names of Richard Pankhurst's wife and daughters. In 1879 Richard Pankhurst married an attractive, intelligent girl more than twenty years his junior who, like himself, had been reared in the Liberal tradition, and had been a suffragist since her school days when she first heard Lydia Becker speak. She was Emmeline Goulden (1858–1928) born in Manchester, the eldest of the ten children of Robert Goulden, the owner of a calico-printing and bleach works.

The marriage was a happy one, domestically as well as politically; and the Pankhursts had five children, two sons one of whom died in infancy and the other as a young man, and three daughters, Christabel (1880–1958), Sylvia (1882–1960) and Adela (1885–1961). Richard Pankhurst stood twice for Parliament in the Liberal interest but was soundly beaten on both occasions. After Gladstone's refusal to insert women's suffrage in the Reform Bill of 1884 he broke with the Liberal Party and he and his wife joined the newly founded Fabian Society. Emmeline Pankhurst had taken Gladstone's advice that women should prepare themselves for the vote by taking civic responsibility; and she had been elected to the Board of Poor Law Guardians for the district of Chorlton upon Medlock.

Her father was furious when his daughter and son-in-law abandoned the Liberal Party; and this was one of the reasons why the Pankhursts migrated to London in the early days of their married life. Later, however, they returned to Manchester. In London and in Manchester husband and wife were active in women's suffrage affairs, and the little girls imbibed suffrage views in their cradles. Money was always short; for Richard

Pankhurst's left-wing views damaged his prospects at the Bar; and Emmeline twice tried her hand at running a fancy goods shop. Her first venture was in a poor, insanitary district off the Tottenham Court Road in London. The family lived in rooms over the shop. It was there that her infant son contracted diptheria and died; and his mother never completely absolved herself from blame, though oddly enough, when her second son was born she gave him the same name—Harry.

The Independent Labour Party came into being in 1893 and the Pankhursts were among its earliest members. Two years later Richard Pankhurst stood for Parliament as an ILP candidate; but, as before, he was decisively beaten. In 1898 he died very suddenly at the age of sixty-two.

When Emmeline Pankhurst was left a widow her two youngest children were still at school; Christabel, the eldest, who was eighteen, was spending a year with friends in Switzerland, and Sylvia, two years younger, was studying art and showing considerable talent. The family was in desperate need of money; and Emmeline was thankful to accept the offer of a salaried post with the promise of a small pension on the Chorlton Board of Guardians as Registrar of Births and Deaths. On acceptance of the post she had to resign her voluntary job as Poor Law Guardian, in which she had been instrumental in making a number of sensible workhouse reforms. Her new post, in a big working-class district, brought her in close touch with the lives of the very poor. When she talked to women with large families who had been deserted by their husbands, or to young girls with illegitimate babies, her reforming zeal turned to hatred of the men who were responsible for so much unnecessary misery. This was undoubtedly one of the reasons why in *her* fight for the vote man was the principal enemy, man who was denying women the vote. In this, as in so many other ways, she was the direct antithesis of Millicent Fawcett and her patient campaign to convert public opinion.

No two leaders could have been less alike. Millicent Fawcett, dignified, idealistic, straightforward and obstinate, never wavering in her faith in ultimate victory; and Emmeline Pankhurst, a woman of quite extraordinary beauty and fascination, a compound of fire and ice, whose fine-drawn face was often to be compared with that of a weary saint. Millicent Fawcett's honesty and rectitude brought converts to her side: Emmeline Pankhurst was a personal magnet and an orator of real genius. She was, said one of her major converts, the musician Ethel Smyth (afterwards Dame Ethel Smyth, 1858–1944), 'as simple as she was complex, as temperate as she was passionate, as loving as she was heartless; who, little as in her bottomless humility she guessed it, was of . . . the breed of heroes and heroines.'[1]

Ethel Smyth, who abandoned her music for two years at Emmeline Pankhurst's command, was one of scores who succumbed to the Pankhurst spell and gladly surrendered to Emmeline the whole direction of their lives. Most of the women had to be content to suffer and to worship from afar; but with Ethel Smyth she had 'the deepest and closest of friendships' which, according to the musician, foundered in the end on the rock of Emmeline Pankhurst's uncritical admiration for her eldest daughter.[2]

After her husband's death Christabel became the object of Emmeline's greatest love and admiration; and it was Christabel who triggered off the militant movement and shared the leadership and the magic with her mother.

When Christabel returned to England after her year abroad she had grown into a buxom, handsome young woman. Even as a girl she had been scornful of what she considered the dilatory efforts of the suffragists to get the vote; and now, apart from attending classes at Manchester University, she spent most of her time at political meetings. Her first impromptu speech was so promising that her mother was told that she had the makings of a fine lawyer. The idea appealed to Christabel, who promptly applied to become a student at Lincoln's Inn, only to have her application refused together with those of several other women: the law was not yet ready to accept women students. She therefore decided to take a course at Manchester University leading to the Bachelor of Laws degree, thinking, as did her mother, that this would make her more useful to the suffrage cause.

Politically, Christabel was growing impatient with the Independent Labour Party; for although Keir Hardie, the leader, who was first returned to Parliament in 1892, was a staunch advocate of women's suffrage his supporters were not all of the same mind. Emmeline Pankhurst who had many Socialist friends had decided to form a women's branch of the ILP and call it the Women's Labour Representation Committee. This was far too cumbersome a title for Christabel, who already possessed considerable powers of argument and persuasion. She insisted—and she got her way—that the name of the new branch should be the Women's Social and Political Union. The Union—or the WSPU as it was generally called—was inaugurated on October 10, 1903. Its objective was immediate franchise: its slogan, 'Votes for Women!', was far more compelling than the suffragist formula—'To extend the parliamentary franchise to women on the same terms as it is or may be granted to men'.

For the first two years of its existence the Union, ostensibly working within the framework of the Labour movement, conducted a preliminary educational campaign at small meetings in Lancashire. Emmeline Pankhurst and her two elder daughters formed the core of the speakers, Sylvia constantly interrupting her art studies to play her part. They were reinforced from time to time by the younger members of the family, Adela and Harry, and by several suffragists whose opinions were more eclectic than conservative. They also enrolled two important recruits, Theresa Billington (afterwards Mrs Billington-Greig, 1877–1964), an elementary schoolteacher with an astute mind and a decisive way with hecklers; and Annie Kenney (afterwards Mrs Taylor, 1879–1953), a cotton factory worker whose enthusiasm and originality soon made up for her lack of political experience. It was Annie Kenney who suggested that the Union should hold open-air meetings on the Sunday before the opening of the Lancashire Wakes Weeks. The Wakes, a kind of travelling fair, was held in the cotton towns; and Sunday was usually spent by the townspeople inspecting the exhibits. Union speakers therefore toured with the Wakes, and after a slow start, as Emmeline Pankhurst recorded, they 'rivalled in popularity the Salvation Army and even the tooth-drawers and patent-medicine pedlars.'[3]

A trickle of old-time suffragists now began to transfer their loyalties to the Union, which potentially was more dynamic than the suffrage societies; but it remained small and insignificant until 1905. A suffrage Bill had been introduced the previous year but had failed to pass its second reading; and by February 1905 Emmeline Pankhurst decided that the time had come for the Union to make itself felt in Parliament. She went to London to stay with Sylvia, who was studying at the Royal College of Art and living in Chelsea. With some of her colleagues and members of the National Union of Women's Suffrage Societies she was present in the Ladies' Gallery of the House of Commons when a Private Members' Suffrage Bill—the second on the list for the day—was deliberately talked out by Labouchère and his friends, who made great and prolonged play with a Bill to provide that all horse-drawn carts should carry a rear-light at night.

At the close of the debate the disconsolate women wandered out into the street and gathered round the statue of Richard I. The aged Mrs Elizabeth Wolsetenholme-Elmy—now a Dickensian-looking figure who wore her silvery hair in ringlets beneath a black bonnet—started to make a speech but was stopped by a police inspector who instructed her to move on. The women dispersed but reformed in Broad Sanctuary where they held a brief indignation meeting with the help of Keir Hardie. This small meeting, which was not even mentioned in the Press, was the real start of the separate WSPU campaign.

A general election was due in the autumn, and the Liberals were confident that they would be able to oust the Conservatives who had been in office for the last five years. The WSPU therefore decided to try and get an authoritative Liberal statement on the suffrage issue at a meeting at the Free Trade Hall, Manchester, which was to be addressed by Sir Edward Grey (afterwards Lord Grey of Fallodon) and by the Liberal candidate for North-West Manchester, Winston Churchill. Christabel Pankhurst and Annie Kenney, who had been more or less adopted by the Pankhursts, were the chosen delegates and they smuggled into the hall a home-made calico banner emblazoned with the words 'Vote for Women' in furniture stain. Women's suffrage was not mentioned in the speeches, and at the end Annie Kenney got to her feet to ask a question. 'Will the Liberal Party, if returned, give votes to women?' There was no reply.

K

Christabel repeated the question, unfurling the home-made banner as she spoke. A hubbub then broke out in the hall during which Christabel was forced back into her seat, with a man's hat pushed over her face. She struggled to her feet again and once more repeated the question. It was not answered; but the Chief Constable of Manchester who, for some reason or other, was on the platform, offered to hand a written question to Sir Edward Grey. The question was written down and handed from one speaker to another; and yet, while Grey and Churchill were personally sympathetic to the cause, they made no attempt to answer it.

The girls then proceeded to create a genuine disturbance. They were hustled out into the street and started to address the people as they left the meeting; and they were arrested for assault when Christabel, who had made several futile attempts to hit a policeman, managed to spit at one. They were released for the night on bail, and at the police court next morning they were ordered to pay a small fine, with the alternative of three days' imprisonment for Annie and seven for Christabel. Emmeline Pankhurst offered to pay their fines, but Christabel indignantly refused.

The prison experience, though brief (Christabel served only part of her sentence) was decidedly unpleasant. The girls had to wear prison clothing, sleep on straw mattresses, and eat coarse, unpalatable food. They met only during the daily exercise march and in chapel, where they huddled close to one another. 'Christabel looked very coy and pretty in her prison cap,' wrote Annie later. 'She took my hand tenderly and just held it, as though I were a lost child being guided home.'[4]

Several sympathizers (including Churchill, it was rumoured) called at the prison and tried, unsuccessfully, to pay the girls' fines. And the Press, which ignored the sober doings of the National Union, really went to town on the incident. 'Our only regret,' declared the *Standard* in its report of the sentence, 'is that the discipline will be identical with that experienced by mature and sensible women, and not that which falls to the lot of children in the Nursery.'[5] And the *Daily Mail* made history by christening the girls 'suffragettes'.

To Millicent Fawcett, the incident at least had the advantage of bringing the issue into the open. The suffrage societies, she wrote, 'had become quite accustomed to holding magnificent meetings . . . with every evidence of public sympathy and support, and to receive from the Anti-Suffrage Press either no notice at all or only a small paragraph tucked away in an inconspicuous corner. The sensation caused by the action of the Women's Social Political Union suddenly changed all this. Instead of the withering contempt of silence, the Anti-Suffrage papers came out day after day with columns of hysterical verbiage directed against our movement . . .'[6]

The first person to greet the girls on their release from prison was Mrs Flora Drummond, a plump little pouter pigeon of a woman, less than five feet tall. Flora Drummond joined the WSPU, where she was familiarly known as the 'General', as a tribute to her dimunitive size and swagger and also to her excellent powers of inventive organization.

Theresa Billington had arranged a welcome-home demonstration at the Free Trade Hall, the scene of the disturbance. Keir Hardie was the principal speaker; and Christabel made a triumphant and sparkling speech. The girls' ingenuity and courage brought a host of recruits to the Union, and helped to launch it on the tide of militant aggression from which it never turned back. The new tactics of interrupting and breaking up meetings masked the less spectacular methods of the constitutional suffragists whose quiet, impressive work was continued throughout the militant campaign.

The Liberals were returned at the General Election of 1905 with a majority of 354 and with Sir Henry Campbell-Bannerman as Prime Minister; and for the first time Labour emerged as a party of some significance, with 52 Members. The WSPU, which had helped Keir Hardie in his election campaign at Merthyr Tydfil, had concentrated its efforts in the North, especially in the North-West Division of Manchester, where Churchill won the seat from the Conservatives. The original Manchester Suffrage Society, following its usual policy of asking each candidate for his views, had received a pointed reply from Churchill in which he stated that while his previous attitude had been one of increasing sympathy, he had 'been much discouraged by the action of certain advocates of the movement in persistently disturbing and attempting to break up both my own meetings and those of other Liberal candidates'. This sort of agitation, he continued, would if it continued prevent him 'from taking any further steps in favour of the cause which you have at heart.'[7]

Churchill, of course, had been thoroughly irritated by the militant tactics, as had a number of his colleagues. Even so, there was a great deal of sympathy for Women's Suffrage in the new Parliament.

Early in 1906 the WSPU descended on the South. Christabel Pankhurst, whose idea it was to attack the Government in Parliament, persuaded her mother to send Annie Kenney on ahead with £2 in her pocket—all that remained after the election campaign—to start 'rousing' London. Christabel reluctantly agreed to remain in Manchester until she had taken her Law degree. Emmeline Pankhurst, having arranged for one of her sisters to take over her job as Registrar, followed Annie to London a fortnight later, to find that with Sylvia's help she had organized a procession of women to march from Caxton Hall to the House of Commons on the occasion of the State Opening of Parliament. Keir Hardie had raised the money to hire Caxton Hall for a suffrage meeting which was attended, among others, by 400 working women—some carrying their babies—who had marched to Westminster from the East End of London.

Emmeline Pankhurst addressed the meeting, revealing for the first time in the South, the full power of her oratory. Annie Kenney spoke next and was still speaking when news was brought in that women's suffrage had not been mentioned in the King's Speech. Emmeline Pankhurst then descended from the platform to lead the women to the House of Commons. The Speaker refused to admit them, and they found the Strangers' entrance barred by the police; but after a good deal of to-ing and fro-ing the Speaker agreed that twenty women should enter at a time. Those who were admitted, some of them having waited for hours in the cold and rain, were fobbed off with pious platitudes; and beyond proving their nuisance value, nothing at all was gained.

The setback convinced Emmeline Pankhurst that an all-out campaign was now essential; and for this she needed money and influence. Keir Hardie was instrumental in providing both when he introduced to the Pankhursts his friends Frederick Pethick-Lawrence (afterwards Lord Pethick-Lawrence, 1871–1961) and his wife Emmeline (1867–1943).

Pethick-Lawrence (born Frederick Lawrence) belonged to a well-known City family. After a brilliant career at Cambridge, where paradoxically, he was President of the Union and represented the University at billiards, he studied for the Bar, became a newspaper proprietor and a prospective parliamentary candidate. Although he started out as a Liberal-Unionist he soon began to veer towards the Left; and after he came down from Cambridge he also took up social work, and went to live at the University settlement in Lambeth.

It was through his social work that Frederick Lawrence met his future wife. She was Emmeline Pethick, who came from the west country, and had early decided to devote her life to the welfare of London's working girls. She worked first in a working girls' club and then, with a friend, founded a second club, and was associated in founding a holiday hostel for girls. In 1899 she met Frederick Lawrence; but she agreed to marry him only after a considerable delay because she did not see how marriage could fit in with the life of a dedicated social worker. In fact the marriage was a genuine partnership; and at the start Frederick Lawrence showed his devoted admiration for the solidly handsome young woman he was marrying by prefixing her name to his.

When Keir Hardie introduced the two Emmelines to one another Emmeline Pankhurst was not impressed. 'She will not help,' she told her daughter Sylvia, 'she has too many interests.'[8] But Emmeline Pethick-Lawrence next attended an informal meeting in Sylvia's rooms and agreed to become treasurer of the recently formed London Committee of the WSPU, which at the moment had no funds at all. Emmeline Pathick-Lawrence drew her husband into the movement; and for the next six years husband and wife proved themselves absolutely invaluable. They were magnificent fund-raisers, and what they could not raise they provided from their own pockets, for time and time again Frederick Pethick-Lawrence went bail for the suffragettes. They also showed exemplary courage, combined with the platform eloquence of the wife and the sound business sense and legal acumen of the husband.

At the beginning of the Pethick-Lawrences' association with the Union Christabel, who had been bracketed first in the LL.B examinations, arrived in London. She was young, brilliant and ebullient, and she appealed to the Pethick-Lawrences even more than did her fascinating mother. It was Christabel, wrote Pethick-Lawrence's biographer, 'who really captured Pethick and permanently transformed his imagination'.[9] She was on the face of it a far more attractive character than her younger sister. Sylvia should really have been an artist, but she was ready to sacrifice everything to the cause and, as time went on, she worked chiefly among the poor in the East End. Adela, the youngest Pankhurst girl, had already thrown up her job as an elementary school teacher to work for the cause in London; but she went to Australia before the end of the militant campaign, settled there, and married a Labour MP.

After the failure of their first assault on Parliament the WSPU began to plan a second. Members were to take part in a representative deputation to the Prime Minister which the National Union was organizing; but instead of waiting patiently for the event the WSPU jumped the gun. Led by 'General' Drummond, a party called at 10 Downing Street and asked to see the Prime Minister, Campbell-Bannerman. He sent out a refusal; and the General put her finger on what she took to be a bell but was actually a knob which opened the front door. Before anybody could stop them the General and Annie Kenney had burst into the house and had almost reached the Cabinet room before they were halted and turned back.

The two women were arrested but no charges were brought against them. They therefore tried something else. In April, 1906, Keir Hardie, who had won a place in the Private Members' ballot, introduced a Women's Suffrage Bill. Several constitutional suffragists were in the Ladies' Gallery to listen to the debate; and so, under the watchful eye of the police, were Emmeline Pankhurst and some of her suffragettes. When it became clear that the Bill, like its predecessor, would be talked out Emmeline gave her followers a signal. 'Divide, divide!' cried the suffragettes in unison as they pushed a crop of little 'Votes for Women' banners through the grille.

The women were hustled out of the Gallery; and the constitutionalists were so indignant at their conspicuous behaviour
that they made an attempt to prevent them from joining their
deputation. Keir Hardie managed to make peace between
them; and a WSPU contingent, led by Emmeline Pankhurst,
joined 300 or so representatives of the suffrage societies, women
graduates, textile workers, and members of the Co-operative
and Temperance movements. Emily Davies led the deputation
and it was introduced by a Liberal MP, Sir Charles McLaren,
whose wife—also present—was a sister of John Bright. Any
deputation led by Emily Davies would be a dignified, orderly
affair; but inevitably the WSPU contingent introduced a dis-
cordant element. Campbell-Bannerman explained that while he
himself was in sympathy with their cause certain members of his
Cabinet and Party were not, and therefore he could take no
action on their behalf. He advised the women, however, to go
on trying to convert the country and, above all, to be patient.

It was now forty years since Emily Davies had helped to carry
the first women's suffrage petition to Parliament; and even
though she was prepared to be patient Emmeline Pankhurst
and her followers were not. Annie Kenney leapt onto a chair, so
that every one could see and hear her. 'Sir,' she shouted, 'we
are not satisfied!'[10]

Later the same day Emmeline Pankhurst addressed a meeting
from the plinth of the Nelson Monument in Trafalgar Square.
As always, she looked elegant and beautiful; and she was
supported, among others, by Keir Hardie, by Annie Kenney
in the clogs and head-shawl of a mill girl and Mrs Wolstenholme-Elmy with her black bonnet and ringlets. Members
pledged themselves to fight until victory was won and to sacrifice their lives if need be. 'Deeds not Words' now became their
menacing motto; and Campbell-Bannerman, who had urged
them to go on converting the country, little knew what dangerous forms of ingenuity he had unleashed.

From this time onwards the paths of the National Union and
the WSPU began to diverge ever more widely, although Millicent
Fawcett was far less censorious about the militants than many
of her followers. Under her presidency the National Union

remained a representative body. But the WSPU, dominated by
Emmeline Pankhurst and the Pethick-Lawrences, and later
also by Christabel, was a virtual dictatorship. Under their
united direction the campaign against the Government was
planned and carried out. In after years Christabel was to suggest
that 'if Mrs Fawcett and Mother had stood together at the door
of the House of Commons, it might have opened. The Prime
Minister could not easily have fought both wings of the Women's
Movement.'[11] This is a very doubtful supposition. It is most
unlikely that the two leaders could ever have combined. If they
had (and many of Millicent Fawcett's friends suggested that
they should) it is probable that Emmeline would soon have
resented the other's cautious tactics, though with all her fire
and vigour she would have found the rock-like Millicent
extremely hard to dislodge.

The Chancellor of the Exchequer, H. H. Asquith (afterwards
Lord Oxford and Asquith), who was known to oppose women's
suffrage, now became the WSPU's chief target. Theresa Billington
and Annie Kenney served a prison sentence (they had the
option of a fine) for creating a disturbance outside his London
house; and in the summer of 1906 Emmeline took a contingent
of women to Nottingham, where he was to speak on the
Government's educational policy. She had carefully framed her
demand for the vote in the guise of a question which implied
that mothers as well as fathers should be enfranchized if they
were to exercise a proper control over their children's education. The question was not answered; and Mrs Pankhurst was
summarily hustled out of the building.

In the autumn of 1906 the Pethick-Lawrences' London flat in
Clement's Inn became the Union's headquarters. It was staffed
almost entirely by volunteers, among them the General, who
had brought her typewriter to London, and Jessie Kenney,
Annie's sister, a boyish looking girl who often went around disguised as a messenger-boy. To the young, it seemed a splendid
adventure. 'As department was added to department,' wrote
Christabel later, 'Clement's Inn seemed always to have one
more room to offer. And so on, daily, weekly, monthly, yearly!
All the time, watching, attacking, defending, moving and
counter-moving! It was indeed a question of "I shall not cease

from mental fight". Yet *how glorious those suffragette days were!*
To lose the personal in the great impersonal is to live!'[12]

In 1907 the Pethick-Lawrences started and took charge of
Votes for Women, the official organ of the WSPU. By 1909 the
journal had a circulation of nearly 50,000 and was bringing in
a steady income from advertisements.

From 1906 onwards monthly 'At Homes' had been held at
Clement's Inn at which the technique of the movement was
discussed and perfected and inexperienced women were instructed in the ways of militancy. Emmeline Pankhurst, who
drilled her followers in the art of heckling, was less adept when
it came to the hurling of missiles. Later, she took lessons from
her athletic friend Ethel Smyth, who once took her at nightfall
to a deserted spot on Hook Heath to throw stones at a tree. 'I
imagine Mrs Pankhurst had not played ball games in her
youth,' wrote Ethel Smyth, 'and the first stone flew back-
wards out of her hand, narrowly missing my dog. Once more
we began at a distance of about three yards, the face of the pupil
assuming with each failure—and there were a good many—a
more and more ferocious expression.' When at length she
managed to hit the target a look of 'such beatitude' stole over
her face that her instructor collapsed with laughter. Mrs
Pankhurst looked annoyed: her sense of humour 'was always
rather uncertain'.[13]

When Parliament reopened in October 1906 Emmeline
Pankhurst led a deputation to the Houses of Parliament and
sent a message to the Prime Minister through the Liberal Chief
Whip to ask if he could hold out any hope that women would
be enfranchised at this, or any future, time. The answer was
'No'. There were loud-voiced protests from the deputation; the
police intervened; and in the ensuing scuffle Emmeline
Pankhurst was flung to the ground. Her angry followers endeavoured to hold a protest meeting outside the House of
Commons: ten were arrested, Emmeline Pethick-Lawrence,
Adela Pankhurst, Annie Kenney and Theresa Billington among
them. They were sentenced to two months in the Second
Division, with the alternative of a fine which, as usual, they
would not pay: and Sylvia Pankhurst, who interrupted the
court proceedings, got a fortnight in the Third Division.

The sentences were severe; and although Sylvia was treated no worse than the others she was segregated from them. Their supporters in the House of Commons made the first of a number of protests against the sentencing of the women to the Second and Third Divisions, arguing that as political offenders they should have been placed in the First Division where they could have worn their own clothes, seen their friends, written letters and read the papers.

Most people considered, however, that they had only got what they deserved: but in the midst of the turmoil was heard the quiet and reasonable voice of Millicent Fawcett, who arranged a banquet at the Savoy for the prisoners on their release. 'I hope,' she said, 'that the more old-fashioned suffragists will stand by their comrades who in my opinion have done more to bring the movement within the region of practical politics in twelve months, than I and my followers have been able to do in the same number of years.'[14]

Several newspapers also showed a modicum of understanding; and Pethick-Lawrence, noting the signs of improvement, publicly made an offer to pay £10 to WSPU funds for every day his wife had to suffer imprisonment. An offer so phrased was open to misunderstanding. At a fancy dress ball at Covent Garden one of the prize winners wore a placard inscribed:

> 'Ten pounds a day
> He said he'd pay
> To keep this face
> In Holloway.'[15]

It was, as Emmeline Pathick-Lawrence's mother remarked, 'a pity Fred put it like that'.[16]

Pethick-Lawrence was not called on to pay out very much: within a few days his wife and one other woman were released for health reasons. In fact, Emmeline Pethick-Lawrence had collapsed from the effects of claustrophobia brought on by the journey to prison in a Black Maria. She was bitterly ashamed of her weakness and set out to conquer it. Later in the campaign she went to prison and suffered the ghastly rigours of hunger striking and forcible feeding with splendid courage.

The publicity given to the prison sentences brought recruits and money to the WSPU; and now that the Prime Minister had shown his hand the Liberal Government became Public Enemy No. 1. Emmeline and Christabel Pankhurst took a party of suffragettes to every by-election campaign, prepared to heckle, break up meetings, assault the police and go to prison, and do anything else they could think of to dissuade people from voting Liberal. There were plenty of by-elections during the next year or so. They were not only caused by the death or ill-health of sitting Members but also because each Minister, on appointment to the Government, had to submit to re-election. It is hard to say what effect the women's intervention had on the results; but they naturally claimed a victory each time a Liberal was defeated or returned with a reduced majority.

Emmeline Pankhurst, supported financially by the Pethick-Lawrences, was devoting her whole time to Union affairs; for she had been dismissed from her post as Registrar and had lost the hope of a pension. She felt now, as Millicent Fawcett felt, that suffrage workers should not support any particular party; and had decided to resign from the Labour Party, a decision which was automatically binding on her followers.

All this time the National Union had been making slow but steady progress; and on February 9, 1907, two days before the State Opening of Parliament, a procession was organized to march from Hyde Park to Exeter Hall in the Strand. In typical February weather Millicent Fawcett led more than 3,000 of her followers on what became known in the annals of the National Union as the 'Mud March'. 'Her small figure ploughed along— a great deal too fast— . . .' wrote her biographer, 'as unperturbed as if she had been walking to church; and neither that nor the great Albert Hall and Hyde Park meetings which followed, seemed to disconcert her at all.'[17]

A few days later Emmeline Pankhurst convened a meeting of her self-styled 'Women's Parliament' at Caxton Hall to debate the King's Speech which, as was only to be expected, contained no reference to women's suffrage. In a dramatic and emotional scene a resolution was carried calling on the Government to rectify the omission; a banner bearing the words, 'Rise up women!' was unfurled, to the answering cry of, 'Now!' Volunteers clamoured for the privilege of carrying the resolution to

the House of Commons; and heard with exultant joy their
leader's warning that they must be prepared to face mal-
treatment and imprisonment.

The leader selected for the mission was a gaunt, elderly, but
statuesque-looking woman, Mrs Charlotte Despard (1844–
1939). Born Charlotte French, she was the daughter of a Naval
captain and elder sister of Field-Marshal Sir John French, who
was to command the British Forces in France at the start of the
1914–18 War. Brother and sister were estranged: they had
probably never been close since the days when Charlotte had
given the small boy his first lessons and found him very dull.
She herself was far from dull, a passionate love of freedom
inspired by Shelley's poems being the mainspring of her life. In
1870 she married Maximilian Despard, a merchant of Irish
extraction who travelled extensively in the Far East for his
firm. During the twenty years of their childless marriage
Charlotte Despard accompanied her husband on many of his
trips and produced an Anglo-Indian romance, which she published under a pseudonym. After his death she retired into a
voluntary retreat for three months, emerging with a fixed
determination to serve suffering humanity in the London slums.
She went to live in Nine Elms, Battersea; and there she served
on Poor Law and Education Committees, founded a dispensary
for women and children and a club for working men. Her
genuine love and sympathy for the underdog drew her into the
ranks of the ILP, and she addressed a great many meetings. The
working men who heard her, we are told, 'worshipped her,
kissed her hand, uncovered their heads when she appeared'.
She was certainly a striking looking figure in her picturesque
uniform of black and white, with a black lace mantilla on her
head, and openwork sandals on her well-scrubbed feet. She
could be practical on occasion, but her working-class audiences
'did not understand the half of the prophetic pledges which
informed her most eloquent utterances'.[18]

They could hardly have been expected to understand very
much. Charlotte Despard was a Theosophist and a strict
vegetarian, 'whose aim was to abolish gradually the mass pro-
duction of other living animals sacrificed to human appetite,
[with] the resultant uplifting of the erring human race to a

higher mental and cleaner physical state. That this would result from universal vegetarianism she was quite sure.'[19]

Charlotte Despard's twin ideals of freedom and service impelled her into the militant suffrage ranks. She had been among the women who had protested at the Prime Minister's curt rejection in the Lobby of the House of Commons in October 1906. And now, preceded by a police inspector, she set out with immense dignity, followed by the chosen deputation and many other volunteers. The women were stopped by police in Parliament Square and told to disperse. They continued marching; and a contingent of mounted police then appeared on the scene to reinforce their colleagues. The foot police now proceeded to push and bump the women; the mounted police scattered them, rearing their horses over those who had stumbled and fallen. It was an ugly scene: women's clothes were torn, their hair pulled down, their faces grimed; but a few of them struggled through to reach the precincts of the House and hold an indignation meeting. They were arrested, together with a number of the demonstrators in Parliament Square. Next day two men and over fifty women were charged at the police court with obstruction and sentenced to fourteen days, Charlotte Despard and the three Pankhurst daughters among them.

A few weeks later a second deputation met with much the same reception; and this time seventy-two people were charged. Three of the women were given thirty days in prison instead of the customary fourteen: for two of them it was a second offence, and the third had had the temerity to hang a 'Votes for Women' banner over the dock.

Emmeline Pankhurst had been away at the time dragooning her forces at a by-election. Whenever she was in London she held a weekly reception at Queen's Hall to welcome new members and congratulate those who had already suffered so much ridicule and contempt, manhandling and imprisonment. The worn beauty of her face, her voice, which Ethel Smyth compared with 'a stringed instrument in the hand of a great artist', and her passionate speeches combined to produce the desired effect. 'I imagine,' added Ethel Smith, 'that it is unnecessary to dwell on the devotion a magical personality like hers was able to kindle when she chose.'[20]

Ever since the start of the militant campaign Emmeline Pankhurst had been so firmly in the saddle that she could demand complete submission to herself, to Christabel and the Pethick-Lawrences; but now, in 1907, there were some murmurings of discontent. Bertrand Russell, son of the Lady Amberley who had inspired Queen Victoria to declare that she deserved a good whipping, stood as a Women's Suffrage candidate at a by-election at Wimbledon and was defeated. He had been supported by the constitutionalists, but because he had made no secret of his Liberal sympathies the WSPU had been forbidden to help him. Some members resented this order; and they also complained that the rank-and-file were given no chance of a hearing at headquarters.

It has been agreed the previous year to hold an annual conference of the WSPU each October. It had been further agreed that there should be an Executive Council composed of the officers of the Union and delegates from the branches, and an emergency committee consisting only of the officers and organizers of the Union and two members appointed by the annual conference. In fact, only one conference was held; and the dissident members of the Union complained that the Executive Council was never convened and that everything was done by the Emergency Committee, on which Emmeline Pankhurst and the salaried organizers (they included Christabel and Sylvia) formed the majority. Charlotte Despard, who by now was secretary of the Union, protested that the constitution was being violated. Emmeline Pankhurst's reply was a threat to tear up the constitution; and she announced at a meeting of the Emergency Committee held in September 1907 that a new committee would be elected, the constitution would be annulled, and the annual conference discontinued.

According to the novelist Naomi Jacob, who was secretary of the Union's Middlesbrough Branch, the delegates to the Annual Conference had actually assembled before Mrs Pankhurst's decision was made known. 'That magnificent woman, Mrs Despard,' wrote Naomi Jacob, who was no admirer of Mrs Pankhurst, 'was to take the chair. The hands of the clock moved slowly to the hour, Mrs Despard rose as we could hear Big Ben begin to strike . . . Her face was expressionless, her voice calm, cool and incisive. She said, "I have a message from Mrs Pankhurst, it reads—there will be no conference". A murmur of dismay, surprise, wonder ran through the hall. Mrs Despard held up her hand. "But there *will* be a conference, and I shall ask you to discuss with me the formation of the Women's Freedom League." '[21]

There were now two militant organizations instead of one. It was implied by the wspu that the dissident members had been expelled: in fact they followed Charlotte Despard, who was a very different kind of leader from Emmeline Pankhurst or from Millicent Fawcett. 'She never argued on controversial issues,' wrote Theresa Billington-Greig, who had followed her into the wilderness, 'merely put them aside'.[22] This did not make for ease of administration; but Charlotte Despard simply went her own way, and anyone who disagreed with her was free to take action on her own. The Women's Freedom League never approached the wspu in influence, numbers or funds although it had more branches than the Union in the provinces,* It also invented some original schemes. One of them was the refusal of house-owners to pay taxes; and Charlotte Despard's admirers grew quite used to haunting the auction rooms to buy back her furniture which had been sequestered for non-payment of tax.

Throughout the debacle the Pethick-Lawrences had remained unquestioningly loyal to the Pankhursts; and, with Christabel, they now formed an unofficial organizing committee which controlled the campaign during Emmeline Pankhurst's absences from London. The leader chose to go to prison for the first time in the early months of 1908. She returned to London after a series of by-elections looking considerably shaken and upset. During one of the campaigns—in which the Liberal candidate had been unexpectedly defeated—some toughs wearing the Liberal colours had bundled her into a barrel and would have rolled her down the street if the police had not intervened. She arrived in London covered in bruises and limping from a sprained ankle, to go straight to a meeting of the

---

* Unlike the wspu, which virtually came! to an end with the outbreak of war in 1914, the Women's Freedom League remained in existence for forty-seven years.

Women's Parliament in Caxton Hall. There was an outcry from the body of the hall when she announced her intention of carrying the usual resolution to Parliament herself. The women were quite prepared to suffer themselves; but they were horrified to think that their beloved leader would also be in danger. Emmeline was adamant; and she was helped into a passing dog-cart by the resourceful General, who had persuaded the driver to stop. Up came the inevitable police and ordered her to dismount and the deputation to walk in single file. Two of her followers rushed to support her; and after a brief tussle Emmeline Pankhurst, the General, Annie Kenney and five other women were arrested. Emmeline was given six weeks in Holloway with the option of being bound over for a year, which of course she refused. She was released before the expiry of her sentence, and reappeared dramatically and unexpectedly on the platform of the Albert Hall to preside over a meeting which had been called to protest against the defeat of a Woman's Suffrage Bill which had already passed its second reading by 271 to 92 votes.

In the course of the debate Herbert Gladstone, the Home Secretary and himself in favour of women's suffrage, had pointed out that men had 'learned the necessity for demonstrating the greatness of their movement and for establishing that *force majeure* which actuates and arms a Government for effective work'.[23]

The National Union and the WSPU both took this as a hint that public demonstrations were in order. The National Union organized a procession of 15,000 men and women to march from the Embankment to the Albert Hall; and among the marchers were Emily Davies, now nearing eighty, and Elizabeth Garrett Anderson, who was over seventy. For once Millicent Fawcett's sturdy composure deserted her. As she stepped onto the platform of the Albert Hall to preside over the huge assembly the girls who were acting as stewards heaped bunches of summer flowers at her feet; and 'everyone could see that she was moved, and found it difficult to open the meeting'.[24] Members of the Women's Freedom League marched in the procession, and Charlotte Despard was one of the speakers. Emmeline Pankhurst and Elizabeth Wolstenholme-Elmy were also present, but the WSPU took no official part in the proceedings, being busy with plans of its own.

About ten days later the 'General' electrified Members of Parliament peacefully taking tea on the Terrace by appearing on the river in a decorated launch, and urging them through a megaphone to 'come to the Park on Sunday . . . There will be no arrests,' she promised. 'You shall have plenty of police protection.'[25] A Member rushed off to call the river police, but by the time they arrived the General had chugged happily away.

On Midsummer Sunday seven processions converged on Hyde Park. Many of the women were decked out in the new suffragette colours of purple, white and green, which had been devised by Emmeline Pethick-Lawrence to dinstinguish them from the constitutionalists whose colours were red, white and green. The Park was crowded, for special trains had been run to London for the occasion; but as the weather was fine a good many of the onlookers (*The Times* correspondent put them as high as 500,000) may well have come to see the sight. Empassioned speeches were made from twenty platforms, and a resolution was sent by special messenger to the Prime Minister— now Asquith, for Campbell-Bannerman had resigned in the spring for health reasons.

Earlier in the year, while still Chancellor of the Exchequer, Asquith had informed a deputation from the National Union that women's suffrage was so important that it could not be introduced without a mandate from the country at a general election. Yet his reply to the WSPU resolution was politely noncommital.

A few days later a deputation from the Women's Parliament led by the two Emmelines was broken up with considerable violence, the police being zealously abetted by a gang of toughs. During the struggle two women got away, went by taxi to Downing Street, and threw stones at the windows of No. 10. This was the beginning of an orgy of organized window smashing.

Although sentences ranging from one to three months were passed on the twenty-nine women arrested that day Emmeline Pankhurst was now determined to commit a crime which carried a longer sentence. She therefore had posters printed urging men and women 'to help the suffragettes to rush the House of Commons';[26] and she repeated the incitement at a meeting in Trafalgar Square at which Christabel and the General also spoke. Warrants for the arrest of the three ring-leaders were issued on the grounds that they were guilty of conduct likely to provoke a breach of the peace. The case was deferred for a week; and during that time there was another skirmish in Parliament Square, which was watched by the Home Secretary and the Chancellor of the Exchequer, David Lloyd George (afterwards Lord Lloyd George) who had his little daughter Megan (now Lady Megan Lloyd George) with him.

Christabel Pankhurst conducted the defence with great verve and expertise at the trial which opened on October 21, 1908. She had subpoenaed the Home Secretary and the Chancellor of the Exchequer and managed to make the latter look extremely foolish. She claimed that there had been no incitement since one of the definitions of 'rush' in *Chambers's English Dictionary* was simply 'an eager demand'; and she asked how Lloyd George, who had made far more violent threats to the suffragettes, could have brought his daughter with him if the child had been in any sort of danger. Emmeline Pankhurst followed her daughter with an outstandingly brilliant and deeply moving speech. 'We are here,' she concluded, 'not because we are law-breakers: we are here in our effort to become law makers.'[27]

There was never any doubt that all three would be found guilty. Emmeline, having appealed unsuccessfully to the Home Secretary against their inprisonment in the Second Division, defied orders by speaking to her daughter, and got this privilege confirmed. Neither she nor the others served their full term (three months for Emmeline Pankhurst and the General and ten weeks for Christabel); and when they were released they were borne triumphantly to a welcome-home breakfast in a carriage drawn by white horses, escorted by suffragettes in purple, white and green.

While they were in prison three members of the Women's Freedom League had chained themselves so effectively to the grille of the Ladies' Gallery of the House of Commons that the grille itself had to be removed before they could be released. Mrs Despard's followers were nothing if not original.

By the end of 1908 militant tactics were on the increase; and more and more suffragettes were protesting their right to be treated as political offenders and placed in the First Division. Certain elegant-looking dowagers now carried hammers and stones for window smashing concealed in their fur muffs; Cabinet ministers were heckled with such persistence that public meetings were declared closed to women; but suffragettes contrived to hide themselves beforehand under the platform or let themselves down through the skylight.

By this time prisoners were adding the hunger-strike to their battery of protests. At first this was a most effective weapon, for they were released as soon as their health began to deteriorate. Soon, however, the authorities resorted to the revolting counter-measure of forcible feeding. A length of rubber tubing was pushed into their mouths or up their nostrils and liquid food was passed through it into their throats. When the prisoners struggled, as most of them did, the process was extremely painful and even dangerous. It so unnerved one of them, Emily Wilding-Davison—an intellectual who had gained a First in English at Oxford—that she barricaded herself into her cell rather than submit to it, and was driven out of hiding by a hose directed onto her through the window in the door.

Many people who had sneered at the suffragettes before now admired them for their courage; and members of the medical and nursing professions joined in the protests. Nevertheless, forcible feeding was continued. A suffragette who had so far escaped it was Lady Constance Lytton (1869–1923), the delicate, retiring daughter of the Earl of Lytton and a friend of Ethel Smyth. Lady Constance had conquered her dislike of publicity sufficiently to throw a brick at a Government car. For this she was sent to prison for a month. She immediately went on hunger strike, but was released without being forcibly fed after three days. Her release was recommended by the prison doctor who examined all the prisoners before forcible feeding because he said that she had a diseased heart and the process would endanger her health. Lady Constance was well aware that her

heart was not strong; but she suspected that had she not belonged to a prominent family she would have been forcibly fed
just the same. She therefore went to Liverpool disguised as 'Jane
Warton, sempstress'. She was arrested for throwing stones and
for inciting people to throw stones at the house of the Governor
of Walton Gaol, and sentenced to fourteen days' hard labour.
She went on hunger strike, was passed medically fit, and was
forcibly fed. In the process she was so distressingly ill that the
doctor in charge begged her to call off her strike: she refused,
and forcible feeding continued. A day or so later, however, she
was suddenly released: the Governor had seen a newspaper
cutting which claimed that the prisoner was not Jane Warton
but Lady Constance Lytton.

After her release Lady Constance protested to the Home
Secretary that the authorities had one set of rules for the rich,
another for the poor. She was one of the cause's real martyrs;
for although she recovered from the illness which followed her
prison experience and continued her Union activities, she never
really regained her strength and remained a semi-invalid until
her death.

Millicent Fawcett, like Constance Lytton, despised a Government which allowed the authorities to pander to private
influence; but on one occasion a friend resorted to wire-pulling
on her behalf. Millicent's elder sister Elizabeth, now over
seventy, had fallen under the Pankhurst spell and—that wise
councellor her husband having died the previous year—had
joined the WSPU as the movement most likely to win the vote.
Millicent, who was deeply distressed by this defection from the
constitutional camp, learned with alarm that her sister had
accepted Mrs Pankhurst's invitation to 'rush' the House of
Commons and joined a 'deputation'. She explained her anxiety
to her friend and colleague Lady Frances Balfour, who went
off without saying a word to ask for—and obtain—an assurance
from the Home Secretary that Mrs Garrett Anderson would not
be arrested. The assurance was scrupulously respected on this
and on future occasions, much to Elizabeth's surprise and
somewhat to her chagrin.

Throughout the entire period of the suffrage controversy
Millicent Fawcett, as has been said, was constantly being urged

by well-meaning friends and sympathizers for the sake of the
unity of the movement to join forces with Emmeline Pankhurst.
She steadfastly refused to make any overtures to her rival; and
at a council meeting of the National Union in 1909 she spoke
her mind most forcibly. 'There are great and obvious advantages
in unity,' she said, 'but I think we should not forget that there
may be disadvantages too. The most striking example of unity
which I know is that of the Gadarene swine, of whom it is
recorded that they "ran violently down a steep place to the sea,
and perished in the waters".'[28]

In the event, of course, these Gadarene swine kept their
heads above water; and the two wings of the movement never
coalesced.

Chapter IX

WOMEN AGAINST THE GOVERNMENT

The year 1910 was known in the WSPU as the year of truce. At the general election held in January the Liberals were returned to power with a greatly reduced majority; and on the eve of the election Asquith had declared that in the event of a Reform Bill being introduced with an amendment on women's suffrage the amendment would be open to a free vote of the House.

After the election a non-party committee—the Conciliation Committee—was set up under the chairmanship of Lady Constance's brother, the then Lord Lytton, to examine the suffrage question and to report on the practicability of extending the vote to some, if not to all, women. During the spring and early summer the Committee prepared a Bill which aimed at giving the vote to women householders and the occupiers of business premises with a ratable value of not less than £10 a year; and it was reckoned that by this means about a million women would be enfranchized.

Emmeline Pankhurst called a halt to militant tactics during the deliberations of the Conciliation Committee: and in honour of the new King, George V, who succeeded his father Edward VII in May, and of the forthcoming Conciliation Bill, the suffrage societies combined in a monster procession through the London streets to the Albert Hall, where Lord Lytton presided over an imposing assembly. The most spectacular contingent— over 600 strong—was made up of suffragettes who had been to prison, each of whom sported a staff tipped with a broad arrow. Among other contingents was the 'Regiment of Portias' with Elizabeth Garrett Anderson well to the front; the Women's Freedom League, led by Charlotte Despard carrying a bunch of arum lilies; and a small detachment of men led by Laurence Housman.

Lord Lytton spoke from the chair of his confidence in the outcome of the Conciliation Bill; Emmeline Pankhurst gave a resounding call for victory; Emmeline Pethick-Lawrence collected £5,000 to continue the educational campaign.

The Conciliation Bill was introduced in the House of Commons on July 12, 1910, and passed its second reading by a majority of 109. It was then referred to a committee of the whole House; but the Prime Minister refused to allow time for the additional stages required for its passage into law; and in November Parliament was dissolved.

Emmeline Pankhurst gave orders for the resumption of millitant tactics in November 1910, when it became clear that the Conciliation Bill was doomed, and after Asquith had infuriated a deputation of Liberal women from his own constituency with a patronizing 'Wait and see'.

On Friday, November 18—'Black Friday' in the annals of the Union—a deputation went to the House of Commons. The women were divided into small groups and told to march in single file in accordance with the law. The deputation was led by Emmeline Pankhurst, impeccably dressed in black, her hat secured by a veil; and the venerable Elizabeth Garrett Anderson, wearing a fur-trimmed cloak and a fur bonnet with white strings. The police, no doubt alerted by the Home Secretary on Dr Garrett Anderson's behalf, ushered the leaders into the House. They were informed that the Prime Minister was not available, and so they assembled on the steps of the St Stephen's entrance as their followers began to converge on Parliament Square. And there, hemmed in by the police, they were forced to look on helplessly while something very like a pitched battle took place. The police, assisted by the usual gangs of toughs, manhandled the suffragettes, punched them in the face and body, tripped them up, knocked them down and kicked them before finally arresting them. Next morning 115 women and two men appeared at the police court. All were released without being charged. To Emmeline Pankhurst this was simply a clever piece of propaganda by a Government which could not afford to alienate any of its supporters just before a general election; for the Prime Minister had announced that negotiations which had been taking place between the Liberal and Conservative leaders had failed and there was to be another election in December. She therefore led the Women's Parliament on a window-smashing raid in Downing Street; but although she was arrested together with more than a hundred of her followers once again no charges were made.

The Liberals were returned to power; and this time Emmeline Pankhurst allowed herself to be lulled by the Prime Minister's assurances that the women's suffrage issue would be considered in 1911 or 1912 and left England for a fund-raising tour of America.

A Conciliation Bill was introduced in the new Parliament and passed its second reading on May 5, 1911, with a majority of 167. Asquith assured the House that there would be facilities for its passage into law during 1912; but in November 1911 the position was reversed by the announcement that a Government Electoral Reform Bill was to be introduced which would not provide for votes for women. A deputation from the National Union was told by Asquith, however, that the Electoral Reform Bill would be so drafted as to admit of an amendment on women's suffrage. He also reaffirmed his undertaking to provide facilities for the passage of the Conciliation Bill.

The constitutionalists accepted Asquith's undertaking and worked conscientiously for the proposed amendment and for the Conciliation Bill. Emmeline Pankhurst was not so trusting and cabled her followers from America to protest. Emmeline Pethick-Lawrence, who had conquered her claustrophic terrors, took charge of a window-smashing raid which ended in prison sentences for 150 women, ranging from five to thirty days. Further outbreaks of window-breaking followed, and damage was done to private as well as Government property. Emily Wilding-Davison, who had a disastrously fertile mind, began an epidemic of arson when she pushed a piece of burning linen through the post office letterbox in Parliament Square.

It was at this stage that Elizabeth Garrett Anderson, who had addressed many meetings as a suffragette, was so shocked by the increase of militant tactics, that she decided she could go no further with the Pankhursts. Her sister Millicent, from whom she had been politically estranged since 1908, wrote to her on December 3, 1911, to say that the National Union considered the attitude of the WSPU towards the Conciliation Bill issue was 'a very big blunder,' and intended to 'lose no opportunity of disowning it and making people understand that we condemn it. It is horrid to do it,' she added, 'but I feel we have no choice . . . I hope we shan't drift apart over this, but I believe the chances of this misfortune (which would be a very great one to me) are less if we are quite frank with one another.' Elizabeth replied at once. 'I am quite with you about the WSPU,' she wrote. 'I think they are quite wrong. I wrote to Miss Pankhurst before (no I think it was the day after) the demonstration but she took no notice. I have now told her I can go no more with them. It is dreadfully sad to have to be divided, but I cannot help it. I have waited several days in case C.P. answered.'[1]

The Conciliation Bill was reintroduced in March 1912, but thrown out by a majority of fourteen. Its defeat was directly attributable to the forthcoming Electoral Reform Bill; for it had been hinted to Members that it would be pointless for them to pass a limited Bill when a complete overhaul of the electoral system was about to take place.

'I felt,' wrote Millicent Fawcett later, 'that what I had been working for for forty years had been destroyed at a blow; but I also felt what beavers feel when their dam has been destroyed, namely, that they must begin all over again, and build up once more from the beginning.'[2]

There was nothing of the beaver about Emmeline Pankhurst who, on her return from America, was arrested for window-breaking in Downing Street, together with Ethel Smyth (who noted that her friend's stones had all gone wide of the mark) and sentenced to two months in Holloway. The news that their beloved leader was in Holloway with them put fresh heart in the other women prisoners who were now so numerous that they occupied a whole wing. In the exercise hour they chanted the suffragette song, *March of Women*, for which Ethel Smyth had composed the music and which she now conducted from her cell window with a toothbrush.

Emmeline Pankhurst was still in prison when in March the police raided the WSPU headquarters at Clement's Inn and arrested the Pethick-Lawrences and the honorary secretary, Mrs Mabel Tuke (she was later discharged) and charged them with conspiring to commit damage to the property of the King's subjects and inciting others to do likewise. Emmeline Pankhurst was included in the charge; and so was Christabel, who was out at the time but was warned by friends and managed to escape in disguise to France. She took an apartment in Paris under an assumed name; and from this fastness proceeded to organize the militant movement while the other leaders were in prison.

The Pethick-Lawrences were refused bail and were lodged respectively in Brixton and Holloway to await trial; and Pethick-Lawrence, who had frequently used his own money to stand surety for the suffragettes, now stepped into the limelight in his own right. 'Beloved,' he wrote to his wife shortly before the trial opened, 'we are very near to a great day, the greatest we have seen in our lives. To me it seems that an honour such as is conferred on only a few in many centuries is about to be conferred on us. We are to stand where the great and noble have stood before us all down the ages. . . .'[3] He was conducting his own defence at the trial and Emmeline Pankhurst was conducting hers; but his wife was being represented by counsel. The Attorney-General, Sir Rufus Isaacs (afterwards Lord Reading) led for the prosecution.

The defendants, who pleaded not guilty, maintained that the real incitement to conspiracy had come from C. E. H. Hobhouse, a member of the Government, who a few days before the renewed outbreak of militancy had sneered in public at women for being less militant than men. The defence was admirably conducted but the result of the trial was a foregone conclusion. Pethick-Lawrence made a dignified appeal to the jury to note the political nature of the alleged offence. 'Speaking for myself,' he said, 'I loathe the idea of any such thing as the deliberate breaking of shop windows. But I know that these women who have taken that course have been driven by the inexorable logic of facts, to do what they did. . . . You are dealing here with people whose life is devoted to an ideal.' He went on to outline the history of the struggle and the specious tactics of the Government; and he reminded the jury that theirs was 'a political fight.' After emphasizing the importance of the Union's educational work he spoke of himself. 'I am a man,' he said, 'and I cannot take part in this women's agitation, but I intend to stand by the women who are fighting . . . I think it is a battle waged for the good of the people of this country, waged by one half of the community whose deeds are valuable to the other part of the country and should not be excluded. . .'[4]

Emmeline Pankhurst followed. She retold the history of the Union's fight and gave a blow-by-blow description of the un-equal battle on Black Friday. She had been ill with bronchitis in prison and her worn appearance added to the poignancy of her words. After her counsel's speech Emmeline Pethick-Lawrence appealed to the judge to consider their right, if convicted, to be treated as political prisoners. The judge, whose summing-up was entirely adverse, disregarded this appeal; and although the jury added to their verdict of 'Guilty' a plea for clemency and leniency, he sentenced all three defendants to nine months in the Second Division and ordered them to pay the whole costs of the trial.

A £2,000 claim for damage to property was later added to the costs; and since the Pankhursts were virtually penniless the entire burden devolved on the Pethick-Lawrences.

The judge's summing-up and the sentences aroused a real outburst of public sympathy. The three prisoners immediately went on hunger strike; and when it was known that Mrs Pankhurst was hunger-striking many of the suffragettes already in Holloway followed suit. Emmeline Pethick-Lawrence hunger-struck for several days and was then forcibly fed: her husband was forcibly fed twice a day for five days. Emmeline Pankhurst had been obliged to listen to the sounds of the struggle, the desperate cries and the vomiting from neigh-bouring cells while she awaited her own turn. But when the doctor and wardresses entered her cell with their apparatus she turned on them with a murderous look and threatened to hurl her heavy earthern water jug at them if they took one step nearer. Completely nonplussed, the doctor mumbled some excuse and backed hastily away.

Next day both the Emmelines were given their freedom: a day or so later Pethick-Lawrence was also released; but not before the subject of forcible feeding had been debated with intense heat and acrimony in the House of Commons. When the Home Secretary declared that it would be applied indiscriminately to all hunger strikers he was asked if he would not arrange for a model to be exhibited in the Chamber of Horrors at Madame Tussaud's; and a Labour Member shook his fist in Asquith's face and declared that he would go down to history as the man who tortured innocent women.

In the absence of the leaders in prison Annie Kenney had been put in charge at headquarters and she received her orders from Christabel in Paris. 'Beloved Annie,' wrote Christabel dramatically, 'The bearer of this note is a good friend of the Cause. She, with another friend, helped me to escape. She will tell you where I am, and give you an address that will find me. Keep this a secret . . . I want you to take supreme charge of the whole Movement during my absence. . . . Come quickly, and bring with you a member who understands the language of the country that I am sheltering in. Disguise yourself, and watch closely for Scotland Yard men. . . . What a day when women win the vote! Press on and give all our loyal ones my love and my faith that each one will obey orders that will be sent through you by me, and by unity we shall win through. Come to me at the first possible moment.'[5]

Beloved Annie needed no urging. At intervals during the spring and summer of 1912 she disguised herself and slipped across the Channel for consultations with Christabel and the invention of new and wilder forms of militantism. Violent protests were planned after June when the Electoral Reform Bill was introduced. The Speaker ruled in committee that if any women's suffrage amendments were carried they would so change the nature of the Bill that it would become, in effect, a different measure and would thus have to be introduced and passed through all its stages. There was no time for the Bill to become law during the session: the Speaker's ruling virtually killed it, for its was withdrawn in January 1913.

During the summer of 1912 Ethel Smyth, who gloried in the cloak-and-dagger stuff, smuggled Emmeline Pankhurst to the coast and on board a Channel steamer. The Pethick-Lawrences were resting in France after their prison experiences; and

Emmeline and Christabel Pankhurst met them by arrangement. The Pankhursts announced that the campaign against private property was to be stepped up; but the Pethick-Lawrences argued that the public sympathy already aroused would enable them to extend the scope of the educational campaign which was far more important. This difference of opinion did not seem unduly serious to the Pethick-Lawrences, who went on to Canada to visit relatives. They were in Vancouver when they received a letter from Emmeline Pankhurst advising them not to return to England but to carry on their educational campaign from Canada and to secure their property against the British Government.

But the Pethick-Lawrences, who had no wish to be thought cowards, were determined to continue the fight at home. Before they left Canada, however, they learned that, since the costs of the conspiracy trial and the subsequent claim for damage to property had not been paid, their Surrey house was in the possession of bailiffs. In the event, Pethick-Lawrence was declared bankrupt and the full amount was taken from his estate.

On their return to London in October the Pethick-Lawrences received an entirely unexpected blow. They found that in their absence the Union's headquarters had been transferred to Kingsway; and next day they were informed by Emmeline Pankhurst that she had decided to sever her connection with them, and that future policy would be directed only by herself and Christabel.

On October 17th she made an announcement to this effect at a meeting at the Albert Hall which, ironically, had been arranged as a welcome-home demonstration for the three ex-prisoners. 'In the Women's Social and Political Union from its initiation until quite recently,' she declared, 'we have had complete unity of purpose and complete unity of policy. When unity of policy is no longer there a movement is weakened, and so it is better that those who cannot see eye to eye as to policy should part, free to continue their policy in their own way. . . . I give place to none in my appreciation and gratitude to Mr and Mrs Pethick-Lawrence,' she added, to loud applause from the body of the hall, 'for the incalculable services they have rendered to the militant agitation for woman suffrage.'

She then explained to an audience which was frankly puzzled by the breach, the new organisation, with Christabel directing affairs from overseas and herself in charge in London when she was not in prison. 'I incite this meeting to rebellion!' she concluded. 'And my last word is for the Government . . . Take me, if you will! . . .'

'And so,' wrote Christabel, recalling her mother's speech in later years, 'in 1912, dedicating herself anew Mother chose, if it should so happen, a convict's grave.'[6]

The Pethick-Lawrences, still stunned by the blow, could not at first believe that Christabel, whom they regarded almost as a daughter, could have been involved; but they soon learned that Christabel was every bit as adamant as her mother. They showed real nobility of character by their refusal to publicize their grievance and by the continuance of their educational work outside the Union, which included the editing of *Votes for Women*. Their departure was the signal for a positive frenzy of militant acts. For almost two years to come there were orgies of arson and window-smashing; and, among other militant acts, telephone and telegraph wires were cut, the orchid house at Kew was wrecked, paintings at Burlington House were slashed, and the Rokeby Venus in the National Gallery was damaged. When a house which was being built for Lloyd George was partially destroyed by a home-made bomb planted (though the culprits were never discovered) by the ever inventive Emily Wilding-Davison and her friends Emmeline Pankhurst boasted publicly of the deed and was arrested for inciting her followers to violence.

She was still awaiting trial when her daughter Sylvia was released from prison. Sylvia, who had been working for the cause in the East End and had been in prison and had hunger struck a number of times for her part in raiding attacks, had refused water as well as food on this occasion and was a pitiful wreck. When Emmeline Pankhurst came up for trial she made great play with the tale of her daughter's sufferings under forcible feeding. Her speech aroused a surge of public indignation; and many people who disapproved of the militant movement were aghast when Emmeline was sentenced to three years' penal servitude.

There was a further outburst of indignation when an article by Sylvia Pankhurst on her sufferings appeared in the *Suffragette*, a paper which Christabel was editing in Paris; and it culminated with the passage in April 1913 of the Prisoners' Temporary Discharge for Ill-health Bill (the Cat-and-Mouse Act, as it was called). Under this Act, which aimed at abolishing forcible feeding, prisoners were allowed to hunger-strike until their health was endangered and then released on licence, with orders to report back to prison at the end of a given period to complete their sentence. Emmeline Pankhurst, Sylvia and a number of their followers refused to accept the licence terms and so were continually under police observation when they were not in prison; and although at first the Act seemed to be succeeding in its object it soon became apparent that the offenders were spending more time out on licence than they were in prison, and so forcible feeding was resorted to again.

To Millicent Fawcett, the Cat-and-Mouse-Act, which was applied solely to one type of offender, was an infamous measure. She was by now convinced that the militants were doing incalculable harm to the movement although she was equally convinced that the Government must share the blame for a hopeless situation. There seemed to her little chance that the militants would refrain from violence. 'I think they would rather lose Women's Suffrage,' she wrote bitterly to a friend in 1913, 'than give up their own way of demonstrating.' And later: 'I never can feel that setting fire to houses and churches and letter boxes and destroying valuable pictures really helps to convince people that women ought to be enfranchised.'[7]

After the bitter disappointment of the Electoral Reform and Conciliation Bills she had set to work like the proverbial beaver to rebuild her dam. This meant persuading the constituent bodies of the National Union to abandon their previous political neutrality. At a Labour Party conference held soon after the scuttling of the Electoral Reform Bill a resolution was adopted which called 'upon the Party in Parliament to oppose any Franchise Bill in which women are not included.'[8] This resolution convinced Millicent Fawcett of the need for an alignment with Labour: and after a good deal of heart-searching (for to many constitutionalists Socialism was allied

with the Devil) it was agreed that the National Union should
endeavour:

'(1) To shorten the term of office of the Cabinet as at present
     constituted, especially by opposing Anti-Suffrage Ministers,
     and
 (2) To strengthen any party in the House which adopted
     Women's Suffrage as part of its official programme.'⁹

A new fighting policy was now worked out for by-elections;
but although the National Union supported Labour it retained its separate identity in every campaign. There were ten
by-elections during the next eighteen months; and the National
Union reckoned that in six of them their intervention had
helped to split the vote and keep the Liberal candidate out.

The National Union combined its by-election policy with
regular appeals to the Government and with indoor and out-
door meetings all over the country. By now it had grown
enormously in strength and numbers and where there had
once been only eighteen provincial societies there were literally
hundreds. In the summer of 1913 a six weeks' 'pilgrimage' was
organized during which women from all parts of the country
converged on London, holding meetings in every town and
village through which they passed. The highlights of the pilgrimage were a huge meeting in Hyde Park and a service in
St Paul's Cathedral. When it was over Millicent Fawcett
wrote to the Prime Minister asking him to receive yet another
deputation. He agreed; but, though extremely courteous, he
was no more forthcoming than usual. 'He amused us by his
politeness, and was quite complimentary about the Pilgrimage,'
she wrote. 'It was then that I could not resist saying to him
that I had never seen a man so much improved.'¹⁰ She felt
sure that if only the suffragettes would leave him alone the
improvement would become more marked. But this, as she
knew, was a forlorn hope.

The suffragettes had orders that however much damage
they might cause to public and private property they must not
endanger human life; but in June 1913 they acquired their
own martyr. She was Emily Wilding-Davison, inventor of
letter-box arson and planter of the bomb which had partly
wrecked Lloyd George's house. Now she crowned her militant

career at the Derby course at Epsom when she rushed forward to clutch at the bridle of the King's horse and was killed.

The Union arranged a solemn funeral procession in which Emmeline Pankhurst intended to take part. She was out on licence at the time, recuperating in a suffragette-run nursing home, but the moment she left the house she was rearrested and sent back to Holloway. This time she copied Sylvia and refused water as well as food, and was released again on licence after three days, for no attempt at forcible feeding was ever made on her after the first abortive effort.

In August she escaped to France and spent two months with Christabel, recuperating and planning still further militant acts. The police could easily have traced her, but she had been so ill and emaciated when she last left prison that they thought it wiser to leave her in peace. In October she sailed for America and another fund-raising lecture tour. When the ship docked she was informed that she would be detained on Ellis Island as a person of doubtful character, pending instructions from Washington. She announced her intention of hunger-striking; but there was no need, for the moment her detention became known the President was deluged with protests from women's organizations and gave immediate orders for her release. The lecture tour was an immense success; and Emmeline returned to England with bulging pockets, only to be rearrested at Plymouth. And so the miserable round of hunger and thirst-striking, release on licence, and rearrest started all over again.

M

Chapter X

WOMEN AT WAR

During the first half of 1914 Emmeline Pankhurst's hold on the militant movement was as strong as ever. 'My splendid ones!' she called the starry-eyed women who cheerfully smashed windows, chained themselves to railings, heckled members of the Government, threw missiles at them, assaulted the police, and committed a hundred other offences in order to get themselves sent to prison. She was well aware, however, that while they shared with her the kicks and the abuse they did not share the limelight.

The Government, though sick and tired of the suffragette agitation, would not yield; but Ministers were now apprehensive at the prospect of appearing in public; and it was said that the King was seriously annoyed by the number of protests which women contrived to deliver into his hands.

The previous December, for example, the King and Queen had attended a gala performance at Covent Garden. There, they were addressed from a box by an elegant looking woman who harangued them through a megaphone on the iniquities of forcible feeding; and the disturbance caused by her subsequent removal had scarcely died down when a shower of suffragette leaflets descended on the audience from the galleries above.

In May, 1914, Emmeline Pankhurst, who was again out of prison on licence and as yet had served only thirty days of the three-year sentence she had been given the previous year, organized a deputation to Buckingham Palace. She did this in defiance of the Home Office, which had refused to advise the King to receive the deputation. The police handled the women as roughly as they had on that memorable Black Friday; but Emmeline had almost reached the Palace gates before she was seized in a bear-hug by a burly police inspector, who picked her up bodily, bruising her ribs. Of the courage of her followers she wrote later to Ethel Smyth. 'I shall never forget how . . . they dashed forward, flinging themselves against [the Wellington Gates] to prevent their being shut, returning again and again to the charge, their tender bodies bruised and bleeding. "She told us not to turn back," said one poor little thing when urged to go away and rest. Bless them!'[1] There is absolutely no doubt that the women displayed an extraordinary degree of courage and indifference to personal suffering on this and on many other occasions; and it is inconceivable that they would have been so inspired by any other leader. Mrs Pankhurst may have been wrong, but she knew perfectly well what she was doing, and the women were proud to follow her.

In June a particularly ingenious and daring verbal assault was made on the King. A debutante in Court dress and ostrich feather gasped out as she made her curtsy, 'Your Majesty, stop forcible feeding!' The girl was hurried away by shocked Court officials. The King gave no sign that he had heard; but he recorded the incident in his diary, adding: 'I don't know what we are coming to.'[2]

Earlier in the year Emmeline Pankhurst had crossed the Channel with her daughter Sylvia for a conference with Christabel. After their continual bouts of hunger and thirst striking and all the privations of prison life they made a strange and pathetic contrast to the expatriate. Sylvia, whose enthusiasm for prison was the equal of her mother's, had formed a number of branches of the WSPU in the East End of London; and, as a convinced Socialist, she had gained a large and devoted following of working men and women. This did not suit Christabel, who had been steadily veering towards the Conservatives as the Party most likely to give women the vote. After a lengthy confabulation Sylvia was instructed to turn her East End branches into a separate organization to be known as the East London Federation. Control of the WSPU was to remain the joint responsibility of Emmeline and Christabel; for the eldest Pankhurst daughter would brook no rivals to herself and her mother.

And so the militant campaign dragged on; and the sense of

fellowship it engendered was stronger than any other tie. As
Annie Kenney put it: 'No companionship can ever surpass the
companionship of the militants.'[3] The movement was their
life; and they squandered everything they had on it. There was
indeed an element of greatness about them, misguided as many
people thought them. 'You see only the folly and the wickedness,' Lord Lytton told his fellow peers in the House of Lords;
'but I also see . . . the pity and the tragedy . . . I have seen
the exhibition of human qualities which I consider to be
as rare and as precious as anything which a nation can possess.
I have seen these qualities given to a cause which in itself is as
great and as noble a cause as you could well find, but given in
such a way as to defeat the very objects that they sought to
obtain. . . . And that to my mind is a tragedy.'[4]

It was nothing less than a tragedy to the constitutionalists,
who had been beavering on out of the glare of public martyr-
dom. By the early summer of 1914 they could point to a
definitely improving attitude towards their patient work both
in Parliament and in the Press, an attitude which impressed
even the anti-suffragists under the banner of Mrs Humphrey
Ward. Millicent Fawcett could scarcely have been expected to
be forgiving towards those women who in 1908 had formed
the Women's Anti-Suffrage League and in 1910 had joined
forces with a similar organization for men led by Lord Curzon.
'Mrs Humphrey Ward's proposal,' she snorted in 1914, 'is
that we as Women's Suffrage Associations should abandon
our main object and purposes in return for her giving her
personal adhesion to votes for women for local parliaments.
It is as if she proposed that the Church of England should
abandon Christianity in exchange for her withdrawing
Robert Elsmere from circulation.'[5]

The constitutionalists were now sure that a change of heart
in the Government could not be long delayed. Millicent
Fawcett, whose thoughts were already turning towards the
part which enfranchised women could play in the happy
years ahead, had begun to study the effect of women's suffrage
in other countries where it had already been achieved, notably
in New Zealand and Australia.

In June Sylvia Pankhurst was given an inkling of this change of heart. Seriously ill as a result of her prison experiences and out on licence once more, she was carried on a stretcher from her home in Bow at the head of a deputation to the Prime Minister from her East London Federation. The women were received by Asquith with politeness verging on respect. He complimented them on the way they had formulated their request; and left them with the impression that he had at length decided to grant it.

Sylvia Pankhurst's work had been exceedingly valuable; but before anything tangible came of it July had passed. With the outbreak of war with Germany on August 4th, the entire suffrage situation was changed; and the suffragists—constitutionalists and militants alike—had to rethink their policy overnight.

Millicent Fawcett was afraid that the longed-for influence of enfranchised women would disappear in war with so much else that was good; but she had no doubt at all where the National Union should stand. 'Women,' she wrote, 'your country needs you. As long as there was any hope of peace most members of the National Union probably sought for peace, and endeavoured to support those who were trying to maintain it. But we have another duty now . . . LET US SHOW OURSELVES WORTHY OF CITIZENSHIP, WHETHER OUR CLAIM TO IT BE RECOGNIZED OR NOT.'[6]

In reply to this message the constituent bodies of the National Union readily agreed to suspend all suffrage activities for the duration of the war: and members joined the Voluntary Aid Detachments, the Red Cross, and other organizations in which women's help was urgently needed including the women's branches of the three armed services. With the recruitment of men into the Armed Forces the unemployment problem among women ceased to exist, and early in August the London Society opened a Women's Service Bureau to recruit women for jobs of all kinds which had hitherto been undertaken only by men. Women now became plumbers, electrical fitters, window cleaners, bus conductors, bargees, signalmen, carpenters, sweeps, and even grave diggers. They were, of course, needed in increasing numbers as nurses and clerks in Government offices and, later, in munitions factories. Initially the War Office had refused to recruit women doctors; but by September 1914 Elizabeth Garrett Anderson's daughter Louisa and a friend, Dr Flora Murray, had opened a hospital in Paris, staffed, equipped and maintained by Englishwomen; and a month later a branch hospital was opened in Wimereux. In 1915 the War Office, having seen the error of its ways, put the two women in charge of a military hospital in London; and in the course of the war with substantial help from the London Society of the National Union fourteen hospital units staffed by women operated for the Allied armies in various parts of the world.

Meanwhile, the National Union had run into trouble. It was clear by the end of 1914 that while Millicent Fawcett carried the bulk of the rank-and-file members with her in her determination to support the war effort, there was an influential opposition on the Executive and among leaders of the constituent bodies composed of pacificists and others who disapproved of her policy. The minority was not only influential but extremely vocal; there was a show-down; and, as a result, all the officers of the National Union—with the exception of the Treasurer and Millicent Fawcett as President—and the majority of the Executive Committee resigned in the spring of 1915. It seemed to many that Millicent Fawcett should herself have resigned at this juncture; but this she refused to do. She stood, wrote her biographer, 'Like a rock in their path, opposing herself with all the great weight of her personal popularity and prestige to their use of the machinery and name of the [National] Union, and they could in no way get the better of her.'[7] And so they went, protesting that she had acted unconstitutionally and had imposed her own will and her personal view-point on the National Union. She was bitterly hurt by the charge, coming as it did from those who had been her chief advisers in the past; but if she resented the implication that she had behaved like a dictator, she remained stubbornly in command of the rump of the movement and set to work once more to reinforce and direct it. She came through triumphantly; and although there were difficult times ahead the National Union survived.

The wartime history of the WSPU was entirely different;

for as an organization it ceased to exist. No one could accuse Emmeline and Christabel Pankhurst of acting unconstitutionally when they called an immediate halt to militant tactics because their word had always been law. The Government responded by releasing all the suffragettes still in prison; and within a month of the outbreak of hostilities mother and daughter were addressing recruiting meetings all over the country; and later Emmeline co-operated with her old enemy Lloyd George in his scheme, as Minister of Munitions, to recruit women for munitions factories.

The martial tone sounded by Emmeline and Christabel and echoed by many individual members of the WSPU was as unacceptable to the two younger Pankhursts as their right-wing politics. Sylvia and Adela were pacificists as well as Socialists. Adela was already in Australia—where women had had the vote since 1902—and was involved in left-wing politics. Sylvia, odd man out at home, spent the war years in the East End helping to organize infant welfare centres, day nurseries, cost-price restaurants and a co-operative toy factory, and any other scheme to offset the ravages of war.

Emmeline Pankhurst, equally anxious to do her bit in this direction, tried to persuade some of her followers to finance a home for war babies. But for once the Pankhurst magic failed to work; and quixotically she resolved to go it alone, causing Ethel Smyth to remark: 'As well try to hold up an avalanche with a child's spade as persuade Mrs Pankhurst out of any idea that had once taken root in her mind.'[8] The net result was that Emmeline was left to support four baby girls, which she did, though precariously, by giving lecture tours and then impoverishing herself by donating a large part of the proceeds to the war effort.

In the summer of 1916 hopes were raised once more that women would not have to wait much longer for the vote. A Bill was introduced in the House of Commons to revive and revise the Parliamentary register, which had lapsed during the first two years of the war. Provision would naturally have to be made for the young men in the forces overseas; but what of the women who had responded with such competence to the exigencies of war? At the instigation of a member of the

Executive of the National Union, the future MP Eleanor Rathbone, a representative Consultative Committee was set up to watch the course of events and, if possible, to influence it. By this time Asquith had been more specific. In the industrial reconstruction which would be necessary after the war, he declared, women would have a 'special claim to be heard on the many questions which will directly affect their interests,' and which might well involve large displacements of labour. 'I cannot think,' he added, 'that the House will deny that claim.'[9]

In January 1917 the issue was considered by an all-Party conference of Members of Parliament under the chairmanship of the Speaker. The Consultative Committee of the National Union was hard at work behind the scenes; but there was no committee of the WSPU to intervene. Emmeline Pankhurst, wrote Christabel later, 'held rather aloof from the negotiations which ended in the Speaker's Conference. . . . She and I believed that a certain detachment on our part would give more effect to the potential post-war militancy which it was the aim of political leaders to avert. We therefore left it to others to discuss such points as the differential age limit for women voters, designed to prevent them from becoming at once an electoral majority.'[10] The Conference recommended that the vote should be extended to all men of twenty-one; and recommended by a majority vote that it should be extended to women over thirty who were on the local government register or were the wives of electors, and to university trained women over thirty who would be entitled to vote as university electors.

Millicent Fawcett welcomed the recommendations as an augury of better things to come. In June the recommendations were embodied in a Representation of the People Bill which passed its second reading with an enormous majority. The third reading went through on December 7th; and in January 1918, after a three-day debate, the Lords accepted the inevitable by sixty-three votes.

The Representation of the People Act, with its modified form of women's suffrage, became law on February 6, 1918. Ironically, it was a moment of extreme Allied peril on the Western Front; and the natural rejoicings of both wings of the suffrage movement were muted by the national emergency. Emmeline Pankhurst, who appeared with Christabel on the platform of the Albert Hall that evening, spoke not only of the triumph but of a future in which women would still have to fight for equal opportunities in the professions and better conditions in the home. Yet although she spoke of the future her audience could not really respond to any rallying-cry save 'Votes for Women!'

The National Union held a thanksgiving meeting at Queen's Hall in March. Millicent Fawcett had always planned to celebrate victory with the music of freedom—the last movement of Beethoven's Fifth Symphony and the Leonora Overture No. III. But she could not cry 'freedom' with the war not yet won: instead, the suffragists sang a new setting by Sir Hubert Parry of Blake's *Jerusalem*, which in its old setting had been their battle hymn.

Millicent Fawcett, who was given a great ovation, spoke precisely as her followers had predicted: they knew her far too well to think she would spring any surprises. 'We do not triumph over our opponents,' she declared; 'it is much better than that. But the great searchlight of war showed things in their true light, and they gave us our enfranchisement with open hands.'[11]

Within a few weeks of the Allied victory in November 1918 a Bill was rushed through Parliament which enabled women to stand for Parliament in the General Election on December 14th. Seventeen women came forward, including Christabel Pankhurst, who stood as a Coalition candidate for Smethick; Charlotte Despard (now seventy-four) and Emmeline Pethick-Lawrence, who stood as Labour candidates for North Battersea and the Rusholme Division of Manchester respectively. Christabel came top of the sixteen candidates who were defeated. The only successful one was the enigmatic Countess Markievicz (formerly Constance Gore-Booth), who fought in the Irish Citizen Army and was imprisoned many times. Countess Markievicz was elected as a Sinn Feiner for the St Patrick's Division of Dublin and, like the other Sinn Feiners elected, she refused to take her seat in the House of Commons.

Emmeline Pethick-Lawrence, who succeeded Charlotte

Despard as President of the Women's Freedom League, continued the campaign for equal citizenship. Charlotte Despard
herself, who lived to be ninety-five and became more and more
left-wing in politics, reappeared next in Dublin as a colleague
of the Irish revolutionary Maud Gonne and a sore trial to her
brother,* who was Lord Lieutenant of Ireland from 1918 to
1921.

Christabel Pankhurst's defeat was a searing disappointment
to her mother, who had thrown herself with desperate energy
into the election campaign. It would have crowned her life's
work to have seen her favourite child in Parliament. But
Christabel had no further interest in politics. Before very long
she had found a more satisfying cause; and in America, where
she spent most of the remainder of her life, she went about
preaching the early Second Coming of Jesus Christ. Sylvia,
champion of the underdog, also found another cause—a
crusade against the evil effects of Fascism in Ethiopia. Their
mother, now firmly anchored to the Conservative Party, kept
a foot in the political camp; but she was still bedevilled by the
need to support her war babies; and it was not until she gave
up the struggle and found other homes for them (Christabel
adopted one) that she was free to take an active part. By that
time it seemed almost impossible to her friends that this
burnt-out husk of a woman had any fight left in her: yet those
who doubted her ability to make a come-back were wrong.

The end of the 1914–18 War and the return of the armed
forces to civilian life produced a shocking dislocation of labour.
In the distressing period of insecurity and unemployment
which followed a great many women who had been doing
men's work had to acquiesce in a situation which deprived
them of their jobs. Women in industry were the most severely
hit: the majority of them were offered nothing more alluring
than the prospect of domestic service with all its petty restrictions and lack of freedom. In pretty well every occupation, however, the most useful of the women were kept on; and in the
non-industrial sphere more occupations were open to women
than before the war.

* He was made a Viscount in 1916 and created Earl of Ypres in
1921.

A number of organizations were now concerned with the unemployment problem among women. Among them was the London Society for Women's Suffrage, which had placed over 2,000 women in wartime jobs and in 1918 changed its name to the London Society for Women's Service.* The main body, the National Union of Women's Suffrage Societies, was of course also concerned in the solution of peacetime problems. In 1919 it was renamed the National Union of Societies for Equal Citizenship, in order to continue the fight for equal franchise and also to deal with the mass of discriminatory legislation which remained.

In the same year Millicent Fawcett—over seventy but still quietly vigorous and without a grey hair in her head—retired from the presidency of the National Union. She was succeeded by Eleanor Rathbone (1872–1946), a leading constitutionalist and a woman of vision and splendid humanity, who had shown great perspicuity in persuading the Union to ask for an amendment to the Representation of the People Bill which admitted women who qualified for the parliamentary vote to the local government register as well.

Eleanor Rathbone, born in Liverpool in a family with a fine tradition of social reform, came down from Oxford in 1896 and took up relief work in her native city. She was no starry-eyed social worker but a young woman with a clear and penetrating brain. Early enquiries which she made into the administration of the Poor Law led her into an analysis of the economic situation of the family unit, and so on to the work which will probably be her lasting memorial—the case for family allowances. During the war she had formed a small Family Endowment Committee which in the autumn of 1918 set out its demand in a pamphlet, *Equal Pay and the Family*: a Proposal for the National Endowment of Motherhood. Almost immediately Eleanor Rathbone ran into trouble with some of her colleagues in the National Union. The opposition was led by the woman she loved and admired and had succeeded as President. Millicent Fawcett was obstinately certain that any scheme for family allowances would endanger the security of family life. She said so with all the force of her years and influence; and

* In 1966 it is still active as the Fawcett Society.

when it became clear that she was fighting a rearguard action she resigned from the Union, 'in friendliness and without anger, but with absolute finality.'[12] For the rest of her life she concentrated her still formidable energies on the work of the London Society, of which she had been a member since 1867, had been Chairman for many years, and was now President.

Apart from family allowances, Millicent Fawcett was in absolute sympathy with the demands put forward by the National Union. They were: equal pay for equal work; a reform of the divorce law and the laws dealing with solicitation and prostitution; the provision of pensions for civilian widows and dependent children; the extension of the franchise to women on equal terms with men, and the return to Parliament of women candidates pledged to the programme of equality; the recognition of mothers as equal guardians with fathers of their children; and the opening to women of the legal profession and the magistracy.

This final demand was met immediately. On December 23, 1919, Royal Assent was given to the Sex Disqualification (Removal) Act which enabled women to become solicitors, to be admitted to the Bar examinations and to practise as barristers, and also to become magistrates.

The Act secured, among other things, the entry of women to a number of professional and learned bodies, and, after a hard tussle, into the Civil Service. It was anticipated that it would also ensure the admittance of hereditary peeresses to the House of Lords, but this did not happen. In 1922 Viscountess Rhondda, a peeress in her own right, lodged a petition with the Lords' Committee of Privileges. It was considered on two separate occasions; and on the second, with the help of the backwoodsmen peers mustered for the event, it was rejected on the grounds that the Act was meant to remove existing disqualifications, not to introduce new rights.

In the House of Commons, however, the situation was bright. In 1919 the first woman Member of Parliament took her seat. She was a Conservative, American-born Viscountess Astor (1879–1964), who won a by-election in the Sutton Division of Plymouth when her husband, who had held the seat for nine years, succeeded to his title. Lady Astor, a vivid, jewel-like little figure, elegant and witty but often tactless and illogical, was scarcely the type of woman the suffragists would have chosen to represent them in Parliament; yet although she was never a great parliamentarian, she did not let them down; but with a warm heart, generosity and courage battled away for all their causes. As the only woman among 600 men, she needed all her courage to survive; and in after life she maintained that she was so paralysed with fright that she sat through her first five hours in the House of Commons without movement. Everything she did, everything she said, everything she wore, was news. As a political hostess she might appear blazing with diamonds: in the House she was invariably soberly dressed in black with touches of white at the neck.

At first she encountered a considerable amount of hostility from certain Members who resented the presence of a woman and did their best to persuade her not to seek re-election when the time came. When she refused they behaved like spoilt children. 'Men whom I had known for years,' she said, 'would not speak to me if they passed me in the corridors. They said I would not last six months. But I stuck it out.'[13]

She did indeed, with the constant help and advice of her husband. 'If you vote for me,' she told her constituents when she first offered herself for re-election, 'you will be getting tuppence for a penny, because you will be getting me and my husband as your representative. No other candidate can offer you as much. I belong to the tried old firm of Astor & Co.'[14]

In 1921 Lady Astor was joined by another woman, the plump and motherly Mrs Margaret Wintringham, widow of the Liberal MP for Lough, who won her late husband's seat at a by-election. Between 1921 and 1928 nine more women were elected, among them several of real stature, including Miss Margaret Bondfield (1873–1953) who, as Minister of Labour in the second Labour Government, was the first woman to hold Cabinet office.

In 1928, with women Members firmly in the saddle, the Conservative Government made the gesture of equality for which the women's societies had been working and waiting and introduced a Bill to extend the vote to all women over twenty-one. Millicent Fawcett, now over eighty but still spry and intellectually vigorous, and Emmeline Pankhurst, nearing seventy but as worn as a ghost, appeared together on the platform of Queen's Hall at a thanksgiving meeting. Eleanor Rathbone was in the chair, and the suffragette leader moved a vote of thanks to a former enemy, now a friend, the Prime Minister, Stanley Baldwin (afterwards Lord Baldwin).

Emmeline Pankhurst might look like a ghost; but when she started to speak—without the aid of a microphone—she came to life once more and the voice which had thrilled multitudes in the Albert Hall in the past was as clear and persuasive as ever. She had recently agreed to become a Conservative candidate and fight a strongly held Labour seat, Whitechapel and St George's in the East End of London, at the General Election which was to be held in the following year. She had no chance of winning the seat, but her speeches had already made a profound impression. But she did not live to fight this test battle: on June 14, 1928, she died after a sudden illness. A fortnight later the Representation of the People (Equal Franchise) Act became law.

Millicent Fawcett, who had been made a Dame of the British Empire in 1925 and later a GBE, survived her rival for another year. She was naturally elated when Margaret Bondfield was made Minister of Labour in the Labour Government of 1929–31; and took a purring delight in referring to her as 'the Right Honourable Margaret'. In the summer of 1929, still active though by now a little bent, she attended a public luncheon given by the National Union in honour of the new women MPs. A few days later she began to fail; and on August 5th, without pain or real suffering, she died.

Millicent Fawcett's funeral was followed by a memorial service in Westminster Abbey. Two plaques in her honour were later added to the Abbey memorial of her husband. One gave her name and the dates of her birth and death. The other outlined her life and work: 'A wise constant and courageous Englishwoman she won citizenship for Women.'

And yet, in death as in life, it was the dynamic figure of Emmeline Pankhurst which held the limelight. In March 1930 a statue of the suffragette leader* was unveiled by Stanley Baldwin in the Victoria Tower Gardens, Westminster, close to the Houses of Parliament where she had staged her most bitter fights. The speakers at the ceremony included Frederick Pethick-Lawrence and 'General' Flora Drummond. Ethel Smyth, resplendent in her robes as a Doctor of Music, conducted her *March of the Women*: and among the spectators was a two-year-old boy—Richard Marsden Pethick Pankhurst—the living proof of Sylvia Pankhurst's contention that the newly emancipated woman should be free to bear children out of wedlock.

In the course of his memorial address Stanley Baldwin declared: 'I say with no fear of contradiction that whatever view posterity may take, Mrs Pankhurst has won for herself a niche in the Temple of Fame which will last for all time.' It is most improbable that history will prove him wrong. Today, among the thousands to whom Emmeline Pankhurst is a household word there are comparatively few who remember the long, patient, stubborn fight of Millicent Fawcett. To which of the two do women owe the vote? Or do they, as many people maintain, simply owe it to the War of 1914–18 in which women had proved conclusively that they were responsible citizens? The answer is probably a compromise. The militants with their highly coloured methods and their acts of personal courage drew public attention and sympathy to the demand for enfranchisement which the constitutionalists had been quietly making for so many years. And in the end a Government, which had refused to be moved either by violence and threats or by sweet reason, was only too thankful to find in women's war work an excuse to capitulate without further loss of face.

It is easy to see why the WSPU, that close-knit companionship of militants which had been so closely geared to the actual fight for the vote, failed to survive the 1914–18 War as a going concern. It is just as easy to understand why members of the

* In 1959 an addition to the memorial was made in the form of two low walls, each ending in a pier with a bronze medallion. One medallion represented the WSPU brooch worn by the suffragettes who had been in prison: the other was a relief of Christabel, who had been made a DBE in 1936, and had died earlier in 1959.

National Union, who had been alive all along to the importance of educating public opinion and had acquired very considerable political expertise and skill in the process, were able to turn their experience to good account in the peacetime campaign for social reform.

A number of women who cut their political teeth in the National Union distinguished themselves in other spheres. Among the best known names are those of Miss Maude Royden, social worker, preacher, and writer on the religious and ethical aspects of the women's movement; Miss Chrystal Macmillan of Edinburgh, who appeared in the House of Lords in 1908 to plead the right of Scottish women graduates to the Parliamentary vote, was called to the Bar in 1924, and was concerned with all questions concerning women's rights both at home and overseas; Miss Margaret Ashton of Manchester, the first woman to sit on the City Council and a tireless worker for causes connected with international understanding; the Hon. Mrs Ernest Franklin, President of the National Council of Women, 1926–1928, and Honorary Secretary of the Parents' National Educational Union for more than sixty years; Alderman Mrs Rackham of Cambridge, one of the first women magistrates, a member of the Board of Guardians and of the Town and County Councils; Dame Kathleen Courtney, a member of the Executive Committee of the League of Nations and Vice-Chairman in 1949; and Joint President of the United Nations Association; and Mrs Margery Corbett Ashby, Honorary President of the International Alliance of Women and of the British Commonwealth League, and Substitute Delegate for the United Kingdom to the Disarmament Conference of 1931–35, who has lectured on education and land questions all over Europe, in the United States and Canada and the Near and Far East.

After the 1914–18 War the political work which had formerly been undertaken by the National Union of Women's Suffrage Societies was carried on by the National Union of Societies for Equal Citizenship, and in due course the educational and social work was diverted to the newly formed Union of Townswomen's Guilds. Later, the National Council for Equal Citizenship (as the NUSEC was now called) was amalgamated with the National Women's Citizens' Associations; and its influence, though largely indirect, is still felt today in the activities of the various organizations which have stemmed from it. The legitimate heir of the women's movement, however, is the Fawcett Society—originally the London Society for Women's Suffrage.

N

Chapter XI

HEIRS OF THE WOMEN'S MOVEMENT

In 1920—just in time for the old warrior Emily Davies to rejoice before her death the following year—Oxford University at last decided to give women students their rightful due. The decision was a bitter pill for the old guard to swallow. The Vice Chancellor went as far as to tell a friend that he was praying daily that women would not be admitted to the degree, and when asked for the form of words, replied: 'Lord, if it must be, let it not be in my time.'[1] In spite of the Vice Chancellor's prayers the decision to admit women to full University status was honoured on October 14, 1920, when degrees by decree were conferred on the heads of the women's colleges and on those tutors who, as students, had taken their final examinations but had not followed the full degree course. After 1920 women could act as examiners and take advantage of University fellowships and scholarships, although a few minor inequalities remained until the end of the Second World War.

With the exception of Cambridge the other universities, led by London which had opened its examinations and degrees to women in 1878, were well ahead of Oxford. But Cambridge, which condescended to admit women to 'titular' degrees in 1921, made them wait until 1948 for full membership of the University. Needless to say, in all the more recently created universities men and women have been admitted from the outset on terms of absolute equality.

A number of women have made their mark in academic life since the heyday of the great pioneers. Among them are the historian Professor Lilian Penson (1896–1963), the pathologist Dame Janet Vaughan and the scientist Dr Crowfoot-Hodgkin.

Lilian Penson took First Class honours in History at London

University in 1917 and after wartime service in Whitehall she earned a doctorate for her thesis on the history of the West Indies and was appointed Lecturer in History at Birkbeck College. Cononial history was her first love but after her appointment in 1930 as Professor of Modern History at Bedford College she did much to establish the study of diplomatic history, in which she herself had done a great deal of research, at undergraduate and post-graduate levels.

As Dean of the Faculty of Arts in 1938 and a member of the University senate in 1940, administration claimed more and more of Lilian Penson's time at the expense of history. But it was her administrative work which led directly to her election as Vice Chancellor in 1948, an office never before held by a woman in any university. The mere fact that her election caused so little stir was a tribute to her personality and ability; for she was unquestionably the most suitable person in the University to hold its highest office. Even the anti-feminists approved of the appointment. The Vice Chancellor of Oxford, Dr Stallybrass, a confirmed misogynist, conceded at dinner a few days before his death that while he disliked the company of most women and believed that he hated all women dons, he found the company of his colleague Professor Penson enjoyable. His enjoyment was shared by many other people; for Lilian Penson dearly loved good talk round the dinner table and herself enjoyed good food and wine.

In 1948, the year of her election, Lilian Penson—already a DBE—was one of the first three recipients of honorary doctorates at Cambridge University, the other two being the Queen (now Queen Elizabeth the Queen Mother) and Dame Myra Hess.

One of the most valuable by-products of Lilian Penson's work was her concern for the young universities of the Commonwealth, which she visited in turn during the vacations. A country which benefited more than any other from her interest in higher education was the Sudan. From 1946, when she first visited Gordon College, Khartoum, until 1956 when it achieved university status, she followed its progress with enthusiasm, and she was largely instrumental in working out the details of its special relationship with London University. And she derived special satisfaction from watching the number of women students grow from two to about forty, enough to fill a women's hall of residence.

Dr Janet Vaughan, who was made a DBE in 1957, was appointed Principal of Somerville College, Oxford in 1945, becoming the first married woman to be made head of a college. Educated at Somerville, she entered University College Hospital with a Goldwater Entrance scholarship. She was awarded a Rockefeller Fellowship, 1929–30; a Beith Memorial Fellowship, 1930–33; and a Leverhulme Fellowship at the Royal College of Physicians, 1933–4. From 1934–39 she was Assistant in Clinical Pathology at the British Post-Graduate Medical School, and during the War was pathologist in charge of the North-West London Blood Supply Depot. In 1944 Dr Vaughan was a member of the Royal Commission on Equal Pay, which favoured equal pay for teachers, Civil Servants and local government officers; and was one of three women who submitted a memorandum to show that if equal pay were also to be introduced in industry it would not only benefit women workers but their families as well. Since the War Dame Janet—an Honorary DSC of the University of Wales and the first mother and grandmother as well as the first married woman to be head of a college—has been Chairman of the Oxford Regional Hospital Board, a member of the Committee on Economic and Financial Problems of Provision for Old Age, and of the Medical Advisory Committee of the University Grants Committee.

The scientist Dr Dorothy Crowfoot-Hodgkin, a Freeman of her native town of Beccles in East Anglia, is also a mother and grandmother. She has been at Oxford continuously since she first went up to Somerville more than thirty years ago, is a Fellow of her College and Oxford University Reader in X-ray Crystallography, and, since 1960, Wolfson Research Professor of the Royal Society at Oxford. In 1964 she became the third woman to win the Nobel Prize for Chemistry, her predecessors being Marie Curie, who won the Prize in 1911, and her daughter, Irene Joliot-Curie, who won it in 1935. Dr Crowfoot-Hodgkin is best known for her work towards finding the structures of penicillin and, later, of Vitamin B12, a liver extract used in fighting pernicious anaemia. In March 1965 she was the first woman since Florence Nightingale to be appointed a member of the Order of Merit.

Dame Janet Vaughan and Dr Crowfoot-Hodgkin are out-standing products of the fight for higher education and medical education for women. As far as medical training is concerned, the protracted and bitter struggle had been virtually won by the time Elizabeth Garrett Anderson resigned her post as Dean of the Medical School in 1903. Progress after that date was sure, if not always smooth; and the growing reputation of women doctors was greatly enhanced by their efficiency during the 1914–18 War. One of a number of outstanding women doctors was Dame Louisa Aldrich Blake (1865–1925), who was appointed Dean of the London (Royal Free Hospital) School of Medicine for Women—as it had now become—in 1914. Dame Louisa ,who had entered the Medical School in 1887, became in 1895 the first woman master in surgery, and was surgeon to the Elizabeth Garrett Anderson Hospital and the Royal Free Hospital. During the war, apart from her work of guiding the Medical School through the intricacies of its wartime problems, she mobilized women doctors and organized and equipped the women's medical units. A first-rate administrator, Dame Louisa was an ideal woman for the job; and she was ready to sacrifice her skill as a surgeon to the exigencies of the moment and even to study finance and accountancy as an aid to the more efficient running of the School.

The 1914–18 War, which depleted the ranks of the medical profession, had facilitated the entry of women students into the teaching hospitals. After the war several of the London hospitals refused to continue the experiment; and it was reckoned that the decision was not unconnected with the vital need to secure the best possible material for their Rugby football teams. An influential woman who protested vigorously against the decision was Lady Frances Balfour, well known suffragist and champion of her sex, who had saved Elizabeth Garrett Anderson from the danger of arrest. In the uniform she had designed for her own wear—a long, high-collared black gown and a black Mary Queen of Scots bonnet—Lady Frances was a distinctive figure at any gathering; and although she was never a leader of the women's movement she was an outspoken and effective critic of Parliamentary Bills dealing with conditions of female labour and in her later years espoused the cause of the barmaids and the women police. When she died in 1931 women students were still being admitted only to a few London hospitals; but those who were accepted were fully integrated into the medical profession on equal terms with men. It took a second world war, however, to open the remaining London hospitals to women and so bring them into line with the provincial hospitals. Even so, inequalities still exist.

The entry of women to the legal profession, which was accomplished so smoothly after the passage of the Sex Disqualification (Removal) Act of 1919, had begun much earlier in the century when a number of women—Christabel Pankhurst among them—had applied for and been refused admission to one of the Inns of Court. In 1912, after four women had been prevented from taking the examinations of the Law Society, a Committee for Opening the Legal Profession to Women was set up and funds were collected with the object of promoting legal action against the Law Society. A test case was heard, but the Court of Appeal upheld the Law Society's decision. Although disappointed by the setback members of the Committee agreed to keep it in being and to continue to work for their goal. In 1913 and 1914 a Bill to admit women to the profession was on the list of Private Members' Bills; but no time was found to take it although the Prime Minister, the Lord Chancellor and the Law Officers of the Crown were known to be sympathetic. In 1918 a Bill to admit women as solicitors passed without a division in the House of Lords but was not debated in the Commons. In 1919 a Bill covering both branches of the profession passed the Lords; but it became redundant with the passage of the Sex Disqualification (Removal) Act, which automatically achieved the objects for which the Committee had been working.

The Committee then proudly presented the residue of its fighting fund—about £160—to the London Society for Women's Service to be used for the benefit of women law students. As a grand finale it gave a dinner at the House of Commons which, to everybody's surprise, was attended by a group of notable lawyers, who made amiable and flattering speeches of welcome to their future colleagues. Perhaps they were mellowed by the extraordinary variety of the champagne, which had been contributed by friends and well-wishers and was of several different brands. At any rate, the unsuspecting Lord Birkenhead, whose glass had been filled repeatedly from a variety of bottles, complimented the organizers of the dinner on the excellence of their wine.

Champagne or no, the women infiltrated into the legal profession painlessly and with very little effort. Some at once began the study of law with the object of practising in the courts: others were articled to solicitors. 'Everyone,' wrote Ray Strachey in 1928, 'predicted that they would have no luck, and that their entry into an overcrowded profession would be a failure; but in the event it has been found that their prospects are much the same as those of their male contemporaries, and that their appearance in wig and gown has created no revolution in legal circles.'[2]

The first woman admitted as a Bar student in the Middle Temple in January, 1920, soon made an impression. She was Helena Normanton (1883–1957) who, as a schoolgirl in Brighton, had made up her mind to become a lawyer if ever this were possible. She had gone with her mother to consult the family solicitor on some complicated question; and the solicitor, who saw that the daughter and not the mother had grasped the situation, gave her a metaphorical pat on the head and remarked: 'She is quite the little lawyer.'

With this grain of encouragement the girl began to study the law although at the time there was no prospect of her being admitted. She also went to London University where she took First Class Honours in Modern History and later studied at Dijon University, gaining diplomas in the French language, literature and history. By the time Helena Normanton was called to the Bar in 1922 she had married; but unlike the suffrage workers who tacked their married on to their maiden names, she fought a legal battle for her right to be known for professional purposes as Mrs Helena Normanton; and when two years later she argued this right in the American courts she could flourish a passport made out to her specification.

Helena Normanton certainly got away to a good start. In 1922 she was the first woman barrister to be briefed in the High Court, where she secured a divorce for her client in ten minutes. She was also the first woman to be briefed in the Central Criminal Court, and the first to prosecute in a trial on a capital charge. In 1946 she became the first woman to be elected to the General Council of the Bar; and in 1949, with Miss Rose Heilbron, was equal first among women KCs of the English Bar, although another woman, Miss Margaret Henderson Kidd, had beaten them to it at the Scottish Bar.

Although Helena Normanton kept her lead in the women's Bar stakes she was not as well liked as some of her contemporaries and successors. She took infinite trouble with her cases, but was sometimes accused of blowing up minor cases into full-scale State trials and of displaying her literary erudition at the expense of a bewildered Old Bailey jury.

As a leading member of a number of British and international organizations, Helena Normanton campaigned sturdily for women's rights. She was President of the Married Women's Association until 1952 when on her own authority she sent a memorandum of evidence in the Association's name to the Royal Commission on Divorce. The memorandum was heavily criticized for being both anti-man and disruptive of the marriage partnership: the President withdrew it and herself resigned from the Association.

None of the distinguished women lawyers who have followed in Helena Normanton's footsteps can be accused of being ultra-feminist, although they have all taken a very natural interest in legislation concerning women and children. The two best known among them, with the largest number of 'firsts', are Miss Rose Heilbron and Mrs Elizabeth Lane.

Miss Heilbron, one of the first two women to take Silk, was born and educated in Liverpool: she took her LLB with First Class Honours at Liverpool University in 1935 and the higher degree of LLM two years later. She was called to the Bar in 1939 and, although she is married, has continued for professional purposes to be known by her maiden name. During a dazzling career in the criminal courts Miss Heilbron has gained a number of spectacular successes. In one of her most publicized cases she defended the turf accountant Jack Comer (otherwise Jack Spot) who was acquitted of charges which included possessing a knife, causing grievous bodily harm, and fighting. 'If you want something to write about,' declared Mr Comer emotionally to newspaper reporters after the trial, 'don't write about me, but about Rose Heilbron, the greatest lawyer in history.'

Miss Heilbron was the first woman to lead in a murder trial and the first to appear in a case in the House of Lords. Among the cases in which she acted for the defence were two charges of murder in both of which a verdict of manslaughter was returned. After her successful defence at the Old Bailey of three of the dockers in the 'incitement to strike trial', one of the defendants, she recalled, came up to her, shook her hand, and declared with the utmost fervour, 'I'd like to kiss you, but I'm married and that would be adultery.'

In 1956 Miss Heilbron was made Recorder of Burnley, the first woman to be appointed to the position of a borough judge, empowered to try indictable offences in boroughs which hold quarter sessions. It was appropriate that she should have been sworn in as Recorder by a woman mayor, who called on her to take the oath of allegiance and the judicial oath.

Mrs Elizabeth Lane, the first woman Assistant Recorder, and Recorder of Derby in 1962, was called to the Bar in 1940, and is married to a barrister. In 1946 she made legal history as the first woman to argue a murder appeal in the House of Lords. She took Silk in 1960; in 1962 she became the first woman county court judge, an appointment which involved her resignation as Recorder of Derby; and in the same year, when she took her place as a Divorce Commissioner, she became the first woman judge to sit in the High Court. On this occasion a woman barrister, speaking on behalf of the women members of the Bar, declared: 'We shall follow your course onwards and upwards with admiration and affectionate regard.'

Since that time Judge Lane's course has indeed been onwards and upwards. In May, 1965, she was the first woman in the history of the London Sessions (now the Inner London Sessions) to preside over one of the courts, as an acting deputy chairman. 'I imagine you are used to making legal history,' said the acting chairman, 'and you have done it again by being the first lady deputy chairman of this court.'

On August 13, 1965, came the announcement that Judge Lane had done it once again, and had become the first woman to be appointed a High Court Judge in the Divorce and Admiralty Division. 'All those who know Judge Lane,' wrote the Legal Correspondent of *The Times*, 'will feel happy that she has been the chosen one; this is the removal of the last bulwark against female emancipation.' The appointment of a woman—Mrs M. Hall—as Clerk to Mrs Justice Lane makes another piece of legal history, for Mrs Hall is the first woman to hold the post of Clerk to a High Court Judge.

A number of other women have achieved 'firsts' in the legal profession; among them is Miss Lilian M. Hollowell, the first woman coroner, who was appointed in 1951; and there is even on record the first woman solicitor to be struck off the Roll for misappropriation of funds, but maybe she is best left anonymous. On April 4, 1945, a lyrical reporter wrote: 'The trumpet of women's rights must sound for Miss Sybil Campbell, who is the first that ever burst into that eminence so stubbornly held by man, the stipendiary bench.' Miss Campbell, who spent much of her early life in Ceylon and took an Economics degree at Cambridge, was a Trade Board Inspector during the First World War, and found the legal aspect of the work so absorbing that as soon as the law was opened to women she entered the Middle Temple as a student. She was called to the Bar in 1922 and practised on the Midland circuit until in 1945 she was appointed Metropolitan Magistrate, Tower Bridge. 'Her Worship', the Press reporter noted, was soberly dressed in a dark grey suit, and 'took her seat with perfect *sang froid*.'

Miss Campbell proved a somewhat controversial figure on the bench on account of the severity of the prison sentences which she passed on first offenders which, on appeal, were reduced to fines. But while she was, perhaps, over stern in her dealings with lawbreakers she was also deeply concerned with the rehabilitation of offenders. The day she retired in 1961 was enlivened by the presence of a barrowboy who entered the magistrates' room and presented her with a large bunch of flowers as a thank-offering for her services seven years earlier in helping to arrange for barrowboys to get licensed pitches.

Although there is no sex or financial discrimination against women in the legal profession very few women have as yet reached the heights; and no woman has yet been made a Law Officer in the Government.

Women have also scaled the heights of the Civil Service but theirs has been a much harder fight. The permanent Civil Servants, wrote Eleanor Rathbone in 1936, 'loathed the thought of admitting women to their quiet and comfortable preserves. Women were all right in the lower grades, of course, and definitely useful as typists. But in the higher grades they would be dreadfully out of place and inconvenient. . . . They therefore produced with alacrity an Order in Council reserving posts overseas to men, and did nothing about admitting women to the Home Service beyond setting up a Reorganization Committee upon which women were barely represented.'[3]

The publication of the Reorganization Committee's report led to a protracted struggle between the Treasury and the women's societies, chief among them the National Council of Societies for Equal Citizenship and the London Society for Women's Service. The women's societies had the House of Commons on their side, and step by step the Treasury was forced to retreat. In 1925 the competitive examinations to the administrative grades were first opened to women; and after further adjustments had been made in 1931 a Royal Commission recommended, and the Treasury accepted as far as the Home Service was concerned, 'the doctrine of "the fair field and no favour" with its implication of an "aggregated staff." '[4]

Even so, there was a good deal of alarm and despondency at the prospect of women in high places. Women were obliged to resign on marriage, which put paid to a number of promising careers; and almost without exception their salary rates were lower than men's, an anomaly which was not put right until after the Second World War.

Outstanding among the women who have reached the top is Dame Evelyn Sharp who in 1948, at the age of forty-three, was the youngest woman to be made a DBE. The daughter of a London clergyman, Dame Evelyn was educated at St Paul's School, and entered the Civil Service in 1926 by the competitive examinations which had been opened to women the previous year. Miss Sharp, who came seventh out of 400 candidates, was the only woman to be placed. Her subsequent climb through the administrative grades was steady, the result, as she said at a later date, of hard work and an inborn interest in the processes of government. With the exception of four years in the Treasury the whole of her service was passed in Departments primarily concerned with local government. In 1946 when she was made Deputy Secretary—or second in command—of the Ministry of Town and Country Planning she was the first woman to hold a comparable post and to receive the recognized salary for the job. In 1955, after serving in the same capacity at the Ministry of Local Government and Planning, Dame Evelyn was appointed Permanent Secretary of the Ministry of Housing and Local Government, and so became the first woman to be head of a Government Department. Her appointment was welcomed by the local authorities who had worked most closely with her and had been impressed by her habitual perspicuity and sense of justice.

When her forthcoming retirement was announced in 1965 Dame Evelyn had some harsh remarks to make about the Civil Service which, as she said in a newspaper interview, 'needs overhauling from top to bottom. The way it has to conduct its business is Victorian. It does its best, of course,' she added; but while she had nothing but praise for the way it has struggled for efficiency since the war, she felt that a major transformation would be needed to enable it to cope adequately with the problems of the future.

The Sex Disqualification (Removal) Act, which had unlocked the Civil Service to women and ensured their grudging acceptance, had been less than fair to aspirants to the Foreign Service; for it had reserved to men 'all posts in the Diplomatic Service and in the Consular Service, in the Government Services of His Majesty in India, and in the Commercial Diplomatic Service and the Trade Commission.' This stipulation effectively kept women from being established in any of the higher grades; and once again it took a second world war to put things straight.

There was a fluttering of the dovecots in 1942 when it was announced that Miss Mary Craig McGeachy, who had been acting as liaison officer in Washington for the Ministry of Economic Warfare, had been given diplomatic status, although there was a rumour afoot that the authorities had been hoodwinked into thinking that 'Craig McGeachy' was a man. Miss McGeachy, born in Canada and educated at Toronto University, worked first in the Dominion section of the League of Nations Secretariat, and was transferred to the Ministry of Economic Warfare after the outbreak of war. Her service in Washington, was of a very high order; and it was said of her that nobody had presented a finer picture of the British people at war.

The fact that Miss McGeachy had been given diplomatic status did not automatically mean that she was now an established member of the Foreign Service, since no admissions were made until 1946. But the precedent which she established was followed by a regular break-through into this hitherto closed reserve. In 1943 Mrs Betty Gibbs, a young widow with two small children, and a member of the British Embassy staff, was also given diplomatic status. Two years later Mrs Marjorie D. Spikes, who had been doing welfare work in the Ministry of Labour before her transfer to Washington, became the first woman to be appointed Attaché of Women's Affairs.

A Foreign Office announcement made on March 5, 1963, to the effect that the appointment of Miss Barbara Salt as British Ambassador to Israel had been cancelled was to many people the first intimation that ill health had put paid to a brilliantly earned triumph.

Dame Barbara Salt—as she became the same year—had spent several years in Germany and Switzerland after leaving school; and after some years of business experience she entered the Foreign Office soon after the outbreak of war. In 1942 she was appointed Vice-Consul in Tangier and remained in this key post until 1946, acquiring a reputation for thorough, efficient and highly intelligent work. In 1950, after a period in the Foreign Office, she was sent as First Secretary in the Commercial Diplomatic Service to Moscow; and later, in her capacity as First Secretary in Washington, she was known as a negotiator of great skill and competence. Between 1957 and 1960 Dame Barbara served as Consul-General in Tel-Aviv, and was then made deputy to the leader of the British delegation to the disarmament conference in Geneva. In 1962, while on leave from her next post as British representative on the Economic and Social Council of the United Nations, she was appointed Ambassador. It would have been singularly appropriate for Britain's first woman Ambassador to have gone to Israel, a country which for some years past had had a woman Foreign Secretary.

So far no other woman has been named as British Ambassador. And in certain other spheres, notably in science and technology, industry, commerce and finance, very few women have gained the higher reaches. In all fairness it must be said that the women are partly responsible for their own exclusion, since comparatively few are attracted by these subjects and many doubt their ability to make good in them. The opportunities which exist for women today in engineering and electrical work were created originally by a remarkable woman, Dame Caroline Haslett, who was the first secretary of the Women's Engineering Society which was founded in 1919, and the founder in 1924 of the Women's Electrical Association. Dame Caroline, who died in 1957, was the only woman member of the council of the British Institute of Management and of the British Electrical Authority which was formed in 1947. She was the first woman Chairman of the British Electrical Development Association; and the first woman Vice-President of the Royal Society of Arts. Her pioneering work for the admission of women to the engineering and electrical professions was not confined to this country; for she was Chairman (later President) of the British Federation of Business and Professional Women and the first British President of the International Federation of Business and Professional Women.

In 1965 the Women's Engineering Society had a membership of slightly less than 300. The majority of the members are employed on the electrical side although some are working in allied professions such as metallurgy, physics and chemistry.

In no sense, therefore, has the same break-through occurred in engineering or in the other professions mentioned above as has occurred in the law, the Civil Service, medicine and in Parliament.

Chapter XII

WOMEN IN PARLIAMENT

It was not only because Lady Astor was the first of the women
MP's that she will be remembered: for while many of them have
surpassed her not one has made quite such an individual mark.
Her speeches were never dull: they were always brief and sometimes brilliant; and although she had a tiresome habit of
interrupting other Members, her remarks, if sometimes insult-
ing were often very much to the point. She made her maiden
speech on temperance, a subject on which she had strong
opinions, for her early first marriage, which had ended in
divorce, had been to an alcoholic. In 1923 she introduced and
piloted through the House the Intoxicating Liquor (Sale to
Persons under Eighteen) Bill,* which was carried with only
ten dissentient votes and remains the law today.

When in 1921 she was joined in the House by Mrs Wintringham, who was billed everywhere as the first British-born woman
MP, Lady Astor showed no trace of jealousy towards her
popular rival. Putting aside their party differences the two
women worked well together on questions affecting women and
children. Mrs Wintringham's Bill on the Guardianship of
Infants became law in 1924; and their joint efforts helped
towards the introduction of nursery schools and women police.

Working closely with Mrs Wintringham on the Guardianship
of Infants Bill was Mrs Eva Hubback who, as Parliamentary
Secretary to the National Union of Societies for Equal Citizenship, was also largely responsible for initiating other reforms
affecting the position of women and children. Legislation
springing directly from the efforts of the women's organizations
has included the Summary Jurisdiction (Separation and

* See Appendix for list of Bills introduced by women Members.

Maintenance) Act of 1925, which embodied reforms in the position of the unhappily married woman; the Legitimacy Act of 1926, which provided for the legitimization of children on the subsequent marriage of their parents; and the Inheritance (Family Provision) Act of 1938, which prevented the complete disinheritance of widows and children.

Among the interesting women elected to Parliament between 1921 and 1928 were one Conservative, the Duchess of Atholl, and three Socialists, Margaret Bondfield, Susan Lawrence and Ellen Wilkinson.

The Duchess of Atholl was the half-sister of Agnata Ramsay, who in 1887 as a student of Girton College, Cambridge, headed the classical Honours list and was placed alone in the 1st Division of the 1st Class. The Duchess, who married in 1899, was a graduate of the Royal College of Music. She taught herself to speak in public by campaigning for her husband, who entered Parliament before the First World War. After the war she was persuaded by Stanley Baldwin to stand for Parliament; and was elected for Kinross and West Perth in 1923, holding the seat until 1938. Originally an anti-Suffragist, in her first Parliament the Duchess spoke in favour of extending the vote to women of twenty-one; and wherever possible she worked with her women colleagues in the other parties on questions of special importance to women and children. She had a somewhat wry comment to make on the dilemma of the women Members who were sent to the House of Commons by the votes of both sexes. 'But when you get there,' she said, 'the women of the country have a charming habit of thinking that it is they who have sent you there and that you are only responsible to them!'[1] Maybe this possessive attitude had done something to change the Duchess's views on the suffrage question!

As Parliamentary Secretary to the Board of Education from 1924–29, the Duchess of Atholl was the second woman to hold Government rank, the first being Margaret Bondfield, who as the first woman Cabinet Minister, had fought her way up from almost impossibly difficult beginnings. This eager, intelligent woman was the tenth child of a Somerset lace-maker, and although her parents did not know grinding poverty it was no

o

easy task for them to bring up a family of eleven. In 1887, at
the age of eleven, Margaret Bondfield started work as an
assistant in a Brighton draper's shop. Wages were deplorably
low: living-in conditions were drab and sordid. The women
slept in a bleak, bare dormitory; they had no privacy, and
nowhere to keep their belongings except in a box under the
bed. It was most fortunate that the girl who in later life did so
much to improve the pay and conditions of shopworkers
should have met at this juncture a middle-aged widow whose
concern for the underprivileged had led her to keep open
house for Brighton shop assistants. She was Mrs Louisa Martindale, mother of two daughters one of whom became a doctor,
the other a high ranking Civil Servant. Louisa Martindale, as
Margaret Bondfield wrote after her death, 'had the gift of
drawing out the best from others:'[2] and she herself never forgot
the sympathetic help she had received.

At the age of twenty, with £5 in her pocket, Margaret
Bondfield went to London. After three frightening months of
unemployment she found a living-in job in a shop where she
had to work a 65-hour week for an annual wage of £15, rising
by stages to £25. Chancing to see a letter in a newspaper from
the Secretary of the Shop Assistants' Union urging employees
to combine in an effort to secure better conditions, she hurried
round to the Union's headquarters. From that time onwards
she spent all her free time on Union work; and when in 1896
she was invited by the Women's Industrial Council to undertake an enquiry into shop conditions, she accepted, realizing
that never again would she be allowed to work in a shop. The
enquiry, which lasted two years, formed the basis of evidence
which was later submitted to the Royal Commission on Shop
Workers. In 1898 Margaret Bondfield was appointed Assistant
Secretary of the Union, and devoted several years to campaigning for shorter hours and better pay and conditions; and
in 1899, as the only woman delegate to the Trades Union
Congress, she spoke in support of the resolution which led to
the creation of the Labour Party. She was also on the committee
of the Women's Trade Union League which had developed
from Emma Paterson's Women's Protective and Provident
League; and she worked under the women's labour organizer

Mary Macarthur (1880–1921) who in 1906 welded the local unions of women workers into the National Federation of Women Workers. By 1923, when Margaret Bondfield was elected to Parliament, considerable improvements had been made in shop and factory conditions. In 1923 she was elected Chairman of the Trades Union Congress; but her appointment to the Government as Parliamentary Secretary to the Ministry of Labour prevented her from presiding over the 1924 conference. She lost her seat at the General Election the same year but was re-elected in 1926. But with the fall of the Labour Government in 1931 'the Right Honourable Margaret' left politics and returned to Trades Union work, representing the Government or the workers on a number of missions overseas. In 1948 she was made a Companion of Honour, a tribute to her ability and achievements, her integrity and downright common sense.

Although Margaret Bondfield was no orator she was gifted with a very fine speaking voice. This vital asset was unfortunately not shared by Susan Lawrence (1871–1947) who was also elected to Parliament in 1923 and had worked under Mary Macarthur. Susan Lawrence had a very different background. The daughter of a solicitor, she was awarded an exhibition for pure mathematics at University College, London, and finished her education at Newnham College, Cambridge. She started out as a Conservative, and as such was co-opted to the education committee of the London County Council and was elected to the Council as a Municipal Reform candidate in 1910. To Socialists this dashing looking, slim young woman, who wore a monocle and drove round Hyde Park in a dog-cart, was a reactionary of the deepest dye. Her conversion to Socialism which occurred in 1912 was as sudden as it was complete. She had taken part with Mary Macarthur in an enquiry into the conditions of women cleaners; and was so horrified by what she learned that she switched from Right to Left almost overnight, to become the most sincere and hard working of social reformers.

Susan Lawrence's first attempts at public speaking were painfully inadequate. Margaret Bondfield, who at Mary Macarthur's request, had agreed to take the chair for her at an open air meeting in the East End of London, reported that her voice in moments of emotion ran up into a high falsetto and her middle-class accent reduced the audience to screams of laughter. But Susan Lawrence had plenty of courage. She took great pains to make her voice acceptable (she had already put away her monocle and her dog-cart): and she won excellent opinions for her work for the Women's Trade Union League.

In 1913, as member for Poplar, Susan Lawrence was the first Labour woman member of the LCC. Some years later she and her Poplar colleagues were sent to prison for refusing to collect the Poor Rate, which they considered far too heavy for the borough to carry alone. Margaret Bondfield, who visited her in Holloway, found her out in the corridor smoking a cigarette, and was told that the whole affair was nothing but a great lark. But the Poplar members' protest bore fruit; for the burden of Poor Law relief later became more centralized.

Susan Lawrence first held Government office in 1924 as Parliamentary Private Secretary to the President of the Board of Education; and in 1929, in the second Labour Government, she was Parliamentary Secretary to the Ministry of Health. She lost her seat in the General Election which followed the financial crisis of 1931 and did not stand again. She had, however, become a byword for the clarity and caustic humour of her speeches; she was the only woman MP of her day who never missed a division or an all-night sitting; and she made a small piece of history when she defied the Speaker's ruling by refusing to cover her close-cropped grey head when she raised a point of order.

Susan Lawrence returned from an official visit to Russia in 1924 to plaster the walls of her study with hammers and sickles and embarrass her middle-class friends by addressing them as 'Comrade' on social occasions. She was not a Communist: but the third member of the Socialist triumvirate, Ellen Wilkinson (1891–1947), joined the Communist Party in 1920 and visited Russia as a Communist the following year.

Known as 'Red Ellen', for her flaming red hair as much as for her politics, Ellen Wilkinson was the third of the four children of a Manchester cotton operative; and she passed by way of scholarships from elementary to secondary school and thence to Manchester University. When she came down from the University Ellen Wilkinson became a pupil-teacher, but her inclination was towards journalism for which she had a very decided gift. In 1913 she became an organizer of the National Union of Women's Suffrage Societies, although the aggressiveness and emotional force of her later speeches seem to suggest that she might have been more at home among the militants. In the same year she was made National Organizer of the National Union of Distributive and Allied Workers. In 1924 her flirtation with Communism came to an end; she severed her ties with the Party and was elected to Parliament as Socialist Member for Middlesbrough East; and for the rest of her life she fought Communism within her Trade Union. After serving as Parliamentary Private Secretary to Susan Lawrence at the Ministry of Health, Ellen Wilkinson lost her seat in the 1931 debacle; but in 1935 she was elected Socialist Member for Jarrow and held this seat until her death. It was fitting that this loyal and vital woman who could seldom resist a fight should represent Jarrow at the time of the slump. In and out of Parliament she laboured for the depressed areas of the north-east; and in 1936 she led the unemployed Jarrow marchers to London, walking most of the way herself, and cheering the 2,000 men who marched behind her. 'Come on, let's have a song,' cried Miss Perky, as she was often called. 'We may be wet but we don't have to look it.' Three years later in her most important book, *The Town that was Murdered*, Ellen Wilkinson gave a detailed history of the shipyard closure and its disastrous consequences.

Inside Parliament Ellen Wilkinson scored a notable success in 1935 when she introduced a Private Members' Bill designed to stop certain flagrant abuses of the hire purchase system and carried it through with support from all three Parties. She was a member of Winston Churchill's Coalition Government, first as Parliamentary Secretary to the Ministry of Pensions and then as Parliamentary Secretay to the Ministry of Home Security. She took her responsibilities for Civil Defence very seriously, and the lack of adequate air-raid precautions in London and the other large cities galvanized her into a tremendous burst of activity. She drove her own car through the blitz to spend her nights in uncomfortable air-raid shelters and did much to counteract Communist efforts to spread dissaffection. She survived two narrow escapes from bombs; but the energy she expended after a long day's work and the nervous tension engendered by her shelter activities seriously affected her health: it had never been good, and all her life she had to battle with asthma and bronchitis.

In 1945 Ellen Wilkinson became the second woman to reach Cabinet rank, as Minister of Education in Mr (now Lord) Attlee's Labour Government. She had already been concerned with the changes made in the structure of education by the Education Act of 1944: now she had the task of carrying on from Mr R. A. (now Lord) Butler. It was tragic that she should have died at the age of fifty-five, just when her loyalty to people and causes and her fighting instincts might have been canalized into real statesmanship.

Another Member for whom people and causes mattered most was Eleanor Rathbone, who entered Parliament in 1929 as Independent Member for the Combined English Universities and retained the seat until her death seventeen years later. Had she cared to sacrifice her independence there is little doubt that Eleanor Rathbone would have been offered a Government post; but she remained free from party alignment and her independence enabled her to do work in and out of Parliament which might otherwise have been impossible. Her finest achievement was probably her long and faithful advocacy of the case for family allowances, in the course of which she published two notable books, *The Disinherited Family* (1924) and *The Case for Family Allowances* (1940); and she lived to see the reform made good in the Family Allowances Bill which became law in 1945.

Among her other achievements, Eleanor Rathbone, as President of the National Union of Societies for Equal Citizenship, kept the suffrage issue alive until equality was gained, and she continued to press for reforms affecting the legal and economic position of women. Her reforming zeal, which touched home conditions at so many points, was not confined to this country. Her concern for the pathetic plight of Indian women dated from her reading in 1927 of Katherine Mayo's sensational indictment, *Mother India*, and was one of the chief reasons why she decided to go into politics. In 1934, after making a personal enquiry on the spot, she published *Child Marriage: the Indian Minotaur*, a book which encouraged the authorities to make the Sarda Child Marriage Restraint Act really effective.

Eleanor Rathbone's intense sympathy for personal suffering also led her to take up the cause of the Jewish refugees from the Nazi terror, both before and after the Second World War. To her, the Government White Paper of May 1939, which severely limited Jewish immigration into Palestine, was the indirect cause of the death of tens of thousands of Jews in Axis-dominated Europe. She harried the Government for pandering to the dictates of the Arab communities; and in 1945, with the White Paper still officially in operation, she identified herself with the Zionists who were demanding the creation of a Jewish state.

With her ardent crusading Eleanor Rathbone was too tenaciously dedicated ever to become a really popular figure in the House. 'Benign and yet menacing,' wrote Sir Harold Nicolson of her in 1946, 'she would stalk through the lobby, one arm weighted with the heavy satchel which contained the papers on family allowances, another arm dragging an even heavier satchel in which were stored the more recent papers about refugees and displaced persons; recalcitrant Ministers would quail before the fire of her magnificent eyes. . . . Yet although in attack she was pertinacious as a flying bomb, in the moment of victory she was amazingly conciliatory. While the battle was on she displayed all the passion of the fanatic; when the enemy yielded, she advanced towards him bearing the olive branch of compromise. . . .'[3]

Had she been born later and lived till 1958, Eleanor Rathbone might well have been among the first of the Life Peeresses created in the autumn of that year with the passage of the Bill which enabled women to sit in the House of Lords: she would certainly have been a splendidly original addition to their ranks. None of the first four Life Peeresses had sat in the Commons though all were distinguished for their public service. The first to be introduced in the House of Lords in October 1958 was Baroness Swanborough, better known as the

Dowager Marchioness of Reading, GBE, Chairman and founder of the Women's Voluntary Services and a member of a number of Government committees, including the Ministry of Housing and Local Government Sub-Committee on Slum Clearance, and the National Advisory Committee for the Employment of Old Men and Women. Lady Swanborough played her part in the ancient ceremonial, robed in the scarlet, gold, and double-banded miniver of a baron, with a gilt rosette in her black tricorn hat. According to a Press report, she took the customary oath 'in ringing tones, promising to "be faithful and bear true allegiance to thee, Queen." A solemn hush filled the chamber as [she] appended her signature and thus became the first woman in British history ever to sign the great Book of Peers. A long, warm murmur of applause signified the Peers' welcome.'

Lady Elliot of Harwood (better known as Katherine Elliot, widow of the Rt. Hon. Walter Elliot, a former Conservative Secretary of State for Scotland and Minister of Health) came to the House of Lords with an excellent reputation for her work in local government affairs in Scotland, especially in the educational and probation services. A former Chairman of the National Union of Conservative Associations, and Chairman of the National Association of Mixed Clubs and Girls' Clubs, Baroness Elliot had been United Kingdom delegate to the United Nations General Assembly in 1954. In 1960, when she moved the second reading of the Public Bodies (Admission of Press to Meetings) Bill Lady Elliot made history as the first woman to sponsor legislation in the Upper House. The Bill had been introduced in the House of Commons by a woman, Mrs Margaret Thatcher, Conservative Member for Finchley. In 1962 Lady Elliot became the first woman to move the Loyal Address in the House of Lords; but she shook her head decisively when Lord Hailsham (now Mr Quintin Hogg) suggested that her business-like black dress should be preserved in the London Museum as a historic relic of the occasion.

Baroness Ravensdale,* who was introduced as a Life Peeress in October 1958, was also a peeress in her own right, the title having devolved on her by special remainder on the death of

*The death of Baroness Ravensdale at the age of seventy was announced on February 9, 1966.

her father Lord Curzon. Lady Ravensdale, a former suffragette and champion of women's rights, and Vice-President of
the National Association of Mixed Clubs and Girls' Clubs, had
said some irreverent things about those peers who had
prevented the hereditary peeresses from taking their places in
the Lords. The peers, she declared to a Press reporter,
resembled 'a drowsy lot of flies in a very hot room,' and a
peeress would be regarded as 'an excited bluebottle coming in
to disturb their sleep.'

In November 1958 the fourth Life Peeress was introduced,
the Socialist Baroness Wootton of Abinger (or Mrs Barbara
Wright, better known as Barbara Wootton), an expert on
economic and social affairs. Lady Wootton made history at
her introduction as the first Life Peeress to refuse, on conscientious grounds, to take the Oath, and to exercise her
prerogative to declare and affirm her allegiance to the Queen.
Lady Wootton's contributions in the House of Lords always
command respect; and in 1962 she was the first Life Peeress to
bring about a Government defeat in the Lords, in a division on
the Children's and Young Persons' Bill. The Bill sought to
retain the minimum age at which a child could be brought
before a juvenile court at eight: Lady Wootton wanted to see
it raised to twelve, and she was supported by forty-two votes to
forty-one.

The Life Peeresses quickly found themselves at home in the
Upper House. The House of Lords, declared Lady Swanborough
at a party given by the Fawcett Society to the first four Life
Peeresses, 'is a delicious place to be in. I listen with my ears
flapping.' Lady Elliot admitted that she found the House
'great fun. Their lordships,' she added, 'are extremely kind to
us.'

One peer above all others made them welcome, the veteran
Lord Pethick-Lawrence, who had fought the suffrage battle so
nobly in the past.

'There they are in our midst,' he wrote proudly in 1960,
'making speeches in the Chamber, joining in our committees
and taking their part with us in all the intricacies and common-
places of our daily life. All of them are women of wide know-

ledge and experience and every one of them has made contributions of value and importance to our discussions. Needless to say they have not disturbed the decorum of the House or ruffled its susceptibilities. In a word, they have certainly made good. . . .'[4]*

Several of the more recently created Life Peeresses came to the Lords from the Commons. Among them is a former Conservative Cabinet Minister, Baroness Horsburgh, who was made a Life Peeress in 1959 and who, as Miss Florence Horsburgh, bore a heavy administrative burden during the Second World War as Parliamentary Secretary to the Ministry of Health, a job which involved the supervision of the casualty services and the evacuation of children from dangerous areas. Lady Horsburgh, who entered Parliament in 1931 as Member for Dundee, was the first woman to move the Loyal Address in the House of Commons; and when Lord Hailsham suggested that Lady Elliot's dress should be preserved he was thinking of the precedent created by Lady Horsburgh, whose dress is now in the London Museum. In 1945 Lady Horsburgh was appointed Parliamentary Secretary to the Ministry of Food, at a time when rationing was most severe; and in 1951, with the Conservatives in power, she was made Minister of Education. When she resigned office in 1954 she was awarded a GBE, thus becoming the first woman to be both a Privy Counsellor and a Dame Grand Cross of the Order of the British Empire. In 1961 she added to her list of 'firsts' when she was appointed one of the three Lords Commissioners who form a Royal Commission and who, seated in the House of Lords, give the Royal Assent to new Bills on the monarch's behalf. There was a certain amount of speculation as to whether the Lady Commissioner would conform to tradition and raise her hat at stated intervals. In the event, her neat velvet tricorn remained in place and, as one newspaper put it, she 'simply nodded regally at the appropriate moments.'

* The first woman to hold a ministerial position in the Lords is Lady Phillips, widow of the former General Secretary of the Labour Party. In December 1965 Lady Phillips was appointed a baroness in waiting (Government Whip).

The Socialist Life Peeress Lady Summerskill is better known as Dr Edith Summerskill. As a practising doctor and a married woman with two children, she first entered Parliament in 1938, after serving on the Middlesex County Council for four years. She was Parliamentary Secretary to the Ministry of Food, 1945–50, and of the Ministry of Pensions and National Insurance, 1950–53, and Chairman of the Labour Party Congress, 1954–5. Renowned for her forthright speeches, Lady Summerskill's maiden speech in the House of Lords, delivered within a week of her introduction in February 1961, was in a Vote of Censure debate on the Government for increasing payments under the National Health Service. Her intervention based, as it was, on experience of the Health Service, was particularly devastating. 'By tradition,' wrote a newspaper reporter, 'maiden speeches are non-controversial, and though Lord Taylor tried later to explain that by Summerskill standards Lady Summerskill's had indeed been a non-controversial speech, no Tory peer—to judge from the fierce unsmiling faces—believed him. And when Lord Taylor went on to promise that the Baroness's contribution was "but a small foretaste of things to come," the frost in the House was chilling. . . .' Since her introduction Lady Summerskill has been engaged in a determined campaign against the continuance of professional boxing; and by 1965, more in line with the feminists of old, as a private member of the House of Lords, she was drafting a Bill to give a deserted wife the statutory right to live in the matrimonial home.

In December 1964 a woman with a brilliant mind, a great public speaker with an enviable reputation for wit, was introduced in the House of Lords. She was Baroness Asquith of Yarnbury (better known as Lady Violet Bonham Carter), devoted daughter of the Prime Minister who had once been the bane of the suffragettes. All her life Lady Asquith has remained faithful to the Liberal tradition and although she stood for Parliament she was never elected. In 1963 she became the first woman to give the Romanes lecture at the Sheldonian Theatre in Oxford. She chose for her theme 'The Impact of Personality in Politics', using as two of her examples her father and her lifelong friend Winston Churchill, of whom she has since given an affectionate but not uncritical appraisal in her book *Winston Churchill as I knew Him*. A reporter, eyeing her 'as she took the oath, knelt loftily to the Labour Lord Chancellor and strode through the Chamber,' remarked that the Lords 'will now have to establish whether its members are fit to regard themselves as her peers.'

Illness has unfortunately kept Lady Asquith much away from the House of Lords; but in July 1965 she rose from her sickbed to make an eloquent and moving plea for the abolition of capital punishment. When Baroness Wootton introduced the Murder (Abolition of Death Penalty) Bill in the House of Lords there was a 99 per cent muster of Life Peeresses: all save two—Baroness Horsburgh and Baroness Northchurch (better known as Viscountess Davidson) voted for the Bill, which passed its second reading by a majority of a hundred.

On this occasion hereditary peeresses were also represented—though sparsely—for after a good deal of stone-walling they had at last been admitted to the House of Lords in November 1963. Three times during the past few years the Lords had declined to admit them. In 1959, with Lord Pethick-Lawrence fighting for their rights on the floor of the Chamber, an excited listener in the public gallery applauded his remark that it was 'foolish to try to fight a rearguard action against the complete equality of one sex with the other.' To some of the other veterans present the sound must have been strangely reminiscent of the suffragette warfare of the past.

In 1963 some twenty hereditary peeresses were entitled to sit in the House of Lords; but by the summer of 1965 only three had taken their seats. The first to do so, and to vote for the Abolition of the Death Penalty Bill, was Lady Strange of Knokin (Viscountess St Davids). Two years earlier her son, Viscount St. Davids, had spoken against any extension of the hereditary principle. When he first opposed it, he said, he had regarded himself as ungallant, since both his aunt and his mother were hereditary peeresses. 'The position is still worse today,' he added in March 1963, 'because my aunt having died, her titles have been scattered. I am now opposing the entry of my mother and three girl first cousins. I only hope all these ladies will forgive me.' Despite his misgivings Lord St

Davids was present on July 7, 1965, when his mother at the age of eighty-one made her maiden speech, a brief but pleasing intervention in a debate on community care. When she resumed her seat on the Conservative benches her son intervened from the Labour benches to congratulate 'one whom the conventions of the House' made it necessary for him to describe as "my noble relative" '; and, to the sound of sympathetic cheers, he concluded that this was the first occasion in the House of Lords that a son had been able to congratulate his mother. 'The Noble Lady must be supremely happy,' said Lady Summerskill; and indeed she was.

In the Labour Government which took office in 1964 a record number of seven women were given Government posts, three of them with ministerial responsibility—Mrs Barbara Castle, Minister for Overseas Development and the first woman Cabinet Minister for ten years; Miss Margaret Herbison, Minister of Pensions and National Insurance; and Miss Alice Bacon, Minister of State, Home Office.

Mrs Castle, Oxford educated and a journalist specializing in foreign and colonial affairs and wartime Administrative Officer in the Ministry of Food, has been Member for Blackburn since 1945. From 1945–51 she was Parliamentary Private Secretary to the President of the Board of Trade; and she has been a member of the Labour Party National Executive Council since 1950 and Chairman, 1958–9. Her present post,* a newly created one, emphasizes the Government's concern to forge strong links with the underdeveloped countries. In November 1964 Mrs Castle was elected Chairman of the Colombo Plan Conference held in London at which twenty-one countries were represented; and in August 1965 her Ministry published a report, *Overseas Development*, promising further aid to underdeveloped countries. It cannot have been fortuitous that the report was timed to appear one day after the publication of a Government White Paper severely limiting the number of immigrants allowed to enter the country.

Miss Margaret Herbison, a miner's daughter, began life as a teacher. She has represented North Lanark in Parliament since

* In December 1965 Mrs Castle was appointed Minister of Transport.

1945, is a member of the National Executive Council and was Chairman, 1956–7; and in 1951 she was joint Under Secretary of State for Scotland.

Miss Alice Bacon, who also entered Parliament in 1945 and has represented North-East and South-East Leeds, went into politics, like Miss Herbison, from teaching. She has been a member of the National Executive Council since 1941 and preceded Miss Herbison as Chairman, in 1950–1. In August 1965 in a fresh effort to reduce juvenile crime she introduced a White Paper which included among its proposals the creation of a system of family councils and courts to replace the existing juvenile courts.*

The best known of the other members of the Government is Miss Jennie Lee, widow of the fiery Aneurin Bevan. As Joint Under-Secretary of State to the Department of Education and Science, Miss Lee has a special responsibility for the arts, and in a White Paper published in February 1965 declared her intention of making Britain 'a gayer and more cultivated country.'

Mrs Eirene White, Parliamentary Under-Secretary at the Colonial Office, a graduate of Somerville College, Oxford, has represented East Flint since 1951. A former Ministry of Labour Officer and political correspondent, Mrs White is a member of the National Executive Council. Mrs Judith Hart, Joint Parliamentary Under Secretary to the Scottish Office, is a graduate of London University and entered Parliament in 1955 as Member for South Aberdeen. And Alderman Mrs Harriet Slater a former teacher and MP for Stoke-on-Trent North since 1953, as a Lord Commissioner of the Treasury, was the first woman ever to be appointed a Government Whip.

Two accomplished members of the Conservative Party are Dames Irene Ward and Joan Vickers. Dame Irene, who on February 6, 1962, laid a wreath at Dame Millicent Fawcett's memorial in Westminster Abbey to commemorate the 44th anniversary of the grant of the vote to women over thirty, entered politics in 1931, since when she has only once been defeated—in the landslide general election of 1945. During her political career she has been respected always as a fearless

* Miss Bacon was made a Privy Councillor in January 1966.

fighter in many causes, among them equal pay, compensation to British victims of Nazi concentration camps, the provision of opera for the provinces, higher wages for firemen, and pocket-money for old people in institutions. In 1961 she promoted the Nurses (Amendment) Act and in 1962 the Penalty for Drunkenness Act.

Dame Joan Vickers, social welfare worker and lecturer, and a member of the LCC, 1937–45, entered Parliament in 1955 as Member for the Devonport division of Plymouth, beating Michael Foot who had represented the division for ten years, by 100 votes. She is Chairman of the Conservative Parliamentary Sub-Committee on East and Central Africa of the Commonwealth Affairs Committee, and in 1962–3 was United Kingdom delegate to the Status of Women Commission at the United Nations.

With seven women in the Government and twenty-one women back benchers it might, perhaps, be hoped that the ancient bugbear of equal pay will at last be settled. There is, of course, no discrimination in Parliament, the Civil Service or the professions although it is true to say that a woman has to be considerably better than her male rivals if she is to succeed in any of them. If in the professions there is equal pay but not equal opportunity, there is still very real discrimination elsewhere, notably in trade and industry. In June 1965, for example, the National Woman's Officer of the Transport and General Workers Union, speaking at the annual conference of the Confederation of Shipbuilding and Engineering Unions, challenged the Government to honour its election promises on equal pay which, if implemented, would remove anomalies existing among women workers, among them some bus conductresses, and van and crane drivers. 'Why not be a butcheress?' (odious word!) pleads a notice prominently displayed in certain butchers' shops today. 'A healthy job at highest wages.' Why not, indeed, always provided that the butcheress, after free training which is offered her, can expect her 'highest wages' to equal the butcher's.

It might not be too much to hope also that before very long benevolent minded men will cease to pat the little dears on the head for their masculine achievements or differentiate between masculine and feminine qualities. Yet will they? Commenting on women's place in politics a clergyman wrote to the Press in 1959: 'If I want a piece of imaginative work done in my parish, I look for a man to do it. If I want something done efficiently, I look for a woman. Men have imagination; women have courage. I think we should recognize this and accept it as something fundamental.'

It would be unfair to place the entire blame for this sort of thinking on the benevolent men. 'Being feminine . . . is just the opposite of masculine,' said Miss Margaret Herbison to a newspaper reporter who interviewed her on her appointment as Minister of Pensions and National Insurance. 'I'm not conscious of trying feminine wiles. Maybe unconsciously,' she added, '[but] I don't really think that I use any more guile than you'd find in a man.' When this question was put to Miss Alice Bacon she administered a sharp rebuke. 'A young reporter once asked me if all women MPs wear low heels. I said, there's no such thing as a woman MP. We're all individuals.' The same point was made in a television interview by Life Peeress Baroness Gaitskill, who sensibly remarked that any contribution she might make to the deliberations of the Upper House would be as a person and not as a woman. Wher people stop labouring this question—if they ever do—that indeed, will be the day!

Appendix

BILLS BROUGHT IN BY WOMEN M.P.S

1922–23	Lady Astor	*Intoxicating Liquor (Sale to Persons under Eighteen) Bill*	Royal Assent
1923–24	Mrs Wintringham	*Guardianship of Infants Bill*	Committed to Standing Committee
1926–27	Miss Ellen Wilkinson	*Factories Bill*	Rejected on 2nd Reading
	Lady Astor	*Public Places (Order) Bill*	Dropped
1927–28	Mrs Philipson	*Nursing Homes (Registration) Bill*	Royal Assent
1928–29	Miss Wilkinson	*Offices Regulation Bill*	Dropped
		Offices Regulation (No. 2) Bill	Dropped
	Miss Bondfield	*Children)Provision of Footwear) Bill*	2nd Reading
	Miss Susan Lawrence	*Children & Young Persons (Employment and Protection) Bill*	Dropped
	Miss Wilkinson	*Aliens (Status of Married Women) Bill*	Dropped
1929–30	Duchess of Atholl	*Illegitimate Children (Scotland) Bill*	Royal Assent
	G.* Miss Bondfield	*Unemployment Insurance Bill*	Royal Assent
	G.	*Hours of Industrial Employment Bill*	Withdrawn
1930–31	Dr Ethel Bentham	*Nationality of Married Women Bill*	2nd Reading

* Government Bill

P

	Miss Eleanor Rathbone	*Wills and Intestacies (Family Maintenance) Bill*	2nd Reading
	G. Miss Bondfield	*Hours of Industrial Employment Bill*	Royal Assent
1930–32	G. Miss Bondfield	*Unemployment Insurance Bills (4)*	Royal Assent
	Miss Picton-Turbervill	*Sentence of Death (Expectant Mothers) Bill*	Royal Assent
1932–33	Mrs Ward	*Home & Empire Settlement Bill*	Committed to Standing Committee
	Miss Florence Horsburgh	*Methylated Spirits Bill*	2nd Reading – Dropped
1933–34		*Methylated Spirits Bill*	2nd Reading —Dropped
1935–36	Miss Rathbone	*Inheritance (Family Provision) Bill*	2nd Reading —Dropped
1936–37	Miss Horsburgh	*Methylated Spirits (Scotland) Bill*	Royal Assent
1937–38	Miss Wilkinson	*Hire Purchase Bill*	Royal Assent
	Mrs Tate	*Housing (Rural Cottages) Protection Bill*	Dropped
	Miss Irene Ward	*Poor Law (Amendment) Bill*	Withdrawn
		Poor Law (Amendment) (No. 2) Bill	Royal Assent
1938–39		*Workmen's Compensation Acts, 1925–34 (Amendment) Bill*	2nd Reading —Rejected
	Miss Horsburgh	*Adoption of Children (Regulation) Bill*	Royal Assent
1945–46	G. Miss Wilkinson	*Education Bill*	Royal Assent
1950–51	Mrs Barbara Castle	*Criminal Law Amendment Bill*	Royal Assent
	G. Dr Edith Summerskill	*National Insurance Bill*	Royal Assent
	G.	*Workmen's Compensation (Supplementation) Bill*	Royal Assent

	Mrs Eirene White	*Matrimonial Causes Bill*	2nd Reading —Dropped
1951–52	Miss Elaine Burton	*Disposal of Uncollected Goods Bill*	Royal Assent
	Mrs Jean Mann	*Care of Senile Persons (Scotland) Bill*	2nd Reading —Dropped
	Dr Summerskill	*Women's Disabilities Bill*	2nd Reading —Adjourned —Dropped
	Mrs Eirene White	*Election Committee Rooms Bill*	2nd Reading —Dropped
1952–53	Miss Margaret Herbison	*Foundry Workers (Health & Safety) Bill*	Withdrawn
	G. Miss Horsburgh	*Education (Miscellaneous Provisions) Bill*	Royal Assent
	Dr Summerskill	*Women's Disabilities Bill*	2nd Reading —Adjourned
1953–54	Lady Davidson	*Protection of Animals (Anaesthetics) Bill*	Royal Assent
	Lady Tweedsmuir	*Protection of Birds Bill*	Royal Assent
	Miss Ward	*Rights of Entry (Gas & Electricity Boards) Bill*	Royal Assent
	G. Miss Horsburgh	*Teachers Superannuation Bill*	2nd Reading
1954–55	Miss Herbison	*Workmen's Compensation (Supplementation) Bill*	2nd Reading —Dropped
1955–56	Dame Irene Ward	*Gas Act (1948) Amendment Bill*	2nd Reading —Dropped
1956–57	Miss Alice Bacon	*Death Penalty (Abolition) Bill*	2nd Reading —Dropped
	Miss Joan Vickers	*Maintenance Orders (Attachment of Income) Bill*	Committed to Standing Committee— Dropped
1957–58	G. Miss Mervyn Pike	*Drainage Rates Bill*	Royal Assent
1959–60	Mrs Margaret Thatcher	*Public Bodies (Admission to Meetings) Bill*	Royal Assent

1960–61	Dame Irene Ward	*Nurses (Amendment) Bill*	Royal Assent
	Mrs Barbara Castle	*Public Lavatories (Abolition of Turnstiles) Bill*	2nd Reading
	Dame Irene Ward	*Road Traffic (Trolley Vehicles) Bill*	Withdrawn
1961–62	Mrs Patricia McLaughlin	*Fireworks Bill*	2nd Reading —Dropped
	Miss Joan Vickers	*Guardianship of Infants Bill*	2nd Reading —Dropped
	Dame Irene Ward	*Penalties for Drunkenness Bill*	Royal Assent
	Mrs Joyce Butler	*Planning Conditions for Private Redevelopment Bill*	2nd Reading —Adjourned
1962–63	Miss Joan Vickers	*Guardianship of Infants Bill*	2nd Reading —Dropped
	Mrs Barbara Castle	*Public Lavatories (Turnstiles) Bill*	Withdrawn
	Mrs Patricia McLaughlin	*Public Lavatories (Turnstiles) Bill*	Royal Assent
	Mrs Judith Hart	*Summary Jurisdiction Bill*	2nd Reading
1963–64	Miss Harvie Anderson	*Animals (Restriction of Importation) Bill*	Royal Assent
	Mrs Joyce Butler	*Farm & Gardens Chemicals Bill*	2nd Reading
	Mrs Eirene White	*Films* (Lords) *Bill*	Royal Assent
	Mrs Patricia McLaughlin	*Flammable Materials Bill*	2nd Reading —Dropped
	Miss Harvie Anderson	*Importation of Rare Animals Bill*	Withdrawn
	Dame Patricia Hornsby-Smith	*Nurses Bill*	Royal Assent
	Mrs Joyce Butler	*Town & Country Planning (Land Values) Bill*	2nd Reading
	Miss Joan Vickers	*Young Persons (Employment) Bill*	Royal Assent
1964–65	Mrs Renée Short	*Abortion Bill*	
	Mrs Lena Jeger	*British Nationality Bill*	

Mrs Joyce Butler	*Farm & Gardens Chemicals Bill*	2nd Reading —Dropped
Dame Joan Vickers	*Guardianship of Infants Bill*	Standing Committee— Dropped
Mrs Joyce Butler	*Labelling of Food Bill*	2nd Reading —Dropped
Dr Shirley Summerskill	*National Assistance (Lords) Bill*	2nd Reading —Dropped
G. Miss Margaret Herbison	*National Insurance, etc. Bill*	Royal Assent
Mrs Barbara Castle	*Overseas Development & Service Bill*	
1965–66 G. Miss Margaret Herbison	*Workmen's Compensation and Benefit (Amendment) Bill*	Royal Assent

NOTES

CHAPTER I: *Birth of a Movement*

1. *The Works of the Right Honourable Lady Wortley Montagu* (1803), Vol. IV, p. 161.
2. *Woman not Inferior to Man* (1739), Chap. II, p. 11.
3. *Ibid.*, Chap. II, p. 15.
4. *Ibid.*, Chap. III, p. 27.
5. *Ibid.*, Chap. V, p. 37.
6. *Strictures on Female Education* (1779) Vol. I, p. 6.
7. *Ibid.*, Vol. II, pp. 21 ff.
8. Quoted G. W. Johnson, *The Evolution of Women* (Robert Holden, 1926) pp. 130–1.
9. Ray Strachey, *The Cause* (G. Bell & Sons, 1928) p. 12.
10. *Ibid.*, p. 15.
11. Mary Wollstonecraft, *A Vindication of the Rights of Woman* (1792) (Everyman's Library) p. 197.
12. *Ibid.*, p. 215.
13. *Ibid.*, p. 69.
14. Ed. R. Brimley Johnson, *The Letters of Hannah More* (John Lane, the Bodley Head, 1925) p. 183.
15. Quoted Cecil Woodham Smith, *Florence Nightingale* (Constable, 1950) p. 316.
16. Hansard, August 3, 1832, quoted *The Cause*, p. 32.
17. Quoted *The Cause*, p. 33.
18. Quoted Lucille Iremonger, *And His Charming Lady* (Secker & Warburg, 1961) pp. 102–3.
19. Quoted *The Cause*, p. 37.
20. Quoted *And His Charming Lady*, pp. 121–2.
21. Mrs William Ellis, *The Women of England* (1841)
22. Quoted *The Cause*, pp. 46–6.
23. *The Cause*, p. 43.
24. John Stuart Mill, *The Subjection of Women* (Everyman edition) p. 219.

CHAPTER II: *The Philanthropists*

1. Sarah Trimmer, The *Oeconomy of Charity* (1787) p. 41.
2. Quoted Edwin A. Pratt, *Pioneer Women in Victoria's Reign* (George Newnes, 1897) p. 200.
3. Quoted Millicent Garrett Fawcett, *Some Eminent Women of our Time* (National Union of Women's Suffrage Societies Pamphlet) p. 11.
4. *Ibid.*, p. 8.
5. *Op. cit.*
6. *Pioneer Women in Victoria's Reign*, p. 198.
7. Quoted Margaret E. Tabor, *Pioneer Women* (The Sheldon Press, 1927) pp. 53–4.
8. *Ibid.*, p. 62.
9. Quoted *The Cause*, p. 82.
10. *Op. cit.*
11. *Pioneer Women in Victoria's Reign*, p. 172.
12. Quoted Clara Burdett Patterson, *Angela Burdett-Coutts and the Victorians* (John Murray, 1953) pp. 77–8.
13. *Ibid.*, p. 202.
14. Harriet Martineau, *Biographical Sketches 1852–1875* (Macmillan, 1885) p. 322.
15. Quoted Hester Burton, *Barbara Bodichon* (John Murray, 1949) p. 63.
16. Quoted Geraldine Macpherson, *Memoirs of Mrs Jameson* (Longmans, Green, 1878) p. 44.
17. *Biographical Sketches 1852–1875*, p. 430.
18. *Memoirs of Mrs Jameson*, p. 94.
19. *Ibid.*, p. 300.
20. *Dictionary of National Biography.*
21. Quoted Alethea Hayter, *A Sultry Month* (Faber & Faber, 1965) p. 82.
22. *Biographical Sketches 1852–1875*, pp. 433–4.
23. Quoted *A Sultry Month*, p. 85.
24. Quoted *Memoirs of Mrs Jameson*, pp. 304–5.

CHAPTER III: *The Educationists*

1. *Barbara Bodichon*, p. 1.
2. Quoted *ibid.*, p. 51.
3. Quoted *ibid.*, p. 92.
4. Quoted *The English Woman's Journal*, Vol. I, No. I (1858) p. 12.

5. Report of the Governesses' Benevolent Institution, quoted *ibid.*, p. 2.
6. Quoted *The Cause*, p. 133.
7. Quoted Barbara Stephen, *Emily Davies and Girton College* (Constable, 1927) p. 90.
8. *Op. cit.*
9. Quoted *ibid.*, p. 91.
10. Quoted W. B. Hodgson, *On the Education of Girls*, a lecture delivered 1864 (published 1869) (Appendix G.)
11. Vol. I, No. 4 (1858).
12. Quoted *The English Woman's Journal*, Vol. XII (1863) pp. 278–80.
13. Quoted *Emily Davies and Girton College*, p. 103,
14. Quoted *The Cause*, p. 145.
15. Quoted *Barbara Bodichon*, p. 165.
16. Quoted *The Cause*, pp. 153–4.
17. *Thoughts on some Questions Relating to Women 1860–1908*, ed. E. E. Constance Jones (Bowes and Bowes, 1910) p. 125.
18. Quoted *Barbara Bodichon*, p. 170.
19. Quoted *The Cause*, p. 155.

CHAPTER IV: *The Doctors*

1. Quoted E. Moberly Bell, *Storming the Citadel* (Constable, 1953) p. 44.
2. Quoted *ibid.*, p. 49.
3. 1860. Autograph Collection, Women's Service Library.
4. October 12, 1860. Autograph Collection, Women's Service Library.
5. Quoted *Storming the Citadel*, p. 53.
6. Quoted *ibid.*, p. 58.
7. Quoted *ibid.*, p. 61.
8. *The English Woman's Journal* (1862) Vol. IX, p. 139.
9. *Op. cit.*
10. Quoted *Storming the Citadel*, p. 85.
11. *The Englishwoman's Review* (1871) No. 5, p. 1.
12. Quoted *The Cause*, p. 173.
13. Quoted Margaret Todd, *The Life of Sophia Jex-Blake* (Macmillan, 1918) p. 25.
14. Quoted *ibid.*, pp. 62–3.
15. *Storming the Citadel*, p. 75.
16. Letter to William Gladstone, 1870; quoted Elizabeth Long-

ford, *Victoria R. I.* (Weidenfeld & Nicolson, 1964) p. 395.

17. Quoted Sophia Jex-Blake, *Medical Women: A Thesis and a History* (1866 edition) p. 91,
18. *Ibid.*, pp. 92–3.
19. *Op. cit.*
20. Quoted *The Cause*, p. 181.
21. Quoted *The Life of Sophia Jex-Blake*, p. 299.
22. Quoted *The Englishwoman's Review* (1872) Vol. IX, pp. 32–3.
23. *The Nineteenth Century*, July 1877, quoted *The Life of Sophia Jex-Blake*, p. 450.
24. Quoted *ibid.*, p. 448.

CHAPTER V: *The Ladies' Circle*

1. Quoted *Barbara Bodichon*, pp. 68–9.
2. *The English Woman's Journal* (1858) Vol. I, pp. 201–2.
3. Quoted *Pioneer Women in Victoria's Reign*, pp. 8–9.
4. Quoted *Storming the Citadel*, p. 17.
5. Quoted *Barbara Bodichon*, p. 102.
6. Quoted *ibid.*, p. 107.
7. *The English Woman's Journal* (1862) Vol. X, p. 147.
8. *Ibid.*, Vol. IV, p. 275.
9. *Ibid.*, Vol. V, p. 391.
10. *The Englishwoman's Review* (1876) No. XLI, pp. 373–4.
11. Quoted *The Cause*, pp. 96–7.
12. *The Englishwoman's Review* (1876) No. XXXVII, p. 225.
13. *Pioneer Women in Victoria's Reign*, p. 24.
14. *The English Woman's Journal* (1860) Vol. V, p. 235.
15. *Ibid.* (1863) Vol. XI, pp. 260–2.
16. Quoted *The Cause*, pp. 93–4.
17. *The English Woman's Journal* (1859) Vol. III, pp. 218–24.
18. Quoted *ibid.* (1860) Vol. VI, p. 53.
19. *Ibid.* (1858), Vol. VI, pp. 413–14.
20. *The Englishwoman's Review* (1875), Vol. VI, pp. 285 and 476.

CHAPTER VI: *The Outsiders*

1. Quoted E. Moberly Bell, *Octavia Hill* (Constable, 1942) p. 41.
2. Quoted *ibid.*, p. 55.
3. Quoted *ibid.*, p. 63.
4. Quoted *ibid.*, p. 70.

5. Quoted John Ruskin, *Fors Clavigera*, ed. E. T. Cook & Alexander Wedderburn (1907) Vol. VIII, p. 354.
6. Quoted *Octavia Hill*, p. 122.
7. Quoted *ibid.*, p. 265.
8. E. Moberly Bell, *Josephine Butler, Flame of Fire* (Constable, 1962) p. 12.
9. Quoted *ibid.*, p. 28.
10. Quoted *ibid.*, pp. 45–7.
11. Quoted *The Cause*, p. 268.
12. Quoted *Josephine Butler, Flame of Fire*, p. 200.
13. Quoted *ibid.*, p. 79.
14. *Op. cit.*
15. Quoted *ibid.*, p. 82.
16. Quoted *The Cause*, p. 202.
17. Quoted *Josephine Butler, Flame of Fire*, p. 91.
18. Quoted *ibid.*, p. 97.
19. Quoted *ibid.*, p. 114.
20. Quoted *ibid.*, pp. 163–4.
21. Quoted Ray Strachey, *Millicent Garrett Fawcett* (John Murray, 1931) p. 111.
22. Quoted *ibid.*, pp. 112–13.
23. Quoted *Josephine Butler, Flame of Fire*, p. 181.

CHAPTER VII: *The Constitutionalists*

1. Quoted *The Cause*, p. 103.
2. Quoted *Octavia Hill*, pp. 270–1
3. Quoted *The Cause*, p. 105.
4. Quoted *Barbara Bodichon*, p. 149.
5. Quoted *The Englishwoman's Review* (1866) No. I, p. 42.
6. Quoted *ibid.*, pp. 48–9.
7. Quoted *Barbara Bodichon*, p. 151.
8. Quoted *The Cause*, pp. 108–9.
9. Quoted *Barbara Bodichon*, p. 153.
10. Quoted *The Cause*, p. 101.
11. Quoted *Millicent Garrett Fawcett*, p. 27.
12. Quoted *The Cause*, p. 121.
13. Quoted Roger Fulford, *Votes for Women* (Faber & Faber, 1957) p. 75.
14. Quoted *The Englishwoman's Review* (1872), No. XI, p. 207.
15. Quoted *Votes for Women*, p. 80.

16. *Millicent Garrett Fawcett*, p. 99.
17. Quoted *The Cause*, p. 279.
18. Quoted *ibid.*, p. 285.
19. Quoted *Millicent Garrett Fawcett*, p. 100.
20. Millicent Garrett Fawcett, *Women's Suffrage* (undated) p. 34.
21. *Millicent Garrett Fawcett.* p. 186.

CHAPTER VIII: *The Militants*

1. Ethel Smyth, *Female Pipings in Eden* (Peter Davies, 1933) p. 189.
2. *Ibid.*, pp. 191–2.
3. Quoted *Votes for Women*, p. 119.
4. Quoted *ibid.*, p. 129.
5. Quoted *ibid.*, p. 128.
6. Millicent Fawcett, *What I remember* (T. Fisher Unwin, 1925 edition) p. 179.
7. Quoted *The Cause*, p. 296.
8. Quoted Vera Brittain, *Pethick-Lawrence* (Allen & Unwin, 1963) p. 44.
9. *Ibid.*, p. 45.
10. Quoted *The Cause*, p. 301.
11. Dame Christabel Pankhurst, *Unshackled: the Story of How We Won the Vote* (Hutchinson, 1959) p. 83.
12. *Ibid.*, p. 78.
13. *Female Pipings in Eden*, pp. 208–9.
14. Quoted *Votes for Women*, p. 151.
15. Quoted *ibid.*, p. 152.
16. Quoted *Pethick-Lawrence*, p. 49.
17. *Millicent Garrett Fawcett*, p. 230.
18. Theresa Billington-Greig, unpublished biographical sketch, Women's Service Library.
19. *Op. cit.*
20. *Female Pipings in Eden*, pp. 195 and 192.
21. Naomi Jacob, *Me and the Swans* (William Kimber, 1963), p. 152.
22. Theresa Billington-Greig, Women's Service Library.
23. Quoted *Votes for Women*, p. 179.
24. *Millicent Garrett Fawcett*, p. 230.
25. Quoted *Votes for Women*, p. 181.
26. Quoted *ibid.*, p. 186.
27. Quoted *ibid.*, p. 190.
28. Quoted *Millicent Garrett Fawcett*, p. 219.

CHAPTER IX: *Women Against the Government*

1. Quoted *Millicent Garrett Fawcett*, pp. 220–21.
2. *What I Remember*, pp. 205–6.
3. Quoted *Pethick-Lawrence*, p. 61.
4. Quoted *ibid.*, pp. 61–2.
5. Quoted *Votes for Women*, p. 255.
6. Quoted *Unshackled: the Story of How We Won the Vote*, pp. 227–8.
7. Quoted *Millicent Garrett Fawcett*, p. 268.
8. Quoted *What I Remember*, p. 212.
9. Quoted *ibid.*, p. 207.
10. Quoted *ibid.*, p. 210.

CHAPTER X: *Women at War*

1. Quoted *Female Pipings in Eden*, p. 233.
2. Quoted *Votes for Women*, p. 297.
3. Quoted *ibid.*, p. 303.
4. Quoted *ibid.*, p. 302.
5. Quoted *Millicent Garrett Fawcett*, p. 271.
6. Quoted *ibid.*, p. 276.
7. *Millicent Garrett Fawcett*, p. 291.
8. *Female Pipings in Eden*, p. 238.
9. Quoted Millicent Garrett Fawcett, *The Women's Victory and After* (Sidgwick & Jackson, 1920), p. 133.
10. *Unshackled: the Story of How We Won the Vote*, p. 293.
11. Quoted *Millicent Garrett Fawcett*, p. 323.
12. *Ibid.*, p. 335.
13. Quoted Vera Brittain, *Lady into Woman* (Andrew Dakers, 1953), p. 50.
14. Quoted *And His Charming Lady*, p. 203.

CHAPTER XI: *Heirs of the Women's Movement*

1. Quoted Joan Evans, *Prelude and Fugue* (Museum Press, 1964), p. 114.
2. *The Cause*, p. 377.
3. Ed. Ray Strachey, *Our Freedom and Its Results*, by Five Women (Hogarth Press, 1936), pp. 134–5.
4. *Op. cit.*

CHAPTER XII: *Women in Parliament*

1. Duchess of Atholl, *Working Partnership* (Arthur Barker, 1958), p. 139.
2. Quoted Hilda Martindale, CBE, *From One Generation to Another* (Allen & Unwin, 1944), p. 35.
3. Quoted Mary D. Stocks, *Eleanor Rathbone* (Gollancz, 1949), pp. 142–3.
4. *Calling All Women*, Journal of the National Council of Women (July, 1960).

INDEX

For Product Safety Concerns and Information please contact our EU
representative GPSR@taylorandfrancis.com
Taylor & Francis Verlag GmbH, Kaufingerstraße 24, 80331 München, Germany